FROM
TEXAS TO
THE WORLD
AND BACK

FROM TEXAS TO THE WORLD AND BACK

Essays on the Journeys of Katherine Anne Porter

Edited by
Mark Busby & Dick Heaberlin

TCU PRESS ▪ FORT WORTH

Copyright © 2001 Center for the Study of the Southwest

Library of Congress Cataloging-in-Publication Data

From texas to the world and back: essays on the journeys of Katherine Anne
Porter / edited by Mark Busby and Dick Heaberlin.
p. cm.
"Sixteen essays first presented at a May 15, 1998 conference . . . at
Southwest Texas State University and held in San Marcos" —Introd.
Includes bibliographical references and index

ISBN)-87565-237-9 (alk. paper)

1. Porter, Katherine Anne, 1890-1980 —Journeys—Congresses.
2. Authors, American—20th Century—Biography—Congresses.
3. Women and literature—Southern States —History—20th Century—
Congresses. I. Busby, Mark. II. Heaberlin, Dick.

PS3531.0752 z62 2001
813'.52—dc21
[B]
00-064863

*Jacket: Black-and-white portraits of Katherine Anne Porter taken in Notre Dame des Champs
apartment, Paris, between the Spring of 1935 and the Winter of 1935-36. Courtesy Papers of
Katherine Anne Porter, Special Collections, University of Maryland , College Park, Libraries.
Color photograph by Paul Porter.
Book and jacket design/Margie Adkins Graphic Design*

To Linda and Andrea and to all future writers
from Texas and beyond who aspire to achieve the
skill and grace of Katherine Anne Porter.

Contents

Introduction

Betsy Colquitt

Edited by Mark Busby and Dick Heaberlin, *From Texas to the World and Back: Katherine Anne Porter's Journeys* collects sixteen essays first presented at a May 15, 1998, conference organized by Busby as director of the Center for Study of the Southwest at Southwest Texas State University and held in San Marcos. The conference celebrated both Porter's life and works and the recent acquisition by SWT and the Hays County Preservation Associates of the house in Kyle, Texas, where Porter lived from age two until her early teens when she left Texas to begin her journeys "to the world." The refurbished house, once the home of Porter's paternal grandmother, will become a museum named for the writer and used by SWT writing programs.

After Porter left the state as a young woman, she never again resided in Texas and visited only rarely, but in her essay "Noon Wine: The Sources," she recalls her Texas past lyrically and also acknowledges her Texas heritage as the primary source for her stories and novellas. As this 1956 essay notes, after leaving Texas, she spent "fourteen years in Mexico, Bermuda, Spain, Germany, Switzerland, but, happiest and best, nearly five years in Paris." (*The Collected Essays and Occasional Writings of Katherine Anne Porter*, Delacorte, New York, 1970, 470). Her return to America in 1936 ended her "living abroad except for short visits back to Paris, Brittany, Rome, Belgium" (469). But though she began writing "Noon

Wine" in Switzerland, her story is shaped by the area of Central Texas where she grew up, and her recollections of this place, "the summer country of my childhood, this place of memory" (470) and its people inform her story. These materials—re-imagined, reshaped, and recreated—were her Texas heritage, and whether by chance or design, the recurrent theme in *From Texas to the World* is her connections to and, on occasion, alienations from her native state.

Born in 1890 at Indian Creek, now a ghost town near Brownwood, Porter writes of her years abroad that

> I felt then, and feel now, that it was all entirely right, timely, appropriate, exactly where I should have been. . . . I did not feel exactly at home, I knew where home was, . . . and all the time, I was making notes on stories—stories of my own place my South—for my part of Texas was peopled almost entirely by Southerners from Virginia, Tennessee, the Carolinas, Kentucky . . . and I was almost instinctively living in a sustained state of mind and feeling, and quietly and secretly, compared one thing with another. . . . So my time in Mexico and Europe served me in a way I had not dreamed of: . . . it gave me back my past and my own house and my own people—the native land of my heart." (470).

That Porter in 1956 remembered her Texas so kindly may suggest that her earlier anger at the Texas literary establishment had by then abated. Founded in 1938, the Texas Institute of Letters awarded its first prizes in 1939. The obvious choices for the fiction award were Porter's *Pale Horse, Pale Rider: Three Short Novels* and Dobie's *Apache Gold and Yaqui Silver*. Porter's book attracted national attention, and she expected to receive the prize. She didn't. As James Ward Lee observes in "Porter and Dobie: The Marriage from Hell," that Dobie received the award was fitting considering his contributions to and role in creating a southwest literary tradition. By contrast, Porter's fiction was removed both in style and substance from the "hide and horn" frontier tradition Dobie explored. Porter's Texas looked to the east and the myth of the Old South, which was still vivid to the southerners who'd come to Texas in the GTT migration during Reconstruction. Porter's literary mentors were also southerners, among them Robert Penn Warren, Eudora Welty, Caroline Gordon, and Allen Tate. But despite Porter's displeasure with the TIL, her quarrel had no lasting effects. She continued to write, and her *Collected Short Stories* would later win both a National Book Award and a Pulitzer Prize, and the Texas Institute continues to flourish.

But if her 1939 visit home was less than happy, her return in 1958, as Richard Holland's "Katherine Anne Porter and the University of Texas: A Map of Misunderstanding" shows, did have important effects. Her visit to Austin came after she'd declined an invitation to teach a semester at the university, but subsequently she accepted an offer to give a public lecture there. Her lecture was described as "triumphant." At the time of her Austin visit, a new UT library was in construction, and with some justification from what UT officials told her, Porter thought the library was to be named for her. In fact, it was 1963 before the long-completed building got a name, that of Peter T. Flawn, a former UT president. As Porter's several letters to UT administrators attest, she was delighted by her expected honor and offered to designate the university as the recipient at her death of her literary archive and some other personal properties. Her letters apparently left UT administrators puzzled as to how to respond, and their slowness to correct her misunderstanding aggravated the problem. When Porter finally realized that a room in the library, not the library itself, would have her name, she withdrew her earlier offer to UT and, soon thereafter, designated the University of Maryland's McKeldin Library as heir to this part of her estate. The only

Porter manuscript at UT-Austin is her corrected typescript of "Old Mortality," which she had donated years earlier at the request of a UT librarian.

But if two of Porter's visits home were unhappy, her four-day stay in Brownwood in 1976 gave her great joy, happy memories, and a lasting friendship with Roger Brooks, whose memoir of Porter's visit also includes some details of her last years. Her visit to Brownwood also brought Porter the most public honor she received from her native state during her lifetime. In 1975, Brooks, then-president of Howard Payne University and a longtime admirer of Porter's fiction, proposed that the university award her an honorary degree, and, in 1976, the degree was conferred. Brooks' essay, "Hosting Miss Porter," which is transcribed from his talk at SWT in April 1999 about her visit to Howard Payne, is his memoir of her visit. His moving depiction of the writer's return home suggests that Joan Givner, a Porter biographer, is right to label this journey as Porter's "most important pilgrimage." Porter was then eighty-six, and her health, fragile for much of her life, was a major concern. Brooks carefully planned her stay even to having medical personnel always available, and he and many others in the university and in Brownwood helped with her visit as Lou Rodenberger's "The Prodigal Daughter Comes Home" details. Porter was a gracious guest and appreciated the care and attentiveness of her hosts. At her request, her trip included a visit to her mother's grave in Indian Creek Cemetery. Brooks gives a touching account of this visit, which led to Porter's decision to have her ashes buried beside her mother's grave. In 1983, three years after Porter's death, her wish was carried out.

From Texas to the World and Back is a valuable addition to the Porter studies. Though the scholarly and critical credentials of the essayists are clearly evident, the major contribution of this collection may be its many insights into the ways in which Porter's Texas heritage shaped her life and her fiction. Though supposing what the dead might think is to presume, it's a safe guess that Porter would have loved this collection for the quality of its essays and the occasion it celebrates. At last, Katherine Anne Porter has "my own house" and her name on a Texas building. That her house will be a place for young writers to learn their craft and practice the art to which she made exemplary contributions is also fitting. ❖

Katherine Anne Porter's Journey from Texas to the World

Don Graham

When I first began teaching the stories of Katherine Anne Porter, in the mid-1960s, I gave little thought to the geographical and biographical underpinnings of her writing. I knew that she was considered a grande dame of American literature and that she lived, rather magnificently, one imagined, in a town house in Georgetown, Washington, D.C. I, on the other hand, taught at Southwest Texas State College in San Marcos, Texas, and lived in a nondescript rental house in the obscure little town of Kyle, twenty miles south of Austin. Kyle had a water tower and a Dairy Queen, and that was about all. Revisiting Kyle twenty-five years later, searching for Porter's roots, I was astonished to realize that the house I had lived in was only a half block away from the one where Callie Russell Porter, as she was christened, had spent the crucial, formative years of early childhood, from age two to twelve. In the 1960s there was as yet no Porter historical marker in Kyle, nor was there any identification of the Porter home.

The remapping of Katherine Anne Porter and Texas is an ongoing project to reclaim Porter as the Lone Star State's premier writer of fiction. The past fifteen years have seen a heightened awareness of Porter's connections with Texas: the appearance of a biography and several book-length critical studies, a symposium at Texas A&M, a statue of her at Sea World in San Antonio, the already mentioned historical marker in Kyle, the preservation of her house (recently purchased by Southwest Texas State University, which intends to establish a writing center there), and even an article about her in *Texas Highways* (February 1998). KAP is at present the hottest tourist attraction in Kyle—and the only tourist attraction in its history. A striking, Marlene Dietrich-like photograph of Porter was also featured on the 1998 edition of the poster for Texas Writers Month. Yet benightedness about Porter's Texas roots and artistry continues. In "Lone Star Lit," an article in the British magazine, *The Economist* (April 1998), the anonymous author mentions J. Frank Dobie and Larry McMurtry, among others, but not Porter.

Her journey back to full acknowledgment and acceptance as a major Texas writer has drawn fire from McMurtry, the heir apparent to Dobie's vision of Texas as a western state. In 1981, a year after Porter's death, McMurtry dismissed Porter as an author of minor status. He accused her of a "profound evasiveness, an uncertainty not so much about what she knew as about what she could bring herself to admit about what she knew. For all her trafficking with revolutionaries and mad poets, for all her scorn of middle-class convention, she was genteel to the core" ("Bridegroom" 16). He concludes his critique by paraphrasing Gertrude Stein's famous remark about Oakland, California, that "there was no there there," saying finally, "I feel very much the same way about the fiction of Katherine Anne Porter. The plumage is beautiful, but plumage, after all, is only feathers" (17).

The charge of gentility must, though McMurtry does not quite say so, have to do with reticence about sexual experience. If McMurtry means that Porter lacked an understanding of sex, the charge is palpably ridiculous. She was married four times, and by her own proud admission had many, many affairs. One does not have to write clinically or pornographically about sex to reveal an understanding of the subject. The story "Magic," for example, which deals with the brutal circumstances of a young prostitute working in a New Orleans brothel, reveals a quite adequate knowledge of sex in a particularly sinister context. Another example of Porter's understanding of sexuality is the remarkable passage in a story titled "The Old Order" (later retitled "The Journey"), in which Porter describes the bold act of Grandmother, who against all Victorian taboos and mores of the day, and over the objections of her husband and own mother, elects to breastfeed her newborn child as well as one born to her former black slave and literally bosom friend, Nannie. Porter describes the act in an interesting way: "She sat nursing her child and her foster child, with a sensual, warm pleasure she had not dreamed of, translating her natural physical relief into something holy, God-sent, amends from heaven for what she had suffered in childbed." The passage continues: "Yes, and for what she had missed in the marriage bed, for there also something had failed" (24). In this remarkable sentence rests the entire content of many quite bad modern novels, including, among others, *The Bridges of Madison County* and all of Danielle Steele.

Until quite recently, Porter in her home state has always lived in the shadow cast by tall men, or short men who told tall tales, namely, the legendary aura given off by J. Frank Dobie and company. Folklorist Dobie, historian Walter P. Webb, and naturalist Roy Bedichek, the three "fathers" of Texas literature, in whose honor a statue now stands in Zilker Park in Austin, had little interest in the work of Katherine Anne Porter for the following reasons: 1. She was an expatriate who had left Texas, and they had stayed at home. 2. She wrote about the southern side of Texas experience, and often she didn't write about Texas at all. They, on the other hand, wrote about little else, but the Texas they memorialized was almost entirely western in subject matter and mythology. They located

Texas literature in cattle country, not cotton country. 3. She was not a romantic celebrant of Texas culture, and they were.

The dominant figure in Texas literary mythology is of course male, a leathery and heroic cowboy, from J. Frank Dobie's old-time cowboys to John Travolta's Urban Cowboy. Porter had nothing to say on the subject of the cowboy. It wasn't her subject. She didn't write about cow people, longhorns, mustangs, rattlesnakes, paisanos, or buried bullion, topics that J. Frank Dobie mined so successfully during their long parallel careers that he became known as Mr. Texas, and, in Texas, she became almost unknown. While Dobie loomed large on the Lone Star landscape, Porter was either ignored in her home state or taken to be something else, a southerner.

When Porter began writing in the early 1920s there was no advantage attached to being a "Texas" writer. To the northern mind, Texas meant cowboys and western themes, period; later it meant outsized humor of the Texas brag sort; but it never meant literature. There were, on the other hand, a great many advantages to being perceived as a southern writer, and Porter, in both her self-fashioning in her work and in the self-promotion of her career, portrayed herself as a southerner. In real life she personified the southern belle, a kind of literary Scarlett O'Hara: beautiful, flirtatious, talented, and manipulative. She made friends with some of the leading academic and literary figures of the day: Robert Penn Warren, Cleanth Brooks, Allen Tate. She married one of them, Albert Erskine. Unlike what friends such as Cleanth Brooks believed, Porter was not born to a grand old southern family but was in fact a product of quite meager economic circumstances, a fact that Brooks did not learn until after Porter's death and the publication of Joan Givner's biography.

The circumstances of Porter's early life in Kyle are these. Born in a two-room cabin in Indian Creek, Texas, near Brownwood, in

1890, Porter was just two years old when her mother died. The father, devastated, moved his family of four children into his mother's house—Grandmother in the Old Order stories—on Center Street in Kyle. This meant that two adults and four children lived in that house: all you have to do is visit the house to see the economic level. The rooms are very small. There are no white columns. To see the white columns it is necessary to visit the Kyle Cemetery south of town where the grandmother is buried, her grave marked by an impressive stone with two marble columns. Contemporaries remember the Porter family as closer to poverty than to prominence. One old-timer recalled that her mother felt sorry for the Porter children, who were poor and badly dressed.

Porter herself spoke of the house in a piece titled "Notes on the Texas I Remember" that she wrote in 1975, when she was eighty-five. The house, she says, was "of a style known as Queen Anne, who knows why?" and that it had "no features at all except for two long galleries, front and back galleries—mind you, not porches or verandas"; these, she says, were covered with honeysuckle and roses and provided a wonderful venue for repose and conversation and iced tea and (can this be true?) "tall frosted beakers of mint julep, for the gentlemen, of course" (102). Gentlemen consuming mint julep on flower-embowered galleries is, of course, straight out of southern plantation mythology, and Porter, here and in her fiction about her family, appears to be ratcheting up the social level several notches to attain a grander personal myth. It is true, however, that the grandmother did come from a family of good standing in Kentucky and when Porter claims that Gov. James Hogg visited at the grandmother's house in Kyle, this may be accurate. Still, I have stood on what she calls a gallery on the front of the Porter house, and it is a front porch, nothing more. The same with the back. It would take a stretch of the imagination to see the porches as "galleries."

In the mid-thirties Porter returned to Texas for important visits with her family and especially her father, from whom she had been estranged since her divorce back in 1915. The house in Kyle struck her forcibly during a visit in 1937: "My father and I visited the dreary little place at Kyle, empty, full of dust, decayed, even smaller than I remembered it" (quoted in Grider xviii). Revisiting the past, in actuality as in her fiction, involved a complex awareness. On another trip with her father that year, she attended an Old Settlers' Reunion in San Marcos and was reminded powerfully of what the generation of the Old Order meant to her. In a long letter to Josephine Herbst (August 15, 1937) she recounted the experience:

> It was a valuable time for me; they thanked me for coming and said how pleasant it had been to see me, and I told them truthfully I had got a great deal more than I had given. . . . I took snapshots of Dad with old ladies he had danced with in his youth. The things about these people that struck me was their look of race—real blood features they had, handsome noses, fine heads, and lively young eyes in their wrinkled faces. Our generation looks mixed and indecisive beside them. God knows we have enough to make us indecisive. The problems they handled so competently for themselves were too much for us, the world I was brought up in taught me nothing about the world I was to live in, but as I looked around me, I thought, these people are strong, and they are my people, and I have their toughness in me, and this is what I can rely upon. . . . I loved them, really with my heart. I liked the precision of their old fashioned language, their good simple manners that would be good manners anywhere, and their absolutely innate code of morals that shows itself in their manners. . . . I feel pretty certain that I could live, now, in San Marcos, Texas, and have a good life and go on writing the way I have begun. . . . I'd be willing to risk it.

BUT—they are a disappearing race, soon they will all be dead, and the young people are scattering out as fast as they can go. The land is impoverished, and the young do not care enough for it to bring it to life. I saw all our fields lying full of weeds, (my grandmother owned six thousand acres of good thick black land in that country once, and it was said you could plant a walking stick and it would sprout in that land) and the present owners don't know enough to plant the fields to clover for a few seasons to bring it back . . . that made me unhappy. (KAP to Josephine Herbst, August 15, 1937, in *Letters* 150)

At that time, Porter, forty-seven, possessed the maturity and perspective to look back on her past in Texas and to quarry from those materials some of her best and most lasting work. She had traveled many miles from Texas and visited many places, Greenwich Village, Mexico, Paris, Berlin, and Bermuda, among others, and such journeys were necessary for her to develop as an artist. Had she stayed in Texas she would always have been Callie Porter and never Katherine Anne; this is what she felt deeply. Of her wanderings she said, "So my time in Mexico and Europe served me in a way I had not dreamed of, even, besides its own charm and goodness: it gave me back my past and my own house and my own people—the native land of my heart" ("Noon Wine: The Sources" 470).

The Texas of Porter's youth, however, when she was young and struggling to find herself, was insupportable; it offered no means for her to achieve the kind of life she came to desire. Eventually she felt that leaving Texas was necessary, inevitable. In a letter in 1941 to her nephew Paul she wrote,

When I was your age and younger, it seemed to me I was on a

desert island quite literally. No one to talk to about the things that interested me, and not only indifference, but active hostility to the way my mind was growing, and the direction my life would take. Not only was I not helped in the least, but I was hindered. It took years of the most exhausting effort for me to struggle out of that situation, and all my work and development were retarded and warped; I had to fight almost to the death even to arrive at the knowledge I needed if I were to survive at all; for I hungered for music and all the arts as if they were bread, and they were bread: for their sake for years I had very little of the material food, and I do not regret one day of it . . . . (KAP to Paul Porter, July 24, 1941, *Letters* 203–04)

In a much jauntier tone, in another letter she told fellow expatriate Texan William Humphrey, "I got out of Texas like a bat out of hell at the earliest possible moment and stayed away cheerfully half a life-time" (KAP to William Humphrey, October 8, 1950, quoted in Stout, 36).

These assessments, written in her maturity, are all after the struggle. But what was the actual struggle like? One of the best clues to the dynamics of Porter's family life in Texas can be seen in a long letter of March 23, 1909, written to Callie by her brother Paul. Porter's original letter to her brother has not survived, but from what Paul says, we can well imagine some of the things that young Callie said. At this time, 1909, Porter was a young wife, age nineteen, who had married three years earlier, just after her sixteenth birthday. Her husband was John Henry Koontz from a prominent ranching family near Victoria, Texas. Her brother's letter is something of a masterpiece of prevailing male assumptions of the period:

Dear Callie: I haven't answered your welcome letter for I hardly knew what to make of it at first. You certainly took me by surprise with your vehemence. It must have been written on one of your off days. What was the trouble; had JK [John Koontz] asserted himself in contravention of the laws or rather, rights of woman. Poor old JK. He is probably an h.p. suffragist [h.p. = henpecked?] at home any way if merly [sic] for the sake of peace. You will find that the average man does not activly [sic] oppose the ballot for women, but merly [sic] regards it with uneasy tolerance as liable to disturb the present relation between the sexes. Dear, why should you butt your head against hard facts; there is no practical reason for allowing you the ballot. I admit it would gratify their vanity, but aside from that it would be of no earthly use to women. It would not help the moral or economic conditions and would bring the millenium [sic] no nearer. False pride and ignorance account for a great many of the women who champion the cause, women whose views are inflated because of natures [sic] stinginess in brain and who blindly follow a lead with out the least conception of what it all means. They become bitter from a fanatical struggle for imaginary rights not knowing an effort not directed by common sense will invariably fail. They do not discriminate between bigness and fineness, unable to see that any influence that they could bring to bear along that line would not equal the influence of the feminine in maternal relations of the home. The worlds [sic] greatest need today is of good mothers, which is the master profesion [sic] for women requiring every art and talent to perfect, of women who live close to their children, who will bear impression of her training all through life. The farther away a woman gets from the thought that she was made to be the helpmate of man, and the mother of his children, the farther she will be from her usefulness. Competition

9

between the sexes is unnatural, you should be mans [sic] inspiration, not his competitor. What effort you make for equality renders you unwomanly and consequently less deserving of the deference which is a womans [sic] portion. American women enjoy more liberty than any other nation on the earth and what are the results. Divorces, soul mates, and numerous other evils. If that is equality it would be far better to keep them fettered than to let them turn liberty into license. You say women are slaves; bound by routine and unappreciated labor. I should call them the White Mans [sic] Burden. . . . A man loves a woman on a pedestal, when she comes down he leaves her. It matters little whether women vote or not, as man is boss now will he be then; finis . . . . (McKeldin Library)

Porter's letter must have been fiery indeed to provoke Paul to such a long and vigorous defense of the way things were in their family and in the Texas of that era.

There were other family dynamics at work to make Porter wish to escape family, place, and the corseted straightjacket of gender. Porter's relationship with her father, Harrison Boone Porter, was complicated. Handsome but ineffectual, he appears never to have recovered from the death of his wife. Rightly or wrongly, Porter blamed him for failures to provide comfort and support for his children. For example, she blamed her early first marriage on her father. In a letter to her nephew Paul, written on the fiftieth anniversary of her marriage, she called that decision "the first serious disaster of our lives." She went on to assign blame to her father: "If we had had a father to care for us, and protect us a little, we would never have taken that dreadful step. But we were really quite desperate, and of course, things came out as they do when you take any step in desperation" (quoted in Givner, *A Life* 90).

After her father's death in 1942, Porter, in a letter to a friend, stated

10

once again her feelings about her father's influence upon her life and career:

> For myself, I know very well that I have contributed something worth having to the world, I have done first rate work and I am proud of it, and I have the right to be, for I did it absolutely without any help and without any preparation except what I got for myself, without any encouragement or belief from my family, and without health or money . . . And I think part of my will to overcome obstacles and to use my gifts came out of my real horror at seeing the way our father simply could not, for whatever mysterious reason, use his own gifts. Many thousands of men have had worse obstacles than he, and have overcome them triumphantly . . . . He could not, and that was his misfortune, and ours, but it was nothing to blame him for or to be bitter about. I used to be, but I outgrew it as I went on . . ." (KAP to Mary Alice Hillendahl, February 6, 1942, *Letters* 224)

Reconciliation with her father on trips to Texas in 1936 and 1937 was an important step in Porter's coming to terms with her past.

In the late 1920s Porter began to rummage through her early life for material for fiction. She began an uncompleted novel titled "Many Redeemers," which dealt with family history and remembrance. Much of this material would find its way into stories published in the mid-1930s and on into the 1940s.

Those works would come to be called the Miranda stories, after the protagonist, a little girl much like Porter. Written as early as 1935 and published in various periodicals, six of the Miranda stories were gathered together under the heading, "The Old Order," and published in book form in the 1943 collection, *The Leaning Tower and Other Stories.*

11

Two other stories that featured Miranda are the short novels "Old Mortality" and "Pale Horse, Pale Rider," which along with "Noon Wine," appeared in 1939 in the volume titled *Pale Horse, Pale Rider*, probably Porter's greatest single book and arguably the best book of fiction written by a Texan. Finally, there is another childhood Miranda story, "The Fig Tree," that lay forgotten among Porter's manuscripts until she rediscovered and published it in 1960. There is also an interesting uncompleted and unpublished Miranda story about a lynching titled "The Man in the Tree," written in the mid-1930s. Arranged chronologically, the stories trace the life of a young child growing up in Kyle, Texas, from about the age of five through a near-death crisis of the young Miranda during the influenza epidemic of 1918, a story based on Porter's own experience in Denver, Colorado.

Of *The Old Order* stories, "The Grave" is the most celebrated and by any standard of measurement an American classic. "The Grave" is set squarely in the Kyle milieu. The time is 1903, two years after the death of Grandmother. With the absence of the matriarchal principle of order and discipline, neighbors see the children as running wild, and the family itself as in decline. Against this backdrop, the action turns upon the adventures of Miranda, nine years old, and her brother Paul, twelve. (It is interesting to note here that Porter has not even taken the trouble to disguise her real older brother's name in this story; more about this later.) The two children are wandering through woods and fields, hunting doves and rabbits, when they happen upon a graveyard the contents of which have been recently disinterred for removal to another cemetery. The children scamper into the open graves, where they find "treasure": Paul finds a gold ring—a wedding band—and Miranda, a coffin screw with an embossed dove on its head. Paul wants what Miranda has and entices her to exchange the two treasures. As soon as the tomboy Miranda, dressed in boy's overalls and carrying a .22, puts on the wedding band, she has a vision of an entirely different future. She suddenly sees herself in a completely new light: "She wanted to go back to the farmhouse, take a good cold bath, dust herself with plenty of Maria's violet talcum powder—provided Maria was not present to object, of course—put on the thinnest, most becoming dress she owned, with a big sash, and sit in a wicker chair under the trees . . . ." What she wants, in short, is to become a southern belle: passive, pretty, no longer a tomboy in a man's sphere of action and movement, but a young begowned woman sitting there and waiting—for what?—for a young suitor, of course, for a husband, for marriage.

Porter continues by expanding the girl's desires far beyond the ones she started out with on this day: "These things were not all she wanted, of course; she had vague stirrings of desire for luxury and a grand way of living which could not take precise form in her imagination but were founded on family legend of past wealth and leisure." The first epiphany in the story is the revelation of a traditional gendered future: beauty, femininity, marriage.

The second epiphany is much more disturbing and much more ambiguous. Following their adventure in the graves, the children have a second adventure. Paul kills a rabbit, and upon inspection discovers the rabbit to be pregnant. Previously Miranda had not minded the killing of animals and birds; now she decides that she does not want the rabbit's fur from which to make doll clothes, as she had always done before. Paul shows her the "bundle of tiny rabbits, each wrapped in a thin scarlet veil." The narrative voice compares the rabbits to "a baby's head just washed," and Miranda in a succession of quick inductions understands exactly what Paul means when he says "as if he were talking about something forbidden: They were just about ready to be born." She says, "I know, like kittens. I know, like babies." But she has not known this lesson of life—and death—until now. The revelation is profound, and

Paul recognizes its importance as well. In fact, Paul fears that he will be in trouble with their father if his sister tells on him.

At the point in the story when Paul cautions Miranda not to tell what has happened, Paul's words to Miranda form a kind of crux as to how to read and understand "The Grave." At a conference on women's writing in Texas, held at the University of Texas in 1984, I heard these words read by a professor in a manner that I can only describe as a version of what Simon Legree might sound like dressing down a slave. The following words were read in the most menacing manner possible, with a stage-villain, exaggerated, masculine growl: "Listen now. Now you listen to me, and don't ever forget. Don't you ever tell a living soul that you saw this. Don't tell a soul. Don't tell Dad because I'll get into trouble. He'll say I'm leading you into things you ought not to do. He's always saying that. So now don't you go and forget and blab out sometime the way you're always doing . . . . Now, that's a secret. Don't you tell" (*Old Order* 61).

But what the text of the story actually contains is not quite so melodramatic. First, there are no exclamation marks in the sentences, no hints of such verbal exaggeration. Granted, the verbs are in the imperative mode, the form of command, but overall, Paul's manner seems more worried than overbearing. The most interesting fact is the sentence preceding the little speech to Miranda: "He . . . said to Miranda, with an eager friendliness, a confidential tone quite unusual in him, as if he were taking her into an important secret on equal terms" (*Order* 60–61). In what are almost stage directions, we see that instead of an exaggerated patriarchal imperiousness, Paul is actually adopting a quiet tone, though intense, to be sure, that is both friendly and, in terms of its concession to equality among the sexes, more seductive than threatening. It would seem that the only proper reading of the speech must be in accordance with Porter's narrative instructions as a comment on immutable patriarchal values.

In actuality Porter's brother had good reasons to worry about his father's being told about the day's disturbing events, for when the story appeared, the real Paul read it and wrote his sister. He told her that she'd got it wrong, that in fact she had told their father, and that Paul had received a severe beating for exposing his sister to such knowledge. Katherine Anne said that wasn't the way she remembered it at all (Givner, *A Life* 71).

The story ends with a famous coda. Miranda is a young woman walking in the market of "a strange city of a strange country" (surely Mexico) when she sees an Indian vendor selling little candy animals, and the sight of these, and especially the smell, causes her to flash back to that moment of her childhood, suppressed and forgotten for twenty years. The last image she sees, in the closing line of the story, is that of her brother, "again twelve years old, a pleased sober smile in his eyes, turning the silver dove over and over in his hands" (61). Feminist critics have made much of this. They find in the destruction of the rabbit mother and its unborn babies a symbol of woman's subservience to males, of men denying women knowledge of their bodies, and here at the end, of Paul as a superior, smug male secure in his triumph. The image of Paul, however, is one of love on the sister's part, nothing more, nothing less. And the theory that the incident intended to suppress women's knowledge of their bodies is highly suspect. Miranda may bury the memory because of the painful twinning of birth and death, but she certainly hasn't forgotten the facts of life. Once she knows how babies are made, she isn't likely to forget.

The story has always been taken as an initiation story in which a youthful protagonist discovers a fundamental fact about the human condition: the nature of animal and human birth. Perhaps Porter's memory of that event might have been triggered by something else, by, possibly, the fact of an early abortion that she had in Mexico. Darlene

Unrue of the University of Nevada at Las Vegas, who is writing a new biography of Porter, has uncovered the circumstances of this abortion (E-mail to Don Graham, July 8, 1998). What lends credence to the story's being about not birth but abortion is the fact that the little rabbits are not born, that they die with their mother, and that the instrument of death is first, a bullet (fired by a male), and that the instrument of dissection, of disclosure, is a "bowie knife." The bowie knife bears special attention. A huge knife, its blade is about twelve to fifteen inches long. It is a fearsome weapon, and a boy of twelve, even in backwoods Texas in 1903, would in all likelihood not have been allowed to carry one around. A Case pocketknife is far more likely. Why, then, did Porter choose to call it a "bowie knife"? It is possible that she simply recalled a famous knife she had heard about in her childhood without knowing its actual dimensions. Or it may be that the bowie knife represents an unconscious reference to the enormous psychological size of the surgeon's instrument used in abortions.

If "The Grave" is rooted firmly in Porter's Texas childhood, so is "Old Mortality," the best Miranda story in which to see the shaping of Porter's essential understanding of herself as a Texas artist-in-training. As a child attending a convent school in New Orleans, young Miranda ponders family legends about the impossibly beautiful dead Aunt Amy and encounters the gulf between romantic family myth and actuality as she sees it revealed in the shabby real conditions of the life of Gabriel, Amy's widowed husband, a drunken gambler. The girl Miranda imagines several roles for herself when she grows up: all are masculine—a jockey, a violinist, an airplane pilot, and, her father jokes, a lion tamer—but because of family legend and changing times, she never imagines herself as a southern belle.

In the last section we see Miranda at eighteen, on a train returning to her home in Texas to attend the funeral of Gabriel. We learn that

Miranda has married and is estranged from her father. During the course of the train ride she meets Cousin Eva, an embittered suffragette who has gone to jail for her beliefs and whose whole life has been twisted by a physical blemish, the absence of a firm chin. During the train trip and afterward in her room in her family home, Miranda comes to several decisions. She will leave her marriage, she will leave her family, and she will leave Texas. What she is going to become she doesn't yet know, but the reader can guess: she is going to become an artist, and to do so she has to fly, as James Joyce put it at the end of *Portrait of the Artist as a Young Man*, past the nets of family, religion, and country. The long epiphanous meditation by Miranda, one of the great set-pieces in Porter, ends on this note: "At least I can know the truth about what happens to me, she assured herself silently, making a promise to herself, in her hopefulness, her ignorance." It is that last word, "ignorance," that marks Porter's mature artistry. The struggle to find a life of meaning in the new, disordered modern world because the old order of belief and certitude is dead, buried with Grandmother, will be heroic though it may not yield the certitude of absolute self-knowledge— hence the word "ignorance" (*Old Order* 182). But the struggle is enough; the journey is everything.

The way Porter saw it, she escaped the snares of family, and her brother Paul did not. When Paul died in 1955, Katherine Anne, who was not able to attend his funeral, wrote to a friend: "There was nothing I could do, he did not miss me; poor man, he was swamped and deluged and God knows I think, almost literally smothered to death in family, yet God knows too he loved them and he could not have lived either without them." (KAP to Gertrude Bechtel, September 20, 1955, *Letters* 475).

For Porter there were never any easy answers, another key to her ability to create stories of lasting value. Most of the hard questions rose out of her early life in Texas. Most of them were never solved, but they inspired some literature of enduring merit. ❖

Works Cited

Fowler, Gene. "Katherine Anne Porter," *Texas Highways* Jan. 1998: 18–25.

Givner, Joan. *Katherine Anne Porter: A Life*. New York: Simon & Schuster, 1982.

———, ed. *Katherine Anne Porter: Conversations*. Jackson: UP of Mississippi, 1987.

Grider, Sylvia Ann. "Introduction: A Folklorist Looks at Katherine Anne Porter." *Katherine Anne Porter And Texas: An Uneasy Relationship*. Eds. Clinton Machann and William Bedford Clark. College Station: Texas A&M UP, 1990. xiii-xxiii.

McMurtry, Larry. "Ever a Bridegroom: Reflections on the Failure of Texas Literature." *Range Wars: Heated Debates, Sober Reflections, and Other Assessments of Texas Writing*. Eds. Craig Clifford and Tom Pilkington. Dallas: Southern Methodist UP, 1989. 13–41.

Porter, Katherine Anne. *Collected Essays and Occasional Writings of Katherine Anne Porter*. New York: Delacorte P, 1970.

———. *Collected Stories of Katherine Anne Porter*. 1965. Reprint. New York: Harcourt Brace, A Harvest Book, 1972.

———. *The Days Before*. New York: Harcourt Brace, 1952.

———. *Letters of Katherine Anne Porter*. Ed. Isabel Bayley. New York: Atlantic Monthly P, 1990.

———. "'Noon Wine': The Sources." *The Collected Essays And Occasional Writings Of Katherine Anne Porter*. New York: Delacorte, 1970. 467–82.

———. "Notes on the Texas I Remember," *Atlantic Monthly* 235.3

(March 1975): 102.

————. *The Old Order: Stories of the South*. New York: Harcourt Brace
    Jovanovich, 1958.

Porter, Paul. Letter to Katherine Anne Porter. March 23, 1909.
    McKeldin Library. U of Maryland, College Park, Libraries.

Stout, Janis P. *Katherine Anne Porter: A Sense of the Times.*
    Charlottesville: UP of Virginia, 1995.

Unrue, Darlene. E-mail to Don Graham, July 8, 1998.

Writing Home: Katherine Anne Porter, Coming and Going

Janis P. Stout

Women write letters—personal, intimate, in relation; men write books—universal, public, in general circulation.
— Jane Gallop, "Writing a Letter with Vermeer,"
in *The Poetics of Gender* (1986)

Usually I am an enthusiastic, nay an aggressive, writer of letters. I own most of the vices of my sex, and I believe letter-writing is considered one of the more dangerous of these . . .
— Katherine Anne Porter to Kenneth Burke, October 6, 1930

In an interview published in *McCall's* in 1965, Katherine Anne Porter recounted an anecdote apparently intended to explain her vagrancy— that is, her footloose wandering, the fact that she had strayed from her family and from Texas and gone wandering about the world doing something other than what proper women are supposed to do. She explained this behavior by reference to her father's failure to encourage her as an artist: "My father once said, 'If you want to write, you can write just as well here at home. Besides, what business has a lady writing? Why not write letters to your friends?'. . . "So I did break with my family," she said, "and with my part of the country" (Givner, *Conversations* 109). This excerpt from the Roy Newquist interview is, it seems to me, quite significant. Tied up within it are a great many elements that made Porter what she was—a great many tensions, really, that are important for understanding her: the demand for being a lady versus her defiance of the lady's life; being a writer as compared to being a lady; being a writer as distinct from just writing something; the idea of letters, in themselves; the idea of going out, making a break for it, versus staying home; the idea of family; the idea of Texas. All of that and maybe more is packed into these few lines.

Home was enormously important to Porter—both the idea of home and an actual place where she could feel at home and secure and comfortable. Her life had been disrupted at an early age, not quite two, when her mother died and she and her brother and sisters and father went to live with her grandmother in Kyle. It had been disrupted again when the grandmother died and she lived from pillar to post—for a time, while her father figured out what to do, in the home of some cousins who were the models for the Thompsons in "Noon Wine," and then in a succession of rented places in a succession of Texas towns, scratching together a living for her father rather than haveing one provided for her. When she married, at sixteen, the relationship was not a happy one, and she and John Henry Koontz moved several times. And then after that, as she attempted to make her own way and her own life, she had even less of a secure home. She was forever fixing places up, trying to make homes of them, and then moving away. In her essay "A House of My Own," published in 1941, she makes it very clear how intensely she wanted a house of her own and how persistently she had tried to buy one:

> There was never, of course, much money, never quite enough; there was never time, either; there was never permanency of any

sort, except the permanency of hope.

This hope had led me to collect an unreasonable amount of furniture and books, unreasonable for one who had no house to keep them in. (Porter, *CE* 175)

The essay describes, humorously but at the same time lovingly, the finding of her house and the complicated process of remodeling that had to be done. It ends with the prospect of moving in and lighting a fire in the fireplace—a wonderful, primitive image of nesting and of self-defense. But a footnote added to the essay a decade later states that she lived in the house "just thirteen months"—an uncharacteristically accurate statement. In her typical way, she became dissatisfied with conditions that might have been foreseen and moved on.

Moving on was a habit of Porter's. If home and houses were important to her, so was the freedom to leave them. As she said in the Newquist interview, she broke with family and with Texas in her mid-twenties and set out to find her life—which means that she at least *began* to break with a great deal that goes with family and Texas. In Willa Cather's *The Song of the Lark*, the central character, an aspiring musical artist who has left her small-town home and gone to Chicago to study piano, is told by her teacher, "Every artist makes himself born" (140). That is what Porter was doing: bringing herself to birth as a writer. Becoming a writer meant emergence, separation, not from the body of the mother, but from home.

The act of departing from home is a much more universal symbol than that, of course. As I have recently written in *Through the Window, Out the Door: Women's Narratives of Departure* (University of Alabama Press, 1998), the act of departing conveys not only unhousement and the uncertainty of confronting the unfamiliar spaces out there where one doesn't have a home, but it conveys, too, a range of values associated with self-assertion, endeavor, independence, personal ful-fillment. It is an act of exploration that is intellectual and spiritual as well as physical. In *Through the Window, Out the Door* I argue that the reason women writers, and particularly those of the modernist period in America, have been such powerful voices speaking of the moment of departure is that their history—not simply personal history, but also the history of centuries—has been one of confinement, of being pent up in houses and in the keeping of houses. The moment of breaking out has been a very significant one for many women. But it is also a very ambiguous moment, because it is fraught with such conflicting values. The departure from home is a troubling and difficult act and one that leaves a residue of doubt and nostalgia.

Certainly it was for Porter. And it is that ambiguity, or I should say the ambivalence that results from that ambiguity, that we see reflected in the fact of her enormous correspondence. She did not, as her father advised, stay home and write letters to her friends. She left and wrote letters back to friends and family. By writing letters home, and letters to the figurative "home" that her long-time friends constituted for her, she could maintain ties of security and continuity while also maintaining her freedom of exploration. Letters home were the means of uniting her urge toward *remaining* or *abiding* with her (stronger) urge toward departing; and they were also, I believe, a means of uniting her urge toward enacting the role of the lady that her father demanded of her with her urge toward breaking free of that role and enacting, instead, the role of the unfettered intellectual and artist, which in Porter's case merged with the role of the Bad Girl. Many of us who grew up before, say, the 1980s will remember that a common way of speaking of the Bad Girl was as a woman who "strayed." And Porter did stray, in mul-tiple senses. Her straying, in the common parlance that is used as a euphemism for sexual license, was indeed another way in which she resisted the crippling, constraining role of Lady. By entering into a life of vagrancy, in multiple senses of the word, while maintaining a lifelong habit of letter writing, she could be both free and bound, both a resister of the status quo and a fulfiller of its proprieties. If you look back at an old copy of Emily Post's rules of etiquette, you will see that ladies were expected to write letters and that the rules for doing so were detailed and were fraught with many dangers for the unwary.

Porter's correspondence, as preserved mainly at the University of Maryland but with a scattering of letters elsewhere, is enormous. The Porter Papers at Maryland are one of the largest literary archives in the country. They provide an incomparably valuable resource for understanding a writer of absolutely the highest artistic standards at work, involved in her own more everyday matters and needs and anxieties, and also involved in the historical and intellectual currents of her time. In addition to the study of Porter herself and her work, her letters are also an important resource for cultural studies during the span of years they cover. How the publishing business operated during half a century or more, how the alert intelligentsia of America, in the persons of Porter and her correspondents, perceived the events of the time, how an intelligent and determined woman navigated the complex currents of gender relations during a time when those relations were changing drastically: all these issues and more can be studied in her correspondence. And besides these general issues illuminated there, one can see the thinking, the assumptions, and the activities of a great many particular people of real significance in the intellectual history of the time because she corresponded with so many and such various acquaintances: Glenway Wescott, Monroe Wheeler, John Hermann (active in the Communist Party and involved as a minor player in the Alger Hiss affair), Allen Tate, Ford Madox Ford, Eudora Welty, Kenneth Burke. The absences are interesting, too: I have found no trace whatever of interaction with Willa Cather, despite Porter's noted essay on her; no trace of Mabel Dodge Luhan, another adventurer; no trace of Alfred Stieglitz or of Georgia O'Keeffe; only a small trace of George Sessions Perry, prominent Texas man of letters (but it is an interesting trace and can be seen at the Harry Ransom Humanities Research Center in Austin). It is a huge, rich, stimulating collection of thousands of letters written over a huge stretch of time, and usually with both sides of the correspondence available—a rarity in archives of letters—because at a fairly early stage in her career she started keeping carbon copies of the letters she sent out. So we can see, again and again, the real interaction of these creative minds in contact with each other.

The style of Porter's letters is simply sparkling. When Malcolm Cowley said that her masterpieces were her letters, she was very angry and wrote to Caroline Gordon that even if it were true (which "God forbid!") she heard in his statement "an echo of cheerful masculine voices down the centuries saying, 'On his mother's side also our hero inherited some gleam of literary talent, for she was a writer of delightful letters.'"[1] That is, Porter heard in Cowley's remark an echo of her father's advice. But she went on to concede to Gordon that she did "not despise good letters" and was glad if she could believe she wrote a good one "now and then." Indeed she did. The collection published several years ago by Atlantic Monthly Press, edited by Isabel Bayley, gives a fair indication and is to be commended, so long as one doesn't assume it represents the full sweep of her letters (no one volume could) or that the letters always appear in precisely accurate form. Bayley selected and in some cases silently edited the letters in the volume in order to establish the picture of Porter that she announced, quite openly, as what she believed to be the real and authentic one: a witty but also kind and generous person. That Porter was real. But there were many sides to Katherine Anne Porter, and a fuller sampling of her letters is needed to represent those various sides. Porter's letters ought to be published, if not in their entirety (which would be an enormous undertaking), then at least in a series of complete correspondence of Porter and. . . . At one time there was a plan on the part of Porter's agent, Cyrilly Abels, to get together a volume of her correspondence with Glenway Wescott, but the two parties themselves became involved and between them they talked and edited it to death. It never appeared. But it is a wonderful correspondence that fully merits publication.

Two of the other most remarkable series are those with Robert Penn Warren and with Josephine Herbst. The Warren letters are filled with literary talk of each other's writing, the Herbst letters with politics and with their shared exploration of what it meant to be a woman making her way in the world in endeavors customarily reserved for men, but at the same time maintaining her enjoyment of activities customarily regarded as feminine. The Warren letters begin in the early 1930s; the Herbst letters in the 1920s. Both continue for many years and from many far-flung places. In both cases, reading them one has a sense of a lifeline being thrown out. Porter was indeed writing letters to her friends, as her father had urged her to do, but she was not by any means staying at home to do it. It is more that her long friendships became a kind of home for her; home became a relationship rather than a place; and she kept up her correspondences—which often took time she needed to spend on writing that she not only wanted to do but needed to do, for income—as a way of maintaining her ties to something secure.

In the case of her family, of course, writing home was a way of maintaining ties to something secure in the sense of place as well as relationship. Her identity was very much tied up with her geographic origins as well as her familial origins; the two operated as one. It is in these letters to family members—most notably her father and her elder sister, Gay—that we most clearly see her maintaining her ties to home even while she rambled away from home. These letters begin as early as 1916, when Porter would have been twenty-six, separated from her first husband, and living away from family, but not yet away from Texas. Writing to her father from a tuberculosis hospital in Dallas in 1916, she wishes the family a happy Christmas, reminds him of the unhappy Christmas they had spent two years before, and tells him how she is being a Santa Claus (that is, maintaining a home ritual away from home) for children in the hospital.[2] In 1919, from Denver, she wrote exulting in her expectation of being in New York by the end of the year and in Europe by the next spring—that is, exulting in her geographic mobility.[3] In April 1920, writing from New York, she commented on her father's plans for settling down and slid directly into her own homing urge but also listed her reasons for staying away from home. It is the clearest possible illustration of her contrary impulses:

> Lord, how we do go back to the soil we sprang from as we grow up. I think all the time of a house in the country, a riot of old fashioned growing things all mixed up together. I should love to live here, but I can't imagine settling down in a country where figs and peaches and climbing roses don't flourish. On the other hand, I hate like the devil to think of the south again for a residence. So far as I can see, I am out of that country forever and a day. Here is where I can work, and where I can work, there I live.[4]

On December 31, 1920, she wrote from Mexico City, "I can not tell you how far I have come." She was not referring just to miles, but to inner travel as well.[5]

From Mexico, from Europe, from New York again, from all the many places she went in her much-traveled life, she kept up a stream of letters home, telling her family what she had discovered, what she was doing, how she was feeling, sometimes asking them for money (in one of the classic traditions of the letter home), sometimes berating them, sometimes regretting the strife that had troubled them as a family in the past and continued to do so. Running intermittently through these letters home is the promise that she will come for a visit—a promise she repeatedly broke. Around March 1943, after her father's death, she added another family correspondent, her nephew Paul Porter. That particular exchange of letters, stretching over many years, is one of the liveliest and also the most revealing of her character, for good and for ill. A few of the most remarkable of Aunt Katherine's letters to Paul are printed in the *Collected Essays and Occasional Writings*. But those few are not by any means the only remarkable ones in the series. This is also one of the most painful sequences in the Porter correspondence, demonstrating how her feelings shifted and clashed from time to time and how hurtful she could be toward those she loved. All in all, Porter's huge correspondence provides a lively chronicle of a mind alert, responsive, and always sensitive, always ready to be hurt—or to be touched.

One of the sad things about Porter as a writer of letters is, as I have said, that she seems at times to have used letter writing as a strategy for avoiding the writing of fiction that she wanted and needed to do—the writing that we as readers want her to have done. Her published corpus is rather modest, both because of her high standards for her art and because she was notoriously a sufferer from writer's block.[6] One wonders if she might have written more fiction if she had written fewer letters. On the other hand, her letters may have helped her write by keeping her engaged, during the down times, with the production of words and by maintaining her sense of attachment to the personal structure of security in her life. She was herself keenly aware of the interrelation of letter writing and fiction writing. It is not surprising, then, to see that there are quite a few letters in her fiction; they pop up rather often. When they do, they do so at crucial points.

One of the most familiar of these would be the smuggling of letters in "Flowering Judas," one of the best known and most consistently praised of Porter's stories. Tom Walsh has elucidated this incident, along with the politically dangerous letters of "The Charmed Life," [7] as disguised references to Porter's actually having read and copied letters that implicated General Fernando Vizcaino in a plot against the government and resulted in his execution. The incident was known at the time as the "Oaxaca conspiracy" (Walsh 23–24, 44–46). Crucial letters indeed! But there are others that, if less highly charged in their public import, are nonetheless very important.

In "Old Mortality" Gabriel writes letters to Amy "from Saratoga and from Kentucky and from New Orleans, sending her presents, and flowers packed in ice, and telegrams" (Porter, *CS* 181). These are letters home designed to remind her of his love and to create an illusion that he is doing well. We might read a number of Porter's own letters home in much the same way. Amy leaves a note for her parents when she rides off to the Mexican border with Harry after he has taken a shot at her irregular suitor at a masquerade ball, and she writes letters to Harry while he is there (Porter, *CS* 189–90). Great-Aunt Sally writes to Amy about the shooting incident "in a spidery hand adept at archaic symbols and abbreviations," urging her to repent (Porter, *CS* 189). After Amy abruptly marries Gabriel, she writes a letter home from New Orleans telling her mother what a gay time she is having but revealing, in spite of her brittle good cheer, her sense of doom (Porter, *CS* 191–92). Not long afterward, a nurse writes to Amy's parents telling them that she is dead. And all of these letters are just in Part I! In Part II of "Old Mortality," Miranda's and Maria's father urges them to write him "nice long letters" (Porter, *CS* 205), but we never know whether they do, and indeed at that point in the story the theme is shifting to Miranda's growing estrangement from her father. Letters slip out of the text, at the same time that the text is tracing the process of Miranda's loosening her ties to home. It is a familiar enough story. As Porter said, everything she wrote really happened, only she did something to it.

In "Noon Wine," another work generally numbered among Porter's masterpieces, a letter home leads to the destruction of the taciturn hired man, Mr. Helton. He writes to his mother sending money, and his pursuer, Mr. Hatch, uses the bank on which the check was drawn to track him down (Porter, *CS* 253). An equally terrible irony is attached to letters in "Pale Horse, Pale Rider." Adam leaves notes for Miranda, which she is too sick to grasp, and when she recovers, the only letter that means anything to her is not from anyone she knows but from a stranger, telling her that Adam has died. This, I think, is important. Traditionally, a soldier's superior officer writes to the soldier's home to inform his family of death. In this case, he also writes to Miranda, who is not family at all but has become family-like in importance because of their love. This is the bond that many of Porter's letters to her friends constitute—not ties to home, in any precise sense, but ties to an emotional structure that served her in the place of home, however far she—like Gabriel or Helton or Adam—wandered.

However far she went—and she went very far indeed, in both a geographical and a metaphorical sense—Porter always cared about home. Or it might be more accurate to say that she always cared about the *idea* of home. In a *Paris Review* interview of 1963 by Barbara Thompson, Porter stated she was a member of the "white-pillar crowd."[8] She wanted very much to be able to think of her life as being anchored in a big family home with white pillars. Of course, it wasn't. And so, much as she wanted home, she found home unacceptable. When she returned to Texas in 1936 to visit her family (for the first time in fifteen years), she quickly became restless, and even after she confessed herself moved and warmed by that renewed contact and the visiting of places from her childhood, she preferred to write letters rather than spend extended periods of time near family. With nearly complete freedom to choose where she would live—freedom, that is, within financial constraints, but given the way she made her living these were fewer than for most people—she did not choose to live in Texas. By that time, the 1930s, and after, Texas must scarcely have seemed like home to her anyway; she had been away and moving about for a long time. But it was more nearly home than anything else she had. It represented the *idea* of home.

The idea of home, or of leaving home or returning to home, looms large in much of Porter's fiction—even larger than the idea of letters. It is especially strong and especially redolent of her actual Central Texas origins in the "Old Order" stories, where the grandmother's life is organized between two poles of existence, her home in town and her home at the farm. When she dies, in faraway West Texas, she has been visiting the home of her married son and attempting to make it over her own way—attempting to make another woman's home her own. Givner suggests that the Gays' large town house was modeled on the house Porter rented during her months in Bermuda in 1928, Hilgrove. If so, it is in a sense all the more remarkable how home-centered Porter's imagination was. Occupying that house built in the two-story veranda style of the southern Great House, she thought of it in terms of the home she had always wanted, and transported it, in her imagination, to Texas—or at any rate, to the South, making it a southern family home in a place that sometimes seems like Texas and sometimes seems more like Louisiana or Mississippi.

This strong home-presence is found in much of Porter's other work as well. In "'Noon Wine': The Sources" she speaks with a luxuriance of love and nostalgia of "my own place, my South" and of "my past and my own house and my own people—the native land of my heart . . . the society of my childhood" (Porter, *CE* 470, 472). Here is her paean to that home place:

> This summer country of my childhood, this place of memory, is filled with landscapes shimmering in light and color, moving with sounds and shapes I hardly ever describe, or put in my stories in so many words; they form only the living background of what I am trying to tell, so familiar to my characters they would hardly notice them; the sound of mourning doves in the live oaks . . . all the life of that soft blackland farming country, full of fruits and flowers and birds, with good hunting and good fishing; with plenty of water, many little and big rivers. I shall name just a few of the rivers I remember—the San Antonio, the San Marcos, the Trinity, the Nueces, the Rio Grande, the Colorado, and the small clear branch of the Río Blanco, full of colored pebbles, Indian Creek, the place where I was born.

I don't believe we can find a more lyrical passage in any of her writing, and it is a passage about home. But if home is lyrical, it is also the place where, according to the same essay, she hears the shotgun report "like a blow of thunder echoing and rolling in that green sky" (Porter, *CE* 474) and a scream—the sounds of death. Home, it seems, is a complex place. It is never, for Porter, a *simple* presence.

In the first section of "Old Mortality" some of the most powerful scenes take place in the attic of the family home—that is, the place in the house most fully given to relics from the past, and thus to a sense of home-continuity. But it is precisely this home and the human relationships it represents that Miranda must flee, not once, in the story, but twice. Her imagination may turn back to that place and to the morning quiet there, in "Pale Horse, Pale Rider," but it is also the place where her ride on Graylie is toward death and alongside the "lank greenish stranger" whose rags "flapped upon his bones" (Porter, *CS* 270). Miranda's reminiscence of home is of a place where everyone is "tangled together like badly cast fishing lines" (Porter, *CS* 269).

Again and again Porter is concerned with the inadequacy of home (in "The Downward Path to Wisdom," "He," "Old Mortality") and with people who need to leave home but nevertheless suffer a sense of loss after they do. The final situation in story after story is one of loss. Much of what is lost is home. For all her memories of rides on Graylie and of sitting with Grandmother in the attic and going over old relics of the past, Miranda can't go back home at the end of "Pale Horse, Pale Rider" any more than she can at the end of "Old Mortality." "How I have loved this house in the morning before we are all awake," she recalls (Porter, *CS* 269), but she returns to it only in dreams. At the end of "He" the inadequately loved child (and we know that Porter felt herself to be that) is being banished from home and, contrary to all expectation, knows it. He responds by crying, but there is no cure for his pain or for that of anyone in the family. They are all overwhelmed by the situation presented to them and cannot—even if he were capable of it—communicate their feelings.

No more can Miranda communicate her feeling of loss at the end of "The Grave" as she stands in a faraway place, among strangers and unfamiliar foods that nevertheless remind her of home, looking back toward the home-time of childhood. She sees, in memory, her brother, her link to home, but he looks as detached from her as she is in fact now detached from him. No communication is shown or implied, and we have no reason to believe that her regret or nostalgia or loneliness (whatever this complex emotion is) will ever be communicated to those at home. She writes no letter.

The position of Miranda at the end of "The Grave" is very much the position of Porter herself—far away in Mexico (or one of the other far-flung places she was always traveling to), reaching back in memory with something like fondness or at any rate like longing, but never quite able to convey to her family what she feels about them or how she feels about the past that they shared. Unlike Miranda (or unlike anything we ever see Miranda do) she wrote letters home. By turning so insistently to the writing of self-referential fiction, set in places that were in fact her own (however she may have slanted them toward the Old South), she was in effect writing another form of letter home. And the two kinds intersect. The record of her *actual* correspondence shows her attempts to ensure that her birth family read her fiction. She sent them copies; she called their attention to what she had written. We would all do the same. But not only her actual letters but also her fictions of the South and of home were attempts to write home.

The phrase "writing home" or "to write home" can be read in two very different ways. It may mean to write *to* home, to write a letter to the people at home. Or it may mean to write *about* home. As we have seen, Porter "wrote home" in both senses. She wrote letters home—a great many of them—and she wrote home, created home in words, in her fiction. But what I'm now suggesting is that we can see her fiction as another kind of letter—a series of communications from the safe distance of a perspective located elsewhere, that ponder the meaning of home, and also a series of communications directed home, to the attention of her family. Thinking about Porter's fiction in that way, we might ask what was motivating these "letters." What did she want to say to her family? Her stories may have been disguised attempts to convey to them her feelings about the past and to explain her reasons for absenting herself, and thus to ingratiate herself once more into the family structure.

If read by her family as letters, Porter's stories show again and again how she had felt about home. In "He," in the various Miranda stories, in the miserably unhappy child of "The Downward Path to Wisdom," she told her father and her sisters and brother how unloved and misunderstood she had felt as a child. These stories, even more than her actual and very turbulent letters to them, were her attempts to tell them what home had been like for her and why she had had to leave it. We cannot be surprised that she could not tell them directly. So strong a sense of compulsion as is reflected in Porter's incessant traveling can scarcely be explained in so many words. We know that her family was offended when she failed to return home, for example, when her niece Mary Alice, Gay's little girl, died or when their father died. These stories become, in a sense, her effort to justify herself.

In one sense, Porter's intended audience for her fiction was her fellow modernists, her fellow writers with the discernment and the commitment to art to grasp what she was doing, technically. But in another, it seems to me, her intended audience was home folks, in the most immediate sense of the term. Writing letters home—both actual letters and the "letters" of her fiction—was a way of maintaining her ties but even more her sense of rootedness, all the while she rambled. It was a way of counteracting her sense of disconnectedness. Like John Donne's compass, they were the fixed foot that stayed at the center, while the free foot ranged about.

Maybe Malcolm Cowley was right, after all, when he said that Porter's masterpieces were her letters. Or, to alter his phrasing just slightly, maybe her masterpieces—"Old Mortality," "The Old Order," "He," "Noon Wine," "Pale Horse, Pale Rider"—*were* letters. ❖

Notes

[1] KAP to Caroline Gordon, Dec. 14, 1931, Bayley, ed., *Letters* 70. The letter to Burke that is quoted in the second epigraph is also found in Bayley 23.

[2] KAP to Harrison Boone Porter, Dec. 21, 1916, Maryland. I am grateful to the University of Maryland, College Park, Libraries and to Barbara Thompson Davis, literary executor, for permission to quote from unpublished letters.

[3] KAP to "Baby," no month or day, 1919, Maryland.

[4] KAP to Harrison Boone Porter and unnamed sister (probably Gay), Apr. 1, 1920, Maryland.

[5] KAP to family (probably father and Gay), Dec. 31, 1920, Maryland.

[6] Joan Givner proposes that she had, in the most literal way, a short attention span, and therefore had difficulty completing works of more than a very limited scope; Givner, *Life* 164.

[7] Porter, *Collected Stories* 94, and *Collected Essays* 429.

[8] Thompson, "Katherine Anne Porter: An Interview," in *Conversations*, ed. Givner 83. The interview was originally published in the *Paris Review* in 1963 and was reprinted in *Writers at Work: The Paris Review Interviews*, Second Series, ed. Malcolm Cowley, that same year.

Works Cited

Bayley, Isabel, ed. *Letters of Katherine Anne Porter*. New York: Atlantic Monthly P, 1990.

Cather, Willa. *The Song of the Lark*. 1915. New York: Bantam Books, 1991.

Givner, Joan, ed. *Katherine Anne Porter: Conversations*. Jackson: UP of Mississippi, 1987.

———. *Katherine Anne Porter: A Life.* Rev. ed. Athens: U of Georgia P, 1991.

Porter, Katherine Anne. *The Collected Essays and Occasional Writings of Katherine Anne Porter.* Boston: Houghton Mifflin/Seymour Lawrence, 1970.

———. *Collected Stories of Katherine Anne Porter.* New York: Harcourt Brace Jovanovich, 1965.

Stout, Janis P. *Through the Window, Out the Door: Women's Narratives of Departure.* Tuscaloosa: U of Alabama P, 1998.

Thompson, Barbara. "Katherine Anne Porter: An Interview." *Katherine Anne Porter: Conversations.* Ed. Joan Givner. Jackson: UP of Mississippi, 1987.

Walsh, Thomas F. *Katherine Anne Porter and Mexico: The Illusion of Eden.* Austin: U of Texas P, 1992.

Katherine Anne Porter's Birthdays

Darlene Harbour Unrue

"I love my birthday," Katherine Anne Porter wrote to a friend in the spring of 1924 as she begged for a "little letter" that would reach her specifically on the fifteenth of May. She further explained to her friend, "I was always so happy to have been born!"[1] The tone of the letter, however, may be a contradiction of her state of mind, for Katherine Anne had many reasons for depression and anxiety that spring, including poverty, loneliness, and the likelihood that she was pregnant with an illegitimate child. Her assertion about her birthday's importance to her, on the other hand, was true.[2]

She had come to regard May fifteenth as a mystical day, an occasion for commemoration and personal assessment and a hedge against disaster. It was propitious, she had concluded, because it marked the sunny Thursday in 1890 when she had emerged into the world, the physical manifestation of her mother's sacrificial pain and unconditional love. As a day of personal assessment, the anniversary of her birth was both a Janus-day and a haven-day, on which she could safely look back at the past year's suffering and failure and also look sanguinely forward to the next year of her life. A friend figuratively described such an annual phenomenon as Katherine Anne's shedding of the past as a locust sheds its shell, hanging it somewhere, leaving it finished and done with, and beginning a new life.[3]

For Katherine Anne, May fifteenth also had become a day to remember the mother who gave life to her and likewise a day to suffer guilt. Because she sanctified her dead mother, imagining her a beautiful and purely good woman who personified the domestic ideals of wifehood and motherhood—becoming a martyr to both—Katherine Anne's failure to succeed as either a wife or a mother lingered darkly in her mind as a betrayal not only of her mother but, indeed, of womanhood itself, a theme that runs through her fiction. She would attempt to compensate for the treason by mastering the arts, domestic as well as fine and literary, and until the very end she never completely abandoned her search for a man who would enable her to become a more nearly perfect woman.

No one knows in what year Katherine Anne registered the significance of her birthday. There are no contemporaneous accounts of her birthday celebrations when she was a child named Callie. Her mother, Alice Jones Porter, who died in March of 1892, would have been present only for Callie's first birthday anniversary, spent at Indian Creek, where the family then lived.[4] And Callie's second birthday would have been given only passing notice by her father, Harrison Boone (Harry) Porter, who by May of 1892 was preparing to take his four motherless children to Kyle to move in with his widowed mother, Catharine Ann Skaggs Porter.

Nothing is known about Callie's third through eleventh birthdays, spent in Kyle. No doubt she sorely missed her mother, who would have told her how happy she was that Callie was born and might even have described the drama of the day of birth. In the absence of her mother, whom she had to imagine, the creative child also turned to fantasy as she invested her birth with fictional possibilities. A voracious reader from an early age, she was fascinated by stories about fairies and saints and beautiful, sad heroines—all, one might say, versions of her mother. As she surveyed her prosaic Calvinist existence with her elderly grandmother and disconsolate father, she liked to imagine that she had not really been born to that family, that she was a changeling left at their door by fairies.[5] Although in late childhood she relinquished the details of that illusion, she clung to the part of it that made her a person separate from the rest of her family. She began to create future possibilities for herself that were appropriate to her differences. She thought she might become a nun (beautiful and melodramatically sad, of course) or even a martyr such as Joan of Arc. Or perhaps she might become an actress, as she naively declared to a visiting clergyman, for which announcement she was soundly whipped by her grandmother.[6]

The grandmother made another kind of impression on Callie, who tried to absorb her discipline, security, and well-bred antebellum ancestry by appropriating a version of her name. At the age of fourteen, when her grandmother had been dead three years, Callie informally changed her name to "Katherine," more suitable also, she thought, for the actress she wanted to become. At the age of sixteen, however, abandoning her ambitions to become either an actress or a nun, she married. Although there are those who might say that in the brutal first marriage Katherine nearly fulfilled her childhood ambition to become a martyr, the reality was less grand. Remaining with her violent and abusive husband for nearly eight years, she finally made a bold decision. Defying friends, relatives, and priests who told her she was casting herself into outer darkness, she filed for divorce on May 15, 1915, her twenty-fifth birthday.[7] It was the first recorded instance of her using the anniversary of her birth as a symbolic reassurance, a good omen, a guarantee of safe conduct into her future.

The auspiciousness of her birthday, however, did not protect her during the next four years from more disappointment, further physical suffering, and financial hardship—the result of many failed love affairs, long miserable months in tuberculosis hospitals, a brush with death during the influenza epidemic of 1918, and the loss of a beloved niece.[8] Nevertheless, Katherine *Anne*, as she called herself by then (further strengthening her identification with her indomitable grandmother Catharine Ann Skaggs Porter), emerged from the years of ordeal with a significant writing apprenticeship behind her, a number of devoted and admiring friends, and a newfound purpose in the artistic life she had chosen to pursue. To become an artist, she assured herself and others, would be the noblest of achievements, nobler even than to become a wife and a mother.

Throughout the 1920s and early 1930s Katherine Anne pursued her goal and fought her demons. An abortion in Mexico in 1921 and the stillbirth of the child with whom she in fact was pregnant in 1924 were among traumatic experiences that distanced her from the standard set by her idealized dead mother, the sanctified wife and nurturer of children.[9] Intensifying her private sense of unworthiness was her inability by the mid-1920s to produce a long work of fiction. Linking both kinds of failure to the day of her birth, she wrote in a marginal note in 1927, "Thursday's child has far to go."[10]

Katherine Anne's frustration and depression reached a peak in 1929, when she had yet to publish a book and when still another love affair failed. The predictable physical and emotional breakdown that followed the disappointment in love brought forward sympathetic friends who arranged for her to have a sojourn in Bermuda to recover her health and to get on with her writing.[11] The six months she spent on the island, from March to August, were artistically and personally important, and no days were more significant than those that surrounded her thirty-ninth birthday. May fifteenth was normally a day on which she looked hopefully to the future despite the misery of the year behind her. This year, however, once past her birthday, she was

41

looking toward forty years of age, and she had no husband or lover, as she lamented to a friend in a letter, no substantial or wide literary reputation, and not yet a book to her credit.[12] She would recreate her state of mind for her autobiographical character Mary Treadwell in *Ship of Fools*, who celebrates her forty-sixth birthday during the voyage:

> It was Mrs. Treadwell's birthday, not the first she had spent alone on a train or a ship; she was feeling her age . . . as a downright affront to her aesthetic sense. All the forties were so hopelessly middle-aged, so much too late to die young, so much too early to think of death at all. (247)

As a result of Katherine Anne's depression and profound loneliness in 1929 (and perhaps because she was working then on stories that were deeply personal to her, focusing on femaleness and self-betrayal[13]), she began to yearn obsessively for "home"—vaguely defined in her mind as a place over which her mother hovered protectively, a place of sunshine and warmth, of cape jasmine and wild roses, of berries and melons. She tried to put her deep longing in the form of poems that she tentatively titled "Night Blooming Cereus" and "West Indian Island." In "Night Blooming Cereus" she defined the night as the time the child returns to its mother.[14] In the much longer and more richly developed "West Indian Island," she made a hurricane a metaphor for her turbulent emotions and called upon the Fates to lift her from misery:

> . . . let me return thus
> To a familiar country,
>
> ⌒
>
> This land
> Will receive me as a friend, as a member

Of the family, will not mock at my journeys, nor
recall them to me, nor deny them,
But will say easily, "So daughter, you are late,
But come in, and welcome!"[15]

Both poems may contain a temporary wish for death, but "West Indian Island" also includes an exoneration for her nomadic wanderings that kept her away from a family hearth. Home, as it were, whether Texas or the grave of Alice Porter, promised unconditional love, absolution, and tranquility.

For seven years, Katherine Anne dealt with the compulsion to go "home" to her mother, an urgent desire always felt most severely on her birthday. Among the manifestations of the compulsion was an obsessive interest in her family history and in the circumstances of her birth. As she wrote to her father pressing him for accounts of her ancestry— telling him she wished to have such information because it would be a barrier against her homesickness—she also asked that he tell her the exact hour and other details of her birth.[16] What she did not confess to her rationalist father was that she was trying to find, in the facts surrounding her birth, fixed, astrological, causes for her unconventional life that would absolve her from responsibility.

But there remained more deeply psychological reasons for her obsession with her birth than an interest in astrology. The complexity is glimpsed in a fictionalized account of the event that she recorded during this same period. Katherine Anne was the fourth child born to Harry and Alice Porter. Their third child, Johnnie, had died of typhoid fever a little past his first birthday, several months before Katherine Anne was born. In the fictional version of her birth, Katherine Anne, who already had settled on the name "Miranda" for the most autobiographical of her fictional characters, created a scene that included her father, her pregnant mother, and their first three children. The baby, Johnnie, has been left behind with a black caretaker while the other members of the family go for an afternoon walk. Johnnie sneaks off, however, and runs to catch up with them. The rest of the dramatic account is important enough to quote fully:

> Crying, he stumbled and fell, and sat in the hot white dust, crying. The mother heard and looked back. Struck to the heart at seeing her baby fall, she turned and in her terrible silence that always frightened her husband, she began to run back, heavy and lurching as she went. Harry went back more slowly, irritated, annoyed, determined to take no part in this badly managed domestic muddle. Where was the nigger? Why in all hell couldn't a whole houseful of niggers manage to keep one two year old baby from wandering into the road? When he came up to Alice, she was holding the baby in both arms, bending over a little, and silently, her face like a mad woman's, she was grinding and stamping something under her heel. . . .
>
> A tarantula had stung the child on the neck; but Alice said nothing, only stopped stamping her foot after a few seconds, and placed her mouth to the small wound and began to suck and spit out and suck again, until Harry, quite beside himself, began to curse horribly, took the child away, and finally got a word or two for her—enough to explain. . . . Then he rushed them all into the house, and holding Alice, he forced into her mouth the strongest antiseptic he could find; silently she struggled and fought, her eyes wild, and only gave up when he said, "Oh, Alice, remember the baby," and suddenly she quieted and began to wash her mouth and lips by herself. . . . Then Sam rode out for the doctor, and the other children were sent to the backyard and told to stay there . .

. 3 days later the baby died, and the following day Alice went to
see him buried, sitting in a chair at the head of the grave, her
hands folded on her knees. . . . That night Miranda was born.
(Author's punctuation.)[17]

There are, of course, major differences between the reality and
the fiction, but what is especially significant in the imagined account is
that the relationship between Alice and Katherine Anne is given still
more importance. Alice, the essential mother, sacrifices her living son to
save her unborn, unknown child. It is not only the ultimate sacrifice—
and divine—it is the greatest testament to Alice's extraordinary love
for Katherine Anne. The fantasy may also be another construction of
Katherine Anne's justification of her childlessness, her aborted child of
1921 conflated in her stillborn male child of 1924, both children sacri-
ficed in order that the artist might survive.

Indeed, soon after the crisis of identity in 1929, Katherine Anne's
success as an artist began to be acknowledged by the literary world. Her
first collection of stories, *Flowering Judas*, was published in 1930 to substantial critical praise.[18] As a result, she received a Guggenheim
Fellowship in 1931 and sailed for Europe, making the journey with
Eugene Pressly, whom she would marry in 1933. For four years, from
1932 to 1936, she lived with Pressly in Paris and worked sporadically on
a biography of Cotton Mather and especially on stories in the Miranda
cycle, drawn from her childhood experiences and her grandmother's
stories about the family's past.[19]

Despite such a significant contribution to her artistic goals, her
personal conflicts remained powerful. By 1935 it was clear that her
marriage was failing, proving once again that she could not succeed as
a wife or, by hypothetical extension, a mother, and she frequently was
ill and depressed. Her natural response to such a mental state had long

been to find solace in a ritual of retreat from the immediate source of the misery. Thus in the spring of 1936, she made a journey back to America alone, ostensibly to revisit Boston to do more Mather research, but with the deeply significant purpose of making a pilgrimage to her mother's grave at Indian Creek. Arriving there the week before her birthday, she planted a rose bush near the tombstone, and on a scrap of paper she impulsively composed a poem she titled "Birthday in a Country Cemetery" and buried under the soil of her mother's grass-strewn grave. The poem begins, "This time of year, this year of all years/ Brought the homeless one home again." It ends with no elegiac reconciliation.[20]

During the course of the next six years, in which she divorced Eugene Pressly, married Albert Erskine, and divorced him, she revised the poem several times (in 1940 retitling it "Anniversary in a Country Cemetery") while she searched for that still elusive state of contentment.[21] Her psychological salvation lay primarily in her art, as she had long known. Thus, as her literary reputation increased, her birthdays became more completely celebratory occasions, often marked by parties she gave for herself. One such party, that in honor of her fifty-fourth birthday, is described by the painter Marcella Winslow, with whom Katherine Anne was boarding in Georgetown. "She is spending about $50 on the party" (nearly a month's rent), Marcella reported to her mother-in-law and described the preparations: "Besides a capon [and ham] [Katherine Anne] is ordering a cake at Avignone Freres, pistachio ice cream, candles, nuts, and liquor (brandy!)" "[W]e expect a big evening," Marcella exulted, thankful, as she said, that Katherine Anne had "hired a man to do it all" (62–63).

Perhaps because Katherine Anne had found solace in art, she began to recall with more satisfaction the 1936 visit to her mother's grave. In 1956, twenty years after the pilgrimage, she revised

"Anniversary in a Country Cemetery" again, making it a true elegy in which reconciliation appears in the last lines. Whereas the 1940 version had concluded with the persona's arriving at the graveyard merely as "the shape of her [mother's] pain," sixteen years later Katherine Anne had found comfort as the "shape of her [mother's] love, sweet as the dust of roses."[22]

The affirmation of her art, which made consolation possible, had continued steadily since 1930, and still more validation was to come. In 1962 she at last completed *Ship of Fools,* her only long novel, which brought her financial security. Three years later with the publication of her *Collected Stories,* she gathered in laurels for which she had long been waiting.[23]

After all the accomplishments and pleasures and personal reconciliations, in her eighth decade Katherine Anne began to look toward death and once again began to think of home, her mother, and her mother's grave at Indian Creek. In May of 1976, forty years after the 1936 visit, she made another pilgrimage. The "birthday party" in her "homeland," as she referred to her 1976 trip to Texas, was arranged by faculty and administrators of Howard Payne College in Brownwood. The occasion was celebrated with an excursion to the cemetery, a reception on the campus, an honorary degree at the college's commencement, and a symposium to which scholars around the country had been invited. The high point of the symposium was a banquet at which Katherine Anne gave a talk. Dressed in a white Mexican wedding dress, she reminisced about her birth at nearby Indian Creek, and she told her audience about her trip to the cemetery: "We took flowers," she said, "and we had a picnic. And it was one of the happy times of my life."[24] Those words, however, were an incomplete summary according to the persons who accompanied her to the grave; afterward she had become so overwrought she wept and asked for a doctor. Rather than the happiness of life, it was clear throughout her speech that death was on her mind. She described in detail the Mexican coffin she had bought for her burial next to her mother. And before she left Brownwood, she was reported to have visited an undertaker to explain that she wanted the poem "Anniversary in a Country Cemetery" engraved on her tombstone.

Several months later Katherine Anne suffered the first of the series of severe strokes that for four years would gradually diminish her. For three of those years she nevertheless was able to muster enough spirit to announce to birthday well-wishers that she planned to recover and to finish writing the books she had started. Even in 1979, despite severely limited mobility and strength, she was able to oversee her birthday celebration, planning the menu and giving explicit instructions to her maid, making sure the event was up to her high standard of successful entertaining. In those years, however, there also were indications that Katherine Anne was acknowledging her swift progress toward death. In 1978 she told more than one friend that death would be a comfort.

Katherine Anne's final celebration of her birthday took place May 15, 1980, at the Carriage Hill Nursing Home in Silver Spring, Maryland. Having suffered an especially debilitating stroke a few months earlier, she was frail, bedridden, and unable to form the connected sounds of articulated speech. For this occasion, the ninetieth anniversary of her birth, five of her friends had arranged an afternoon party, which included red and white roses, balloons, and gifts and culminated in birthday cake, ice cream, and champagne wheeled into her small room on a cart.[25]

Katherine Anne, however, seemed preoccupied, unable to manage the champagne even with a straw, and barely touching the cake. The ice cream, usually a favorite, melted uneaten. The friends fell into long hushed silences when she struggled to tell them something at which they could only guess. They supposed her "unordered sounds," as one friend later said, were meant to be a "disavowal of the place in which they found her." With her unparalyzed left hand she gestured an arc that took in the small room but was meant to encompass her diminished life. She seemed to be saying, "I have never lived this way and do not wish to do so now." She clung to one friend who handed her a rosary, while another friend assured her, "We are with you. We love you."

Her birthday had ceased to be a haven-day of good omens. No longer able to create the art that sustained her, she could only look backward, not forward. One friend thought it symbolic that her "writing hand" was the paralyzed one, the kind nurse who gently placed the hand inside the bedcover, with unintentional irony referring to it as the "baby" that had to be tucked in. It was of course the only surviving child she had, but it finally had been enough. Katherine Anne would live only a few months longer. She died on the nineteenth of September.

At some point within the four years after her 1976 visit to her mother's grave, she had changed her mind about her own epitaph, deciding on "In my end is my beginning," words of Mary Queen of Scots quoted by T. S. Eliot. It was appropriate in many ways, as she knew. To be returned to her mother in death was also to return to her own birth, the relationship between the womb and tomb a prevalent theme in her fiction, as more than one critic has observed.[26] Her final journey to that graveyard took place in the spring of 1981. On a day filled with sunlight, roses, and cape jasmine, her ashes were buried in a grave beside her mother's. She was home at last, after a long life's circuitous journey. ❖

Notes

[1] Katherine Anne Porter (KAP) to Genevieve Taggard, May 10, 1924, Katherine Anne Porter Papers, University of Maryland, College Park, Libraries. This letter as well as all other unpublished material from the Katherine Anne Porter Papers and the Isabel Bayley Papers is quoted with permission of the University of Maryland, College Park, Libraries and Barbara Thompson Davis, Trustee, the Katherine Anne Porter Literary Estate.

[2] According to Porter's letter to Taggard of Nov. 14, 1924, she was pregnant with a child due to be born the middle of January. A letter from Porter to Taggard Dec. 18, 1924, reveals that the child, a male, had been stillborn Dec. 2, 1924. Katherine Anne Porter Papers, University of Maryland, College Park, Libraries.

[3] Kitty Barry Crawford to Donald L. Stalling, interview of Mar. 2, 1951. Paraphrased by Stalling 65.

[4] According to her tombstone in the Indian Creek Cemetery, Alice Porter [Mary Alice Jones Porter] died Mar. 20, 1892.

[5] KAP, autobiographical notes, Katherine Anne Porter Papers, University of Maryland at College Park Libraries.

[6] KAP, autobiographical notes; Gay Porter Holloway to KAP, July 25, 1954; KAP to Gay Porter Holloway, Nov. 13, 1961; KAP to Erna Schlemmer Johns, Feb. 5, 1963; Erna Schlemmer Johns to KAP, May 3, 1931; Katherine Anne Porter Papers, University of Maryland, College Park, Libraries.

[7] KAP married John Henry Koontz June 20, 1906; the divorce was granted June 21, 1915 (divorce judgment 19893-C, District Court 68, Dallas County, Texas).

[8] Rumors have persisted for years in Texas that among KAP's failed love affairs between 1915 and 1920 were two additional failed

marriages. Her experience in the flu epidemic provided the raw material for "Pale Horse, Pale Rider," published in 1938. Her beloved niece was Mary Alice Holloway, daughter of her sister Gay. Mary Alice died in July 1919 of spinal meningitis.

[9] KAP's friend Mary Doherty confirmed to Thomas F. Walsh that KAP had an abortion in Mexico in 1921 (64). KAP's diary entries for 1920–21 and certain poems she composed in the 1920s support the supposition.

[10] KAP, marginalia, in Henry Charles Lea, *A History of the Middle Ages*, vol. 3 (New York: Harper, 1888), 500; Katherine Anne Porter personal library, preserved at the University of Maryland, College Park, Libraries.

[11] The love affair was with Matthew Josephson. The friends who made her Bermuda trip possible included especially Becky and John Crawford.

[12] KAP to Josephine Herbst, May 21, 1929, Katherine Anne Porter Papers, University of Maryland, College Park, Libraries.

[13] KAP was working on "Flowering Judas" (1930) and "Theft" (1929).

[14] See *Katherine Anne Porter's Poetry* 29–30, 86.

[15] See *Katherine Anne Porter's Poetry* 29–33, 34, 35, 87–89.

[16] See KAP to Harrison Boone Porter, Mar. 22, 1933, Katherine Anne Porter Papers, University of Maryland, College Park, Libraries. KAP's interest in both her ancestry and astrology had been apparent to some degree since 1927, when she was in Salem, MA, researching the Mather family.

[17] KAP, unpublished notes (Many Redeemers), Katherine Anne Porter Papers, University of Maryland, College Park, Libraries. This passage is quoted as KAP wrote it; the periods that resemble ellipses, irregular in number, appear routinely in her letters and notes as an eccentricity of punctuation.

[18] See, e.g., reviews by Louise Bogan, Margaret Cheney Dawson, John McDonald, Allen Tate, Edward Weeks, and Yvor Winters.

[19] Between 1932 and 1936, KAP published "The Circus," "The Grave," and "The Old Order" (title later changed to "The Journey"). She also completed "Old Mortality," which was published in 1937.

[20] See the first drafts of the poem in *Katherine Anne Porter's Poetry* 170–71.

[21] KAP married Eugene Dove Pressly Mar. 18, 1933. She divorced him Apr. 9, 1938, and married Albert Russel Erskine, Jr., Apr. 19, 1938. She divorced Erskine June 19, 1942.

[22] See this version (No. 5) in *Katherine Anne Porter's Poetry* 171–72.

[23] In 1966 KAP received both the Pulitzer Prize and the National Book Award for her *Collected Stories*.

[24] Transcript of KAP speech; collection of the author.

[25] Account of KAP's ninetieth birthday celebration drawn from the unpublished memoir of Isabel Bayley, Isabel Bayley Papers, University of Maryland, College Park, Libraries. The five friends were Isabel Bayley, Jane DeMouy, Clark Dobson, Jack Horner, and Ted Wojtasic.

[26] See, e.g., Glenway Wescott 36.

Works Cited

Bogan, Louise. [Nothing Is Fortuitous]. *New Republic* 64 (Oct. 22, 1930): 277–78.

Dawson, Margaret Cheney. "A Perfect Flowering." *New York Herald Tribune Books* Sept. 14, 1930: 3–4.

McDonald, John. "Chamber Music." *Boulevardier* 6 (Dec. 1930): 22.

Porter, Katherine Anne. "The Circus." *Southern Review* 1 (July 1935): 36–41.

———. *The Collected Stories.* New York: Harcourt Brace, 1965.

———. "The Grave." *Virginia Quarterly Review* 11 (Apr. 1935): 177–87.

———. *Katherine Anne Porter's Poetry.* Ed. Darlene Harbour Unrue. Columbia: U of South Carolina P, 1996.

———. "Old Mortality." *Southern Review* 2 (spring 1937): 686–735.

———. "The Old Order" [The Journey]. *Southern Review* 1 (winter 1936): 498–509.

———. *Ship of Fools.* New York: Atlantic-Little, Brown, 1962.

Stalling, Donald L. "Katherine Anne Porter: Life and the Literary Mirror." M.A. thesis. Texas Christian U, 1951.

Tate, Allen. "A New Star." *Nation* 131 (Oct. 1, 1930): 352–53.

Walsh, Thomas F. *Katherine Anne Porter and Mexico: The Illusion of Eden.* Austin: U of Texas P, 1992.

Weeks, Edward. "The Atlantic Bookshelf." *Atlantic Monthly* 147 (May 1931): 22.

Wescott, Glenway. "Katherine Anne Porter Personally." *Images of Truth.* London: Hamish Hamilton, 1963. 25–58.

Winslow, Marcella Comès. *Brushes with the Literary.* Baton Rouge: Louisiana State UP, 1993.

Winters, Yvor. "Major Fiction." *Hound & Horn* 4 (Jan.-Mar. 1931): 303–05.

Troubled Innocent Abroad: Katherine Anne Porter's Colonial Adventure

Jeraldine R. Kraver

In Katherine Anne Porter's 1924 poem "In Tepozotlan," one of her "Two Songs From Mexico" (Porter, *Essays* 486), the speaker searches for a glimpse of a young beekeeping girl whom she had once seen: "I should like to see again / That honey-colored girl." Her hands, the speaker recalls, "were kissed by bees," and her "fingers dripped honey." She wonders, "Who can tell me where she is gone / That *un*troubled innocent" [emphasis added]. The sense of longing at the heart of the poet's query, the *ubi sunt* that drives Porter's short verse, also defines her Mexican experience. It is, ultimately, lost innocence that informs Porter's troubled relationship with Mexico.

Describing herself in 1920, Porter recalled arriving in Mexico "all fresh and wide-eyed and taking in everything" (Lopez 121). How she responded to all that she "took in," however, has been a source of some critical confusion. In 1963, Daniel Curley suggested that for Porter there was "a moment when Mexico stood for the promised land. The beauty and dignity of primitive people gave her an insight into human possibilities she had never dreamed of" (Curley 660). Curley's interpretation was the standard for more than a decade. However, his conclusion was based upon incomplete information.

Curley had relied on Porter's erroneous dating of her bleak sketch, "The Fiesta of Guadalupe," as 1923. In actuality, it had appeared in 1920. For Curley, this sketch indicated a change from the more optimistic perspective offered in the (what he believed to be earlier) 1922 story, "María Concepción." The story, Curley argued, was an indication that Porter had, at least initially, achieved "insight into human possibilities" among the Mexicans and recognized "that they were indeed descendants of emperors" (680–81). Thus, the pessimistic tone of "The Fiesta of Guadalupe" signaled for Curley a change in Porter's attitude. However, because "The Fiesta of Guadalupe" had, in fact, appeared three years earlier than Porter indicated—that is, before "María Concepción"—the pessimism of the sketch is, as it turns out, Porter's early response to Mexico. The confusion surrounding the dates of Porter's work invalidates Curley's conclusion.

A second revelation was Thomas Walsh's 1979 discovery of "Xochimilco," a sketch published anonymously in May 1921. "Xochimilco" offers an idyllic and highly romanticized look at Mexican Indians. Like "María Concepción," this essay was also written after "The Fiesta of Guadalupe." These discoveries reveal that Porter did not move from the optimism of "María Concepción" to the fatalism of "The Fiesta of Guadalupe." Rather, pessimism colored even her earliest work. Walsh argues that Porter's early and conflicted responses to Mexico are indicative of her "tragic vision of life," one formed even before her arrival in Mexico (Walsh 641).

In *The Colonizer and the Colonized*, Albert Memmi offers an alternate method for approaching and understanding Porter's response to Mexico, a response that, in many ways, reflects the intellectual and emotional dilemmas faced by colonizers. Porter arrived in Mexico hoping "to assist at"[1] a revolution; her friends from Greenwich Village had advised her, "In Mexico something wonderful is going to happen"

(Lopez 121). She never imagined that in her "familiar country," she would adopt the mindset of a colonizer.[2]

For many colonizers, there is an initial response of revulsion, even anger, at the colonial situation. Memmi explains that sometimes a new arrival is "astonished by the large number of beggars, the children wandering about half-naked . . . ill at ease before such obvious organization of injustice, revolted by the cynicism of his fellow citizens. . . ." (19). These emotions define the opening sentence of "The Fiesta of Guadalupe." Porter writes, "I followed a great crowd of *tired burdened* pilgrims, *bowed* under their burdens of potteries and food and babies and baskets, their clothes dusty and their faces a little stained with *long-borne fatigue*" [emphases added] (Porter 394). When the actual conditions of the colonized confront what Memmi identifies as the colonizer's "humanitarian romanticism," the result is "contradiction which looms at every step, depriving [the colonizer] of all coherence and tranquility" (21, 20). For Porter in Mexico, this contradiction weighed like "a heavy, dolorous dream" as she watched the celebrants at the basilica of Guadalupe: "It is their ragged hands I see, and their wounded hearts that I feel beating under their work stained clothes like a great volcano under the earth and I think to myself, hopefully, that men do not live in a deathly dream forever" (398).

Walsh juxtaposes Porter's description of "The Fiesta of Guadalupe" with a far more upbeat description of the same event that appeared on the front page of the same issue of the newspaper *El Heraldo de México*. The differences, as Walsh presents them, are clear:

> The reporter describes a festive occasion, one almost totally different from what Porter saw. . . . In fact, the words "Indian," "poverty," and "suffering" appear nowhere in his text. But Porter, newly arrived . . . was so overwhelmed by the bowed and burdened Indians that she could see little else. (640)[3]

Porter, like Memmi's newly arrived colonizer, was unable to ignore the poverty and despair of the supplicants at the shrine. Such colonizers, Memmi explains, have yet to embrace the cynicism of their fellow citizens who warn the newcomers, "'Pay no attention to poverty! You'll see: you soon get used to it'" (19). Indeed, most colonizers do, as Memmi notes, "get used to the poverty and the rest" (19). Those unable to do so most often leave. When she penned "The Fiesta of Guadalupe" in 1920, Porter was pessimistic, but she was not yet cynical.

Both the sketch "Xochimilco" and the story "María Concepción" reflect the kind of "humanitarian romanticism" that colonizers must eventually disregard if, as Memmi asserts, they are to remain content in the colony.[4] Struck with the essential injustice of colonialism, as Porter was at the shrine of Guadalupe, the "colonizer who refuses" will look to discover the existential character of the colonized. Porter does just this in the works that immediately follow her sketch of the fiesta. The titled heroine of "María Concepción," for example, embodies the kind of vigor and spirit that Porter found absent in the Indians at the basilica. And, "Xochimilco" offers Porter's vision of "the beauty and dignity of the Mexican people" (Curley 680).

The Indians of Xochimilco, unlike the pilgrims at the shrine of Guadalupe, had maintained a traditional connection to the land. Indeed, the Indians in this idyllic community appeared to Porter as one with the earth. She writes, "They seem a natural and gracious part of the earth they live in such close communion with, entirely removed from contact with the artificial world" (75). For instance, Porter describes an old man steering his barge through the village's canals as one who "lives as a tree lives, rightly a part of the earth" (82). The villagers "get all material for their needs from the earth"; in fact, Porter notes, the maguey is a plant by which "the Indians can live almost entirely" (79). The Indians of Xochimilco little resemble the supplicants at the basilica with their faces "streaked with long-borne fatigue." And, unlike the worshipers with their eyes turned away from the earth toward the heavens, the Indians at Xochimilco "hardly lift their eyes from their task" of gathering vegetables or making flower bouquets (75). They retain their simple life in part as a result of their "voluntary detachment" from the politics of Mexico. They maintain, Porter notes, "an almost unbroken independence of passing governments" (81). Porter warns, however, that the outside world poses a serious threat to the halcyon life of Xochimilco. Because of its beauty, the village is already "in danger of being taken up by rich tourists" (78).

These two early pieces, the sketch of the Fiesta of Guadalupe and the description of Xochimilco, indicate that Porter, the "humanitarian romantic," recognized the importance of the land to Mexico's Indian population. This idea is also apparent in her July 1921 political essay, "The Mexican Trinity," which examines the economic and political issues that defined much post-revolution reform. In challenging the ideologies that permit oppression, Porter once again resembles Memmi's colonizer who refuses to become cynical. Memmi posits that having discovered the "economic, political, and moral scandal of colonization" the colonizer who refuses "[vows] not to accept colonization" (19). Early political essays like "The Mexican Trinity" and "Where Presidents Have No Friends," as well as "La Conquistadora," Porter's 1926 review of Rosalie Caden Evans' letters, indicate that she was very well aware of the economic, political, and moral dilemmas confronting post-revolution Mexico.

Although "The Fiesta of Guadalupe" indicates Porter's frustration with the Indians of Mexico, in early pieces she often tempers her harsh judgment of the Indians by portioning blame to outsiders who had subjected the Mexicans to centuries of slavery. Porter saw land reform as a central challenge for Mexico's leaders. In her reports from Mexico, however, she suggested that the leaders were unable to meet this challenge. The inability of Mexico's post-revolution government to reestablish the Indians' traditional connection with the land became, for Porter, one important measure of the revolution's failure. Another was the failure of the Indians themselves to embrace the opportunities for change afforded by the revolution. In a March 1921 article for the *Magazine of Mexico* titled "The New Man and the New Order," Porter celebrated Mexico's new president, Alvaro Obregón. She asserted that both the people of Mexico and their president were now responsible for effecting change:

> The new president's greatest distinction is in his knowledge that of his own self he can do nothing. He has frankly told his people this and given them the admonition that only by their cooperation could Mexico take its rightful place. . . . So in its last analysis the new order which is beginning with every evidence of permanence and stability rests with all the people of Mexico, from president to peon, each responsible according to his own degree and station in the scheme of destiny. (60)

Such optimism, both in the politicians and the people of Mexico, was short-lived. In the end, Porter would conclude that both groups had failed to assume their respective responsibilities.[5]

Despite Porter's passionate denouncing of the forces that oppressed Mexico's Indians, she, like most "colonizers who refuse," began to resemble more and more the "colonizers who accept." Such a transformation is, Memmi predicts, inevitable once the colonizer recognizes that "he has another civilization before him, customs differing from his own, men whose reactions often surprise him, with whom he does not feel deep affinity" (24). In her early writings, Porter was clearly aware of the causalities and circumstances that created the crisis in Mexico. However, she soon lost sympathy with Mexico's oppressed indigenous peoples. This attitude is apparent even in "The Mexican Trinity," in which she concludes that, because "the revolution has not yet entered into the souls of the Mexican people" and compelled them to rise against their oppressors, the Indians, who are the "very life" of Mexico, appear as an "inert and slow-breathing mass, these lost people who move in the oblivion of sleepwalkers under their incredible burdens; these silent and reproachful figures in rags" (401–02).[6]

Porter's response typifies that of Memmi's colonizers, for, like them, she could not ultimately ignore the differences between the two cultures. Memmi writes,

> [The colonizer] cannot help judging those people and that civilization. How can one deny that they are under-developed, that their customs are oddly changeable and their culture outdated? Oh, he hastens to reply, those defects are not attributable to the colonized, but to decades of colonization. . . . (24)

Porter's observations in "The Fiesta of Guadalupe" and "The Mexican Trinity" suggest that the revolutionary spirit among indigenous Mexicans was, indeed, "under-developed" and their commitment to Catholicism was "outdated." Although in her early work she does defend the Indians as victims of centuries of colonization and exploitation particularly at the hands of Euro-American industrialists and a corrupt clergy, her subsequent work indicates that, like Memmi's colonizer, Porter recognizes that the "distance between [her] commitment" and that of the Mexicans is insurmountable (42).

Because Porter was one who was, as she told Hank Lopez, "dissenting by nature," the apathy of the Mexican Indians must have proved disheartening (122–23). The rapid changes celebrated by her Greenwich Village friends were little apparent among the inert and plodding native population. The Indians had lost their vital connection to the land, and the revolutionary activity seemed long past. Thus, the Mexicans who appear in Porter's later works do not resemble the Indians of Xochimilco; rather, they are the Indians of "The Fiesta of Guadalupe" and "The Mexican Trinity"—an "inert and slow-breathing mass" apparently unwilling to embrace the revolution.

Porter despaired as Mexico's Indians not only embraced the religion of their conquerors but also coveted the Euro-American lifestyle. In "Leaving the *Petate*," a 1931 essay for *New Republic*, Porter describes how her maid Eufemia, a pure Aztec, prizes Japanese tea sets and "toilet articles of imported German celluloid" (392).[7] For Porter, the *petate*, a straw mat for sleeping on the earth, symbolizes the Indians' connection to their native land and traditional ways. Among Mexicans, however, the *petate* is the subject of the derisive proverb, "Whoever was born on a *petate* will always smell of the straw" (388). Interestingly, during the revolution, when it was vogue to celebrate the Mexican Indian, the *petate*, once a symbol of degradation, became a badge of honor. However, in 1931, a decade after the revolution, Porter was convinced that, when the chance presents itself, many of Mexico's Indians would choose to "leave the *petate*." Eufemia reflects this trend: she covets western knickknacks, she cuts her braided hair into a contemporary bob, and she wears high-heeled patent leather pumps that "hurt her feet shockingly" (390). Although Eufemia is well versed in traditional medicine, Porter reports that she "takes up readily with every new thing[,] . . . [including] Lysol, patent toothpaste, Epsom salts, bicarbonate of soda, rubbing alcohol, and mustard plasters" (392). Porter concludes that Eufemia will marry her young man, who is not, as Eufemia boasts, an Indian, and she will never return to her village. Disheartened, Porter can only hope that Eufemia's mestizo children will not become part of the new generation of "conservative right-minded dull people" but, instead, one of the "mestizo revolutionaries, and keep up the good work of saving the Indian" (393).

Porter's frustration with Eufemia and other young Mexicans who covet Euro-American ways is evidence of a departure from her earlier sympathies. Yet, in the end, her expectations were unrealistic given the "centuries of servitude" that she herself had lamented. In fact, Eufemia and her peers behave in a manner typical (and inevitable) of the colonized. Memmi notes that the colonized often exhibit a desire to "become equal to that splendid model [the colonizer] and to resemble him to the point of disappearing in him" (120). Eufemia and her contemporaries are perfect examples of this tendency. Similarly, Eufemia's failure to embrace her history is also a function of the colonial situation. Memmi explains that the colonized are "in no way a subject of history any more.... [They have] forgotten how to participate ... and no longer even [ask] to do so" (92).

At one point, for Curley's "moment" perhaps, Porter understood the plight of the colonized. In that spirit of understanding, she wrote pieces like "The Fiesta of Guadalupe" and "The Mexican Trinity." In the end, however, the fundamental differences between the Mexico that she had imagined and the Mexico she encountered began, after nearly a decade, to wear both on Porter and her sympathies. She had imagined a Mexico populated with "mestizo revolutionaries," only to discover a place of "conservative right-minded dull people." Memmi's conclusion about the colonizer's mindset defines Porter's relationship with Mexico at the end of the 1920s. Memmi writes, "It was really a long time ago that [the colonizer] was certain, *a priori*, of the identity of human nature in every dimension. True, he still believes in it, but rather like an abstract universality or an ideal to be found in history of the future"

(26). The Mexico that Porter had projected onto "Xochimilco" and "María Concepción" was in fact an abstract ideal that little resembled the reality of the Mexican Indians.

By the time Porter visited the Hacienda Tetlapayac in 1931, where Russian director Sergei Eisenstein was filming what would become *Que Viva México*, she was completely disillusioned. Her despair informs her final Mexican story, "Hacienda," a fictionalized account of events that occurred during her three-day visit. The world of Don Genaro's hacienda is antithetical to that of Xochimilco. The "leisurely industry" (81) of the Indians at Xochimilco becomes "just another day's work [and] another day's weariness" (163) on the hacienda. Throughout the story, Porter uses, as a sort of leitmotif, the workers moving between the vat room and the maguey fields, chanting, counting, and rolling barrels. The "closed dark faces" (142) of the Indians on the hacienda suggest that they share little in common with the villagers of Xochimilco where "no strained lines of sleeplessness or worry mar their faces" (82). On the hacienda, the Indians more closely resemble the defeated peasants of "The Fiesta of Guadalupe" or "The Mexican Trinity" than the children of Xochitl.

In post-revolution Mexico, Porter replaces the sweet-smelling world of Xochimilco with the fetid world of Don Genaro's hacienda. By 1931, Porter was convinced that the revolution had failed. In response, her early anger was dulled and her humanitarian romanticism numbed. For the colonizers who refuse, Memmi indicates that their options are few: they can withdraw physically from the colonial situation or remain to fight and change it. Of course, they can always simply accept the reality of colonialism. The closing lines of "Hacienda" make Porter's choice clear—leaving the hacienda, the narrator comments, "I could not wait for tomorrow in this deathly air" (170). Joan Givner suggests that the final words by the narrator of "Hacienda" were also "[Porter's] final words on Mexico." The story was, Givner claims, "a summation of all [Porter's] feelings about Mexico" (241, 239). ❖

Notes

[1] In a 1963 interview for the *Paris Review*, Porter explained to Barbara Thompson, "I went running off on that wild escapade to Mexico, where I attended, you might say, assisted at, in my own modest way, a revolution." Givner, *Conversations* 78–99.

[2] In a 1923 letter to the editors of *Century* titled "Why I Write About Mexico," Porter describes Mexico as "my familiar country." The letter is reprinted in *The Collected Essays and Occasional Writings of Katherine Anne Porter*.

[3] Although the author of the front-page description of the fiesta is unknown, it is clear that he/she views the events of the day quite differently from Porter. In *The Labyrinth of Solitude*, Octavio Paz offers an interesting discussion of the role of the fiesta in Mexican culture. Chapter Three of his study, "Day of the Dead," helps explain two very different visions of the fiesta of Guadalupe.

[4] In May 1921, less than six months after her arrival in Mexico, Porter visited the Indian village of Xochimilco. The *Christian Science Monitor* published an account of this visit titled "Xochimilco." "The Children of Xochitl," a longer essay from which "Xochimilco" was derived, is among Porter's papers at the McKeldin Library, University of Maryland, College Park, and has been reprinted in *Uncollected Early Prose of Katherine Anne Porter*.

[5] Of Obregón, Porter would later say that on the day of his inauguration he was "a ludicrous figure . . . so drunk that he was draped over his podium like a rag doll." See Joan Givner's *Katherine*

Anne Porter: A Life 182.

[6] This, I would suggest, is also at issue in "Flowering Judas," where many of the revolutionary leaders are more interested in wooing Laura than in effecting necessary change.

[7] "Leaving the *Petate*" appears in *The Collected Essays and Occasional Writings of Katherine Anne Porter*, 388–89.

Works Cited

Curley, Daniel. "Katherine Anne Porter: The Larger Plan." *Kenyon Review* 25 (autumn 1963): 680–81.

Givner, Joan, ed. *Katherine Anne Porter: Conversations*. Jackson: UP of Mississippi, 1987.

———. *Katherine Anne Porter: A Life*. New York: Simon and Schuster, 1982.

Lopez, Enrique Hank. *Conversations With Katherine Anne Porter, Refugee from Indian Creek*. Boston: Little Brown, 1981.

Memmi, Albert. *The Colonizer and the Colonized*. Boston: Beacon, 1965.

Porter, Katherine Anne. *The Collected Essays and Occasional Writings of Katherine Anne Porter*. Boston: Houghton Mifflin, 1970.

Walsh, Thomas. "'That Deadly Female Accuracy of Vision': Katherine Anne Porter and *El Heraldo de México*." *Journal of Modern Literature* 26 (spring 1990): 635–43.

———, ed. *The Uncollected Early Prose of Katherine Anne Porter*. Austin: U of Texas P, 1993.

Porter and Dobie: The Marriage from Hell

James Ward Lee

For a number of reasons, Katherine Anne Porter and J. Frank Dobie are united—even in their extreme dissimilarity. What binds them is geography and an insignificant literary prize awarded to Dobie in 1939. What separates them is also literary and geographical. Dobie was a traditionalist, a romantic, a realist, a Texas chauvinist, and a devotee of the Old West—or at least his version of the Old West. Porter was a modernist, an etherealist, and an inventor of an Old South that she had no more inhabited than Dobie had his West. Though they were born a couple of years and about two hundred miles apart, the two writers couldn't have lived in more opposite writing universes. Dobie was the ultimate westerner; Porter transformed herself from small-town Central Texas girl to "moonlight and magnolias" southern woman to internationalist. Dobie spent most of his life in Texas. Porter left Texas early in life and wandered the world for a large part of the twentieth century. Dobie died—in Texas—in 1964; Porter outlived him by sixteen years and died as far east of Texas as you can get and still be on the continent. Despite all their differences, the two remain married in the minds of many Texas commentators—partly because of that obscure literary prize and partly because of a universal desire to proclaim somebody "best of show." As A. C. Greene, author of *The Fifty Best Books On Texas*, once said to me of lists, "Everybody loves a Hit Parade." Greene's comment is borne out by the recent lists of 100 Best Novels, 100 Best Movies, and Greene's own—and latest—*The 50+ Best Books About Texas.* In any case, as each year passes and things should settle down, Dobie-Porter arguments become more bitter, and theirs seems a literary marriage made in Hell.

Literary critic Tom Pilkington, who calls J. Frank Dobie "the father of Texas literature," says, "If Dobie is the father, the matriarch of Texas letters is Katherine Anne Porter"(Taylor 557). Don Graham, who is, ironically, the J. Frank Dobie Regents Professor of American and English Literature at the University of Texas at Austin, is quoted in *The Dallas Morning News* on April 15, 1998, as saying that Porter "stood out among tall men." Graham's comment is quoted in an editorial, which goes on to say, "Translated, that means she fares well against such Texas legends as J. Frank Dobie and Walter Prescott Webb."

Dobie's reputation is fading. This is especially true among the advanced literati. But to many old guard writers and commentators, Texana collectors, historians, and Old West aficionados, J. Frank Dobie is still the king. And the Dobie/Porter wars still heat up whenever the two camps gather. There is no quicker way to start a literary argument than to bring up the *cause célèbre* surrounding the 1939 Texas Institute of Letters literary prize. And it almost always comes up when Texans gather to talk about literature. It is never brought up by the Dobieites, for to them it is an embarrassment. But the Porterites never miss a chance to decry the blindness of the TIL fathers and mothers in awarding the prize to Dobie instead of to Porter. As Dobie's reputation has waned, Porter's has waxed. A passionate dean at the University of Texas at Arlington—in opening a Porter conference—once called Katherine Anne Porter "the only star in the Texas firmament." The distinguished Porter critic Janis Stout of Texas A&M University says in her *Katherine Anne Porter: A Sense of the Times* that "as a literary artist . . . her stature is indisputable" (248). But despite these laudatory comments, Old Guardsman/historian/belletrist/literary commentator A. C. Greene does not list Porter's famous *Pale Horse, Pale Rider* in his latest version of *The 50+ Best Books About Texas*. This omission incenses Don Graham, a Porter devotee despite his credentials as the Dobie Professor. Graham calls Greene's latest 50 "[a] puny pantheon" and "a new, weird update" of the original Greene list (Graham, "Outlaw Heart").

When it comes to Porter, passions run high, higher with each passing year, it seems. The nascent restoration of the KAP home place in Kyle, numerous conferences on Porter, the glamorous photograph of Porter that graces the 1998 Texas Writers Month poster, the ever-increasing stock of articles and books devoted to Porter's rather slender output—all suggest that Porter is indeed the "only star in the Texas firmament." Or at least she was until the recent canonization of Cormac McCarthy by the Texas literary establishment.[1] (It is in "Outlaw Heart" that Graham takes his swipe at A. C. Greene for "booting out" KAP and calls for a "long moratorium on the subject of Texas writing." After Graham has had his say, one presumes.)

Passions indeed run high where KAP is concerned. And none higher than Joan Givner's in her 1982 Simon and Schuster biography *Katherine Anne Porter: A Life*. One of the things that she found most distressing about Porter's treatment by Texans was the fact that in 1939 the barely fledged Texas Institute of Letters failed to give its first "best book" award to *Pale Horse, Pale Rider*, the very book that A. C. Greene "booted out." Instead the TIL gave its first award to J. Frank Dobie's *Apache Gold and Yaqui Silver*. And though almost sixty winters have passed since that first TIL scandal, the wounds with some regularity reopen and bleed as did those of the "mightiest Julius" as he lay in state before all of Rome.

In 1983, at a celebration of the University of Texas' centennial

—in the very heart of Dobie country and not six blocks from the spot where Dobie died—Givner said, in a much quoted passage, that Dobie would have "won out over Jane Austen, Jean Rhys, Eudora Welty, Marianne Moore, Virginia Woolf, and the entire Brönte clan lumped together. And he would have done so even if these writers had been born in Waco." Not quite so often quoted is what comes just before Ms. Givner's catalog of non-winners. She says:

> One hardly needs to invoke complicated arguments to express the difference between J. Frank Dobie and Katherine Anne Porter. His cowboy image and style was as flauntingly and exaggeratedly masculine as hers was feminine. I would suggest that the "indigenous nature" of Dobie's subject matter was that its masculinity conformed more to the spirit of the West. There was none of that tremulous sensibility, that preoccupation with the inner world of the imagination, with relationships between men and women or with what George Eliot has called "the roar on the other side of silence." ("Katherine Anne Porter: The Old Order and the New," in Graham, 59-60)

It is impossible to argue with Givner that Dobie's 1939 winner was "flauntingly and exaggeratedly masculine"; indeed, all of Dobie's work was. Dobie lacked "tremulous sensibility" or "the preoccupation with the inner world of the imagination," and, Lord knows, Dobie's roars were not "on the other side of silence." But I cannot agree that there is no need to offer complicated arguments that might help to explain the difference between J. Frank Dobie and Katherine Anne Porter—or rather the difference between the works of KAP and the works that were written and approved in Texas during the Porter-Dobie era. And I don't think the last word has been said about the controversial 1939 Best Book

Award by the Texas Institute of Letters.

First, a few words about the Texas Institute of Letters in 1939. It was in its third year, and its beginnings had been "tremulous." For one thing, Dobie, the reigning intellectual in the state at the time, had misgivings about joining the rather pompously titled organization. And he was not the only Texas writer to hesitate: folklore collector and college registrar John Lomax objected to a proposed list of charter members by saying that there were too many who "teach English rather than writing it effectively" (Vann 6); and the now almost-forgotten novelist Donald Joseph (revivified in *The Texas Observer* by Dwight Fullingum) wrote the founders to say that "not half a dozen people in Texas are doing nationally recognized creative writing" (Vann 5). Despite the reservations, the new organization, conceived by Billy Vann of Mary Hardin Baylor College, got off the ground more or less during the Centennial Year, but it was still struggling three years later when it was proposed that "the Institute undertake to make suitable recognition of the outstanding Texas book of each year" (Vann 15) Three members—Hilton Ross Greer, Stanley Babb, and Ann Pence Davis—were appointed to "make plans." I am not sure whether the three of them chose Dobie over Porter or whether there was a vote of the members, but Dobie was chosen and the rest, as they say, was scandal.

But think for a second about the masculine versus feminine argument, which seems to be applied today every time the 1939 controversy arises. Here are a couple of facts. For one thing, a quarter of the charter members of the TIL were women. This does not prove conclusively that there was no gender bias among the members, but it is worth some consideration. Another fact: the president of TIL that year was a woman. Poet and novelist Karle Wilson Baker was the second president and third fellow of the organization. In fact, between 1939 and 1946, Ms. Baker, Rebecca W. Smith, and Lexie Dean Robertson had all served two-year terms as president of the organization. Again, not conclusive proof. Another fact: the book that won the award in 1940 was Dora Neil Raymond's *Captain Lee Hall of Texas.*

I am aware that there is no way to prove that the TIL was not masculine-dominated and male-centered and gender-biased, but I have a suspicion that it was not as much a men's club as it has been pictured. Nor am I sure that masculine versus feminine is what was going on in those early years of the Institute. I do think J. Frank Dobie would have won against all comers in 1939—against Welty or Woolf or Mrs. Mary Wortley Montague. Not because he was a male but because he was J. Frank Dobie. The organization, in its years of infancy, was eager to clutch the vain and cannily pompous Dobie to its collective bosom. And what better way was there to do that than to give him an award? This turned out to be one way to help turn Dobie into the literary dictator that he was determined to be. And I don't think anybody questions the fact that Dobie dominated Texas letters in the middle decades of this century. As I have said elsewhere, he did this by force of personality and self-promotion and industry but without literary taste. But because I plan neither to praise nor to bury Dobie here, I will not detail his shortcomings as a critic. But I do have some things to say about him as a determiner of taste and a master publicist of himself and of romantic Texas.

Because Texas literature during the Dobie years was in its last great burst of Lone Star romanticism, what amazes me most about the 1939 imbroglio was that Porter was considered at all for an award by TIL. Perhaps her nomination came from those English-teacher members that Lomax had decried earlier. After all, by 1939, the New Critics were beginning to make inroads into English departments, and Robert Penn Warren and Cleanth Brooks had just published *Understanding Poetry,* the second most influential English textbook ever published in

America. (The McGuffey Readers still hold first place.) *Understanding Poetry* became the Bible—or rather the first of several Bibles—for the New Criticism. And if any writer ever wrote works that fitted the prescriptions of the New Critics it was KAP. Her work was allusive, ironic, often open-ended, and as mystifying as critics and English teachers demand. The most admired of the Porter stories—"Flowering Judas" is a perfect example—cry out for explication. A common reader is left in the dark, and it remains for the critic to untangle the images, symbols, allusions, patterns of reflexivity, and what sophomore students are given to calling "hidden meanings." Teachers can spend several days with "Flowering Judas" or "Pale Horse" and still not exhaust the possibilities. Critics can spill words over hundreds of pages in attempts to "explicate the last verse" of either of those works.

Someone once remarked that for the New Critics to appreciate a poem, it had to be as close as possible to the works of the seventeenth-century Metaphysicals. T. S. Eliot, in many ways the father of New Criticism and Modernism, devoted a great deal of space to reviving the Metaphysicals—Donne, Herbert, Marvell, Crashaw, and others. As the British and American New Critics gained ascendancy in the literary world, Shelley and Wordsworth and Tennyson were consigned to dim poetic corners; Keats was transformed into a demi-Metaphysical; and new writers began writing to the fashion of the day—John Crowe Ransom's poetic reputation rests on his ability to write mock-Metaphysical, which he did superbly. The tensions and ironies of the poets fed over into fiction, and writers like Joyce, Lawrence, Woolf, Faulkner, Katherine Mansfield, and Porter wrote novels and stories requiring the same deep analysis as Donne had needed. Virginia Woolf once noted that a novel should be "at least as well written as a poem." I think that means that fiction should have the same density, the same impenetrability, as the poems being admired at the time. As for writers like Trollope and Tennyson and Dickens, there was hardly a place for them in the new pantheon. Someone once dismissed Tennyson by referring to "the glutinous syllables of the poet laureate." No more "glutinous syllables," no more focus on story.

I think, given the temper of the times—and Porter's friendships with many of the Southern Agrarians/New Critics—it is easy to see how her works became very models of metaphysical, ironic, decadent twentieth-century writing. And it seems to me that such works were not playing well in Texas in 1939 among any but the most advanced critics and belletrists. What obtained in Texas letters in 1939 was not tinged with what Ms. Givner calls "tremulous sensibility."

Maybe European and American letters had moved from Romanticism to Modernism, but Texas was still more than a generation behind. Everyone has a theory about the movement of artistic periods, but most agree that they move from primitive to decadent—here "decadent" is a descriptive rather than a pejorative term. Decadence in literature comes toward the end of a period, and its quality is often superior to the works produced during the high tide of the period. Northrop Frye's argument that western literature has, over 1500 years, moved from myth to irony is an example of the path from primitive to decadent. As is Wylie Sypher's anatomy in *Four Stages of Renaissance Style*. Sypher traces the style of the Renaissance from its primitive beginnings to its classical apogee to its decadence—"mannerist" and "rococo" are two useful terms he uses in this description of the decadence of the period. But perhaps the simplest way to look at the progress of a movement from primitive to mature to decadent is to think of the three capitals that top Greek columns. In grammar school we learned of the movement from Doric to Ionian to Corinthian—from simple to complex, from plain to ornate, from primitive to decadent. These progressions constantly repeat themselves. What, after all is Modernism but the decadence of Romanticism? If we have Blake and Wordsworth, we are almost certain to have Tennyson and Browning and later Hardy and Housman and Wilde and Faulkner and Woolf and Joyce and Katherine Anne Porter.

The Modernist movement, which I argue is the decadence of Romanticism, was in full flower when Porter shook the dust of Tarrant County off her feet, denied she had ever worked for the *Fort Worth Star-Telegram* or had been married to a Texan, and set out for what many inferiority-complexed Texans at the time called the "civilized world." As she put it in a letter to William Humphrey, ". . . I got out of Texas like a bat out of hell at the earliest possible moment and stayed away cheerfully half a lifetime" (Stout 36). Unlike Huck Finn who "lit out for the territories," KAP lit out *from* the territories.

While Katherine Anne Porter was establishing cosmopolite credentials and writing stories that attracted the attention of the New Critics, James Frank Dobie was staying at home promoting the Texas of his imagination—and his Texas was expansive, optimistic, filled with certainty; in short it was romantic by almost any definition. Dobie represented Texas as it saw itself in the twenties and thirties. It was in full flower. It was the finest flower of the American West. Never mind that Texas was a southern state where cotton was the principal export and that the majority of its inhabitants saw themselves as southerners, Dobie and Hollywood were projecting Texas as the gunslinger West, what Owen Wister once called a "playground for young men." This view of Texas as the Wild West was as old as the dime novels, but it was working toward a fever pitch in the 1930s. The Centennial was on the horizon, and it hardly needs to be said that Dobie was on the Advisory Panel on Texas History for the hundred-year celebration. He was ubiquitous in those days. By 1932, he had already begun on a weekly radio show called "Longhorn Luke and His Cowboys" from station WOAI in

San Antonio. (He got paid $25 a program plus expenses to and from Austin.) In 1939, he began his syndicated newspaper column "My Texas." Lon Tinkle says that by the time Dobie won the first TIL award, he was already being called "Mr. Texas."

Not only was Dobie the main intellectual spokesman for Texas, he was both a shaper and a reflector of Texas writing. And the writing of that time had little that was decadent or ironic or Modernist about it even when it was not written about Dobie's "West of the Imagination." There was little in Texas literature that was touched by irony and "tremulous sensibility." The Texas pictured by Lone Star writers was not always tinged with the romanticism of Owen Wister and Frank Dobie, but there was little irony in those pre-war days. Writers like Dorothy Scarborough, Ruth Cross, Barry Benefield, Clair Ogden Davis, and Karle Wilson Baker were producing fiction that was as unlike Virginia Woolf's experimentalism or KAP's interiority as Dickens was unlike Proust. The thirties in Texas was the time of Berta Harte Nance's poem that begins "Other states were carved or born,/But Texas grew from hide and horn." These years produced Sallie Reynolds Matthews' *Interwoven*, a nostalgic and romantic family history, and George Sessions Perry's *Hackberry Cavalier, Walls Rise Up*, and the great *Hold Autumn in Your Hand.*[2]

The main line of Texas literature remained straightforward, un-ironic, un-decadent throughout "the War Years" and through most of the fifties—and remains so in the works of writers like Elmer Kelton today. Tom Pilkington wrote that in 1961 Larry McMurtry dragged "southwestern fiction kicking and screaming into the twentieth century" with *Horseman, Pass By* (Taylor 511). Another way of stating Pilkington's thesis is to say that McMurtry's first novel lays to rest the romantic West as Dobie and his followers saw it. But before *Horseman, Pass By* appeared, Texas fiction was well on the way toward its ironic mode, its decadence. Madison Cooper's *Sironia, Texas* (1952) is hardly in the Texas mainstream as Dobie knew it; instead it bears the marks of decadent writing in its ironic and almost Faulknerian treatment of Waco society. William Humphrey's dark and Porter-influenced stories were being written as early as 1949 and his important *Home From the Hill* came out in 1958. Another Porter devotee, William Goyen, began publishing parts of what would become *The House of Breath* as early as 1949. It was not long before a great many anti-romantic works began to appear: writers we associate with the 1960s and early 1970s like Bud Shrake, Bill Brammer, R. G. Vliet, Bill Casey, and John Irsfeld portray a Texas that Dobie would have found unappealing if not unrealistic.

None of this is to say that Texas writing today is totally given over to "the roar that exists on the other side of silence," but when I look at a Texas tradition of existentialism and despair and decadence that begins with Porter and continues through Goyen and Humphrey to Cormac McCarthy, Edward Swift, and James Crumley, I feel called upon to echo Yeats on Ireland: "Romantic Texas is dead and gone, it's with Frank Dobie in the grave." But it was not in 1939. And I don't find it all that strange—or even inappropriate—that *Apache Gold and Yaqui Silver* won the first award given by the Texas Institute of Letters. ❖

Notes

[1] *Texas Monthly,* July 31, 1998

[2] I don't suppose this applies in the context of the Porter/Dobie flap, but *Hold Autumn in Your Hand* won the TIL Award in 1941 and the National Book Award in 1942. I can't help but wonder how it would have fared against Porter and Dobie had it appeared two years earlier. But I suspect that Dobie would have won against Perry because the TIL needed Dobie as an ally.

Works Cited

"Dallas Diary: Porter Established Standard for Texas Literature." *Dallas Morning News*. Apr. 15, 1998, natl. ed.: 24A.

Givner, Joan. *Katherine Anne Porter: A Life*. New York: Simon and Schuster, 1982.

———. "Katherine Anne Porter: The Old Order and the New." *The Texas Literary Tradition*. Ed. Don Graham et al. Austin: U of Texas College of Liberal Arts, 1983.

Graham, Don. "Outlaw Heart: Cormac McCarthy's Border Trilogy." *The Texas Observer*. July 31, 1998: 5–7.

Pilkington, Tom. "Texas." *Updating the Literary West*. Fort Worth: TCUP, 1997.

Stout, Janis P. *Katherine Anne Porter: A Sense of the Times*. Charlottesville: UP of Virginia, 1995.

Taylor, J. Golden, et al. *Literary History of the American West*. Fort Worth: TCUP, 1987.

Vann, William H. *The Texas Institute of Letters, 1936–1966*. Austin: Encino Press, 1967.

Katherine Anne Porter and the University of Texas: A Map of Misunderstanding

Richard Holland

Katherine Anne Porter's biographers present convincing evidence that her natural ambivalence toward Texas was hardened into hostility by two events that she perceived as slights on the part of arbiters of culture in her home state. The first was the snub of *Pale Horse, Pale Rider* by the Texas Institute of Letters in 1939 when the fledgling writers organization chose instead to honor *Apache Gold and Yaqui Silver*, TIL founder J. Frank Dobie's second compilation of mining yarns. Bookending the TIL rebuff were the events precipitated by Porter's first return to the state in twenty years to speak at the University of Texas in the fall of 1958—a seemingly triumphant return that raised expectations both on her part and on the part of the university.

It appears that expectations were always full of drama in the case of Porter, whose status as one of America's masters of short fiction was achieved partly as a result of her carefully tending her literary reputation step by step, adroitly choosing opportunities that would enhance her career and quickly discarding offers that appeared to be less promising. Likewise, the University of Texas, led by the ambitious Harry Huntt Ransom, was emerging from the shadow of censure by the American Association of University Professors and with deep pockets for gifted faculty and purchases in rare books and manuscripts, was entering a golden era not matched in the history of the school. Just beginning a period of heroic library collecting, Ransom felt that a beneficial relationship with Katherine Anne Porter could only help further his literary goals for the Austin campus.

Anyone familiar with the operations of universities and particularly special collections in academic libraries knows of the pitfalls in the area now euphemistically called "donor relations." Porter was a potential literary donor and Harry Ransom was a special collections builder who, at least in this part of the world and in the time frame of the late 1950s and early 1960s, transcended all others. It should come as no surprise that the eventual result of their contact resembled a train wreck more than a glorification of a lifetime of literary art or the wisdom of an institution embracing the best of its own culture. Institutions, even those as eager to please as was the University of Texas in the late 1950s, seldom fulfill the desires of any individual, particularly one with needs as deep as Miss Porter's.

The archives relating to what may or may not have been promises made and broken by both sides in this episode are well-thumbed by scholars, but nothing that I have read fully takes into account the dynamic happenings at the University of Texas under the leadership of Ransom.[1]

As her biographers make clear, Katherine Anne Porter had already formed some opinions of the university by the time of her triumphant visit to the campus in the fall of 1958. Almost twenty years earlier she had been contacted by Donald Coney, generally regarded as the most distinguished head librarian in the history of UT. Coney's letter, dated June 9, 1939, was mailed to Baton Rouge and used both Miss Katherine Anne Porter and Mrs. Albert R. Erskine, Jr., in the address. The librarian's letter is a bold and elegant pitch for Miss Porter to contribute the "Flowering Judas" and "Noon Wine" manuscripts to the university library.

Interestingly, his approach is strictly regionalist—he is requesting the manuscripts for the Texas Collection. He says:

> My dear Miss Porter:
> I am trying to bring together for the Library a collection of manuscripts and related materials of important books bearing on Texas. Your "Noon Wine" seems to me to be of this kind and—to make a brazen story a short one—I covet its manuscript for this collection. As a matter of fact, Texas is so much a part of the background of the three stories of *Pale Horse, Pale Rider* that I'd like the entire manuscript.

The letter goes on to explain the utility of authors' manuscripts and typescripts to literary study and then lists works of Dobie, Webb, Laura Krey, and Karle Wilson Baker that had recently been added to the collection. Two and a half weeks later, Coney's brazenness was rewarded when on June 27 he acknowledged receipt of the first draft of "Old Mortality." To me this indicates that early on Miss Porter was interested in her literary legacy and chose not to turn aside a charming request. It is important to remember that her rejection at the hands of the TIL did not occur until later in the year—the group's 1939 meeting was on November 17-18, held in Dallas' Cokesbury Bookstore. The group's prize to Dobie for "Best Texas Book" was the first one awarded by the organization.

The correspondence reveals that fourteen years passed before KAP's next official contact from the university, this time a form letter from another UT librarian, the hapless Winnie Allen, archivist at the Texas Collection. Miss Allen writes Porter a letter similar to that of Coney in intent, but a world apart in knowledge and style, which I think meant very much to Katherine Anne Porter. Miss Allen's perfunctory inquiry dated June 4, 1953, again mentions the Texas Author collection at the Barker Center and rather unconvincingly states that she has over the years "taken great pride in you as a native Texan." She does not once indicate that she is aware of the generous 1939 gift to the collection (McKeldin). Miss Porter's response is a well-known letter that bluntly states her belief that the university has lost the typescript of "Old Mortality":

10 June 1953

Dear Miss Allen:

A good many years ago, maybe ten or even twelve, the then archivist of the University of Texas Library asked me to give a manuscript to the Library. I did, a typewritten, hand-corrected draft of "Old Mortality" with a note saying the scene was that country lying between San Marcos and Austin, in Hays County . . . .

I can only suppose that this document has been lost in the shuffle, and I may say if so it is a pity, for I have collectors who are happy to pay me several hundred dollars for even very small mss. and when a great institution like the University of Texas asks for such gifts from living writers who are not best sellers or expect to be, they—the administrators—are quite literally asking the writer to give them free something which has a positive cash value. Many times I have been rescued from real financial distress by the timely purchase of a manuscript for five hundred dollars by a collector. Now what I wish to say is this: I have always heard, whether it is true or not, that the University of Texas is one of the richest in this country, and in the world. BUT that its resources are all bound by rule to be devoted only to building and physical expansion; nothing for faculty salaries or for education; that is to say, nothing at all generous or at all in keeping with the University income and the physical show. Of course, all educational institutions expect authors to give away their substance; it never occurs to them that it might be a service to living literature if they purchased such items while the author lived, in order to help him live and work. It is all very well after he is dead to accept bequests, if his heirs and executors are willing to donate them. But somehow I do not feel under obligation to give anything negotiable to the University of Texas, or any other, considering the astronomic difference between their resources, and mine. (McKeldin)

The letter ends with a request to see if indeed the "Old Mortality" typescript is on the premises, and she ends "If you don't want it, I should be delighted to have it back! It would be ready money for me!"[2] I found no record of a response to this articulate outcry either from Winnie Allen or any other university officer. We now know, of course, that nine years later, with the publication of *Ship of Fools*, Katherine Anne Porter would have as much popular acclaim and financial reward as any mid-century American writer.

By 1958 literary matters had taken on a completely different cast at the University of Texas. Riding high on the campus was the liberal young literary scholar Harry Huntt Ransom, who quickly progressed from being chair of English to vice-president and provost. Under his dynamic leadership the humanities on the campus in Austin shone as never before or since. In his impatient push for excellence, he threw over formal procedures in many departments and brought in exciting young scholars to UT as "University Professors," who were hired outside the formal requirements of advancement in their departments. This group included John Silber in philosophy, Roger Shattuck in French, and William Arrowsmith in classics, who rose with Ransom in the late 1950s, but who all fell ten years later under the regime of regents chairman Frank Erwin, who characterized their special status after he fired Silber as "birdnests on the ground."

One of Ransom's lasting legacies was the creation of new journals—one of which, the *Texas Quarterly*, featured first-class criticism, fiction, photography, and design. In the late 1950s and early 1960s Toscanini, Count Basie, and the Modern Jazz Quartet performed in Gregory Gym, Aldous Huxley read from his psychedelic writings in Batts Auditorium, and T. S. Eliot appeared to be delighted in his appearance on the campus when he was presented with a Stetson hat.

One of the ways that Ransom broke with what he thought was mediocre about the status quo on campus was in turning his back on the libraries. After Donald Coney had left Texas to begin a brilliant career as head of libraries at the University of California at Berkeley, the UT libraries languished. Ransom, who was a book man through and through, devised a plan to perform an end run around the regular library system and create his own. To this end, beginning in about 1957, he was able to divert significant funds into rare books and manuscripts outside the purview of other libraries on campus.

Standing by Ransom as he raided the literary treasure houses of America and Britain were his secretary, Frances Hudspeth, who in many ways oversaw the day-to-day operations of the university, and a number of faculty and staff sympathetic to his bookish pursuits, including Mody Boatright, Tom Cranfill, and Warren Roberts in English, and Frank Wardlaw, the brilliant editor-in-chief of the university press. Of the library staff, Ransom did appear to respect the formidable Fannie Ratchford, who had written an important book on the T. J. Wise forgeries, but Miss Ratchford was close to retirement during the period of Ransom's ascendancy.

Ransom's great year of coming out as a national and international literary power was 1958. Not only did the year see the commencement of his long-awaited *Texas Quarterly*, it marked the publication of the first Humanities Research Center monograph, D. H. Lawrence's *Look! We Have Come Through!* and, November 17, the opening of the first of many ambitious literary exhibits, this one titled "An Exhibition on the Occasion of the Opening of the T. E. Hanley Library." The fabulous contents of the Hanley collection were stored, along with Ransom's other treasures, in some set-aside floors of the Texas Tower, just above the top of the Main Library's closed stacks. The informality of security for these great collections and the lack of any systematic conservation for them would make present-day special collections personnel swoon.

One of the youngest of Harry's Boys—as they were known around campus—was William Handy, an assistant professor of English whose outstanding teaching in American literature gained him a following among bright students. Handy and his wife had been T. S. Eliot's Austin hosts during his visit, and it was natural that he would contact the next big-name writer to be invited to the campus, Katherine Anne Porter. Acting as director of the Texas Program in Criticism, on October 8, 1958, Handy issued a formal invitation to Miss Porter to lecture at the university for a fee of $600. She replied quickly, writing on October 12, 1958, to William Handy and setting a date of October 22. Her handwritten note states that she would read her essay "Noon Wine, the Sources," calling it her first attempt to "account for a story." The entire second page of the letter deals with the physical aspects of her lecture: a microphone to be sound tested before her talk regardless of the size of the hall, and most importantly the right sort of lighting. "A rose-color or amber spotlight full into the face, no overhead or footlight lighting. Lights at back if needed but full front certainly! I wear evening dress and try to make a pleasant evening for the people who are so good as to come to hear me" (CAH). Indeed, her carefully planned presentation created a sensation, and I doubt if Austin has ever seen quite such a literary spectacle as Miss Porter decked out in evening dress, opera-length gloves, and lorgnette.

Miss Porter's trip to Austin only lasted two days, but it had the appearance of being a momentous reunion on both sides—her first trip to Texas in twenty years and an opportunity for Ransom's university to impress a prodigal daughter with their non-provincial accomplishments. An indication of her sentiment is the story of her being met at the Austin airport by English professor Frank Lyell, a Mississippian who was a dear friend of Eudora Welty. Accompanying Lyell for the meeting was another Mississippian, Willie Morris, just back from a stint as a Rhodes Scholar at what he called "the other Oxford." In a 1980 interview, Morris recalled:

> I went with Frank and we met her at the airport and we were heading back to the University, and she saw the state capitol, a beautiful building all illuminated against the horizon, and she said, "Frank, do we have time to stop in the capitol for a minute?" We went into the rotunda, and there were tears coming down her face. Frank said, "Katherine Anne, what's wrong?" She said, "My daddy brought me to this building when I was ten years old, and it was the first real building I ever saw." (*Conversations with Willie Morris*, 68).

After the lecture there was a party in her honor, more than likely at the home of Lyell, whom she later wrote asking if he had found her copy of the *Yale Review* she had misplaced in Austin. Miss Porter was gratified by the attention of so many Texas English professors, and apparently at the party someone broached the idea of her literary papers finding a home on the UT campus. Also during her whirlwind visit she held forth to Winston Bode for a long article in *The Texas*

Observer, delivering her opinion on regionalism and bluntly stating that "Texas has no serious writers. I am the first serious writer that Texas has produced." Don Graham has, correctly I think, placed Porter in a tradition of southern writing, and she did point out to Bode that she looked kindly on the literary efforts of two young East Texas writers, William Humphrey and William Goyen, the next generation of the Texas "southern" school. To place this in context, it was two more years before three notable "non-southern" Texas literary landmarks were produced, these being John Graves' *Goodbye to a River,* Bill Brammer's *The Gay Place,* and Larry McMurtry's first novel, *Horseman Pass By.*

Follow-up correspondence after the trip concentrated on three discrete but somehow interrelated topics: her placing a portion of the forthcoming *Ship of Fools* in *The Texas Quarterly,* an offer from the university for a visiting professorship to commence in the fall of 1959, and an implied promise that President Ransom would honor her in some significant way in a forthcoming library building linked with the implied promise that she would gather together her literary papers for the university. Two days after her lecture, on October 24, Ransom's assistant Frances Hudspeth wrote concerning *Ship of Fools:* "This morning the Editorial Committee of the Texas Quarterly asked me to write you at once and ask that you permit us to publish the portion of *A Ship of Fools* about which you spoke to Dr. Cranfill and Dr. Handy. We are able to offer you a modest stipend of $500 for the serial publication rights to about 30,000 words from the book." Commenting that Dr. Ransom was in Houston attending a regents meeting, she concludes, "He is more eager even than the young men you met to secure your work for the *Quarterly*" (CAH).

Miss Porter's response reflected a quandary about which portion of *Ship of Fools* to excerpt, because she saw the book as a whole, but she did send two passages, one that she called "the Jewish episode." The last paragraph of this letter dated "All Saints 1958" reads:

> My visit to the University of Texas was delightful and exciting to
> me, and the welcome I received quite melted my heart: that is the
> country of my beginning in this world, my earliest memories, and
> it is wonderful to find that the bonds which seemed no stronger
> than spider web are tough as steel thread! I am very happy about it.
> Please give my remembrances to all who were so merry with me
> there. (McKeldin)

Two weeks later, after receiving volume one, number one, of *The
Texas Quarterly*, she wrote in a p.s. to a letter to Ransom:

> Did I say before, that the priceless first number of *The Texas Quarterly*
> came to join the others, and I have them carefully curated from this
> abusive world. It is a most beautiful magazine, with the life and bold-
> ness and variety with elegance that I love best in anything at all, but I
> think these qualities become best the arts! It was splendid reading, all
> of it, and I hope it prospers, and that no evil eye shall be allowed to
> look at it. . . .

> Long life to *The Texas Quarterly*!
> (January 1, 1959, McKeldin)

Frank Wardlaw handled publishing Ransom's *Texas Quarterly*,
and after Mrs. Hudspeth had passed on to him the sections of *Ship of
Fools*, he happily reported to Miss Porter in a letter dated December 30
that it was in the hands of the editorial committee. In a letter to him
dated January 24, 1959, Miss Porter indicated her uneasiness about part
of *Ship of Fools* being out of her hands:

Now it comes to me that possibly your editors and yourself have found it not suitable for your Quarterly and are hesitating to say so? I appreciate always tact and friendly manners, but also I am a very professional writer, and know something of the trials of editing and publishing. So please don't hesitate for a moment to say so, if you can't use the mss. . . . We shall always meet as friends in the future with no regard whatever for this decision, I hope. I am just not the kind of author you have to baby along. So please let me know your decision as soon as you are able. (CAH)

Publication was delayed until the August issue, and the *Quarterly* file at the HRHRC demonstrates what Miss Porter's approach to editorial suggestions was: forget it. A debate over moving the placement of a comma was won hand's down by the writer when she wrote back in capital letters a resounding "<u>NO</u>!"

Harry Ransom had the reputation, and still does, of promising potential donors special treatment in exchange for their literary archives, and it is clear that certain conversations may have transpired during Miss Porter's visit to Austin, but none of the conversing was from Ransom, who, as we have seen was out of town, as was English chair Mody Boatright. That being said, I do believe that in writing neither Ransom nor Mrs. Hudspeth ever directly promised to name any building after Katherine Anne Porter and that at first Porter knew what the university's intentions were and were not. In a carefully worded letter dated November 7, 1958, Dr. Ransom wrote to Miss Porter: "I know Texas. I think that you know it too. Therefore I believe you will understand the sincerity and conviction with which the Administration has voted to establish in the new library Center the Katherine Anne Porter Library" (CAH). Her response, dated November 16, is similarly clear about the proposed honor:

Your decision to establish in the Library Center a library in my name is the kind of honor I never imagined for myself, not being much concerned with honors, but now it is bestowed, I am enraptured with it, it seems now to be just what I should have chosen for a moment in my life—if I had been choosing! It is a gentle, lasting kind of glory, as if one had managed to merit well of the Fatherland without quite knowing how. . . . (CAH)

The sincerity of the offer and its acceptance are clear. If there was a sin committed, it was not a sin of commission but of omission on the part of the university, when it became obvious that Miss Porter had expanded in her mind the subtle notion of having a named library area within a building to the much grander notion of the university constructing a new library in her honor. The first hint of this different thinking on her part is in her answer to English chair Mody Boatright's offer for her to have a visiting professorship in the fall of 1959. In this letter dated December 26, 1958, she says:

I am still somewhat overwhelmed at the decision to name the Library Center for me. That for me is such an honour as shall do me nicely for life, I need no other, and I have never dreamed of this! I have been thinking what I might do as a token of my feelings, and I shall offer the library my entire literary estate, whatever it may be—at present it consists of several thousand books, bushels of papers, mss. unfinished, notes and hundreds of letters; this store grows almost visibly day by day; I also have a trunkful of photographs made at all times and occasions of my whole life, and in fact, I shall leave to the University—if the University would like to have it—the entire history of my life and works. I offer this only provisionally, and if you think it would be acceptable, I should be glad for you to tell me how to make the offer in form to the proper person; and as soon as I know, I must make a new will. (CAH)

To Dr. Ransom dated January 1, 1959, she inquires: "What am I to do between my good news and the actual laying of the cornerstone? I know a great occasion when I see one, and I wish deeply to carry myself in every way befitting it, and not to do or say anything at all untactful or untimely" (CAH). On the same day she wrote Professor Frank Lyell, "of having the Library of the new Center named for me in full—I always loved glory and never wanted anything else. . . ." (Handwritten note cited in Wade). In neither of these letters, one formal and one a letter to a friend did she refer to her literary estate (CAH).

Two months later, it was clear that Miss Porter's fantasies about a shrine on the Austin campus had gotten pretty much out of control. Frances Hudspeth had written her that "plans for the new library continue apace." In her answer dated March 1, Miss Porter, in a handwritten p.s. signed KAP, states: "I am quite mad for news of my Library. I want to see plans, I want to be buried under a marble slab in the floor! I'd rather have this honor than the Nobel Prize and a Congressional Medal rolled into one! Nobody in the world was ever so in love with a Library as I am with this one!" (McKeldin). Faced with this thanatopic reverie, the university perhaps would have been discreet to remind Miss Porter gently that the idea for the Porter Library was to be an area inside the building highlighting her works and archives and to suggest that she leave the cornerstones and floor materials to the experts.

The Ransom files at the Center for American History do reveal that both Mody Boatright in an undated memorandum and Frank Lyell in a 1960 handwritten note congratulating Ransom on his ascendancy to become president of the university refer to Miss Porter and encourage

Ransom to act directly. Boatright says: "Dear Harry—I thought you might wish to write Miss Porter, especially about her book collection," and Lyell asks, "In the new undergraduate library, is there to be a KAP wing, room, niche, or shelf—or will the whole shebang be named for her as she seems to think?" (Handwritten notes, CAH).

As late as August 1959, Ransom dropped her a short note saying that the university was acquiring materials in southern history and literature to be placed in a "Porter Library," and in 1962 he sent a wire to her publisher Little Brown congratulating her on the publication of *Ship of Fools*. Some of the tremendous publicity surrounding the publication of her only novel mentioned the university, including an article in the March 8, 1962, *Christian Science Monitor* that makes a little fun of her primitive roots by saying: "Uncooked Texans are reminded that Miss Porter was born at Indian Creek, Texas, and her voice still sounds a little like it. The University of Texas is building a $2,000,000 library for contemporary literature to be called the Katherine Anne Porter Library." Even faced with this prominent press coverage, there is nothing in the Texas or Maryland files that show any follow-up to these announced plans by either Ransom, Hudspeth, or Porter.

The Academic Center and Undergraduate Library opened in 1963. Students rightly called it "Harry's Place," and up on the fourth floor there eventually were several named library rooms, including the Blanche and Alfred Knopf Library, the J. Frank Dobie Library, a special room reproducing Erle Stanley Gardner's office, and a large area that housed the Humanities Research Center's considerable collections of art and photography. The Ransom staff now reports that there are roughly twenty named rooms or discretely housed collections within the HRHRC. In the 1980s these special rooms were closed under the administration of Decherd Turner, and now they are open by appointment. A few months before he died, in the summer of 1964, KAP's *bête noire*,

J. Frank Dobie, stated forcefully in a letter that he was so sick of thinking about his still-unfinished monument in the Academic Center, he didn't care if it happened or not.

The university did eventually get around to naming Ransom's 1963 building twenty-two years later, in August 1985—it is now called the Peter T. Flawn Academic Center, honoring a former UT president. Harry Ransom as chancellor held a grand opening of the Academic Center in the fall of 1964, with a major exhibit of the university's literary rarities installed on the fourth floor of the building. This exhibit and catalogue, titled *A Creative Century: Selections from the Twentieth Century Collections*, was an announcement to the world that great things had happened in book and manuscript collecting at Texas. The word century was used to designate one hundred collected authors as well as the modern time period. Two Texas writers were represented in an array that included E. M. Forster, D. H. Lawrence, James Joyce, and Virginia Woolf. These were J. Frank Dobie and Katherine Anne Porter, whose corrected typescript for "Old Mortality" was given a place of honor.

The final act between Miss Porter and Dr. Ransom was initiated when she presented her literary archive to the University of Maryland in December 1966. Texas newspapers got hold of the story and Miss Porter, then seventy-six years old, appears to have been misquoted by a reporter for the *Fort Worth Star-Telegram* named John Mort (December 18, 1966). Two weeks later, *The Dallas Morning News* book critic, Lon Tinkle, ran a long column about what he termed a "stunning blow" to culture in Texas, lamenting "if only this state had a longer tradition and a 'civilized ambience' or style about how to honor its creative spirits" (January 1, 1967). Tinkle milked the situation for all it was worth, listing the number of times that Miss Porter had almost died, including a bout with pneumonia in Dallas in 1964 when her illness led to her cancellation of a talk to the Texas Institute of Letters. It was this non-performance that led Larry McMurtry to call her "the Elizabeth Taylor of Texas letters." In fact she lived sixteen more years.

The end of the correspondence between Porter and Ransom was initiated by Miss Porter, when on January 20, 1967, she states: "Dear Dr. Ransom: You have been quoted lately in several Texas newspapers as saying that my claim that you had asked me to give my library, books and papers to the University of Texas was 'simply not true.' You are quite right, and I wish to assure you that I said nothing of the sort to the reporter." She goes on to say that she remembers his idea for a library room and that she had offered him her literary estate, and that "from that day to this I have not received an answer to that letter." Well, as we have seen, this letter was actually sent to Mody Boatright, who sent a memo to Ransom reporting on Porter's informal offer. I would guess that in the wake of the sentiments expressed in the "marble slab in the floor" letter, Ransom and others at the university thought that negotiating with Miss Porter about her literary estate would put them in an impossible *quid pro quo* position and that they passively withdrew from her bluntly emotional need to be honored in her home place.

By the time Ransom received Miss Porter's letter of January 20, he had undergone almost six weeks of negative publicity about the incident and finally had the opportunity to address her directly. In a remarkable three-page letter dated February 1, he says:

> Dear Miss Porter:
> As I telegraphed you yesterday, I am deeply grateful for your letter.
> Having typed these sheets myself, I will see them into the post office because I believe that the mails are responsible for many unhappy misunderstandings. As for your final suggestion that the plans for the Porter Library "shouldn't concern either of

us further," I firmly agree that you should not be disturbed again by either the rumors or realities in Texas. In my thirty-one years at the University, no distinguished visitor has roused greater admiration, affection, and enthusiasm than you stirred among young students, members of the faculty, and officers of administration during your unforgettable visit here. The plan made then still stands at Texas. Because of our pride in you and our gratitude, we proposed a Katherine Anne Porter Library that was to reflect the best that had been written in modern fiction and the best critical opinions about it.

Ransom goes on to list in an almost rambling way his changing duties during the eight years that elapsed between her campus talk and the Maryland announcement.

Listing Professors Handy and Roberts and Mrs. Hudspeth and Mary Hirth as part of his collection team, he says, "Roberts has been on repeated leave abroad and Handy, after many tragic family difficulties, left Texas for Oregon. I set down these particulars because I can imagine—but only with difficulty—that changing assignments here may have caused confusion." The remainder of the letter is a pained apology and defense:

One point I must emphasize. Having written you about our initial plan, I did not receive any word directly from you. Both Mrs. Hudspeth and Handy gave me reports from time to time, none of which intimated your wonderfully generous intention of giving the University your own collections. During the December meeting of our Board of Regents in Houston, I received the only direct communication from a newspaper reporting your displeasure. A young woman representing the *Houston Chronicle* interrupted the meeting to inform me that you had announced from Washington that after having sought your collection, I had ignored letters from you (I believe her word was "snubbed") and because of the University's—and my—continued discourtesy you had decided to give your collection to Maryland.

After stating to the Houston reporter that it was "simply untrue" that he had ignored any letter addressed directly to him, Ransom says, "I have had every file in the University searched. I have found no letter contradicting that single public statement of mine. For what must have seemed to you unpardonable rudeness [and what would seem to the academic community manifest stupidity as well as calculated bad manners] I am deeply sorry." In closing, Ransom says, "Try to remember the University happily. After all, you and your great work belong to a wider and longer-lived company than twentieth-century Marylanders and Texans. Sincerely yours. . . " (Carbon copy in CAH).

Later in the year it was left to the straight-shooting Frank Wardlaw to vent a little anger toward Miss Porter, which must have been building during the eight years since his dealings with her working on the *Ship of Fools* excerpt. Early in 1967, Wardlaw was focused on the publication of *Three Men*, a tribute to J. Frank Dobie, Roy Bedichek, and Walter Prescott Webb, to be edited by Ronnie Dugger. Porter pulled her contribution to the book at the last minute and the university press at some expense had to reset the type. In his letter dated April 21, 1967, Wardlaw says:

Dear Miss Porter:

Whom do you think you are deceiving—besides yourself, of course? You tell me that the permission you granted Mr. Dugger to use your letter had nothing to do with the book on Bedichek, Webb, and Dobie which we are publishing. This is simply not true. Well, I am taking the disputed passage out of the book, at consid-

erable cost to the Press. I am doing it not out of consideration for you, for you are entitled to none in this matter, nor out of fear of legal proceedings, since you haven't a leg to stand on, but in deference to the wishes of Ronnie Dugger, who has behaved with great decency throughout this episode. Besides the excised passage is quite unimportant and adds very little to the book. To me, who for a quarter of a century believed (on rather slender evidence it must be admitted) that the author of *Pale Horse, Pale Rider* was a transcendent figure in American Literature, this episode is almost as big a disappointment as was *Ship of Fools.*
Sincerely,
Frank Wardlaw. (CAH)

This powerful blast was, as far as I can tell, Katherine Anne Porter's last official contact from the University of Texas in the 1960s. ❖

Acknowledgments

Grateful thanks for permission to quote unpublished materials are extended to Barbara Davis, literary executor of the Katherine Anne Porter Estate, to the Center for American History and the Harry Ransom Humanities Research Center at the University of Texas at Austin and to Mrs. Rosemary Wardlaw. Additional thanks go to Beth Alvarez at the University of Maryland Special Collections, to Ralph Elder at the Center for American History, to Cathy Henderson at the Ransom Center and to Steve Davis at Southwest Texas State University's Southwestern Writers Collection, who verified the date and place of the 1939 TIL meeting.

Notes

[1] My sources are those mentioned by Sally Dee Wade in *Katherine Anne Porter and Texas*—the Ransom Papers at the Center for American History at UT and Miss Porter's University of Texas file at Maryland. In addition I examined the *Texas Quarterly* files at the Ransom Center, which provide insight into the earliest publication of a portion of *Ship of Fools*. Future references in the text will refer to letters as held either at the McKeldin Library at the University of Maryland, College Park, or the Center for American History in Austin (CAH).

[2] In *Katherine Anne Porter: A Sense of the Times*, Janis Stout quotes KAP's letter to Paul Porter dated Aug. 14, 1948, in which she sarcastically says: "Oh yes, and the Library of Texas recently asked me to contribute another manuscript to their collection. Pore lil old thaings. But I haven't got one handy. Filthy little bastards, the lot of them" (Stout, 35). I found nothing from this period in any UT files indicating any formal approach to her regarding a manuscript and likewise there is nothing listed in Sally Dee Wade's thorough bibliography of letters in *Katherine Anne Porter and Texas: An Uneasy Relationship*.

Works Cited

Bales, Jack, ed. *Conversations with Willie Morris*. Jackson: UP of
      Mississippi, 2000.

Katherine Anne Porter and Texas: An Uneasy Relationship, edited by
      Clinton Machann and William Bedford Clark. College Station:
      Texas A&M UP, 1990.

Stout, Janis P. *Katherine Anne Porter: A Sense of the Times*.
      Charlottesville, UP of Virginia, 1995.

Trapped by the Great White Searchlight: Katherine Anne Porter and Marital Bliss

Larry Herold

Katherine Anne Porter considered the matter of marriage carefully and issued her opinion from Paris: "I know, always have known, that marriage is not for me under any circumstances whatever" (*Letters* 76). She knew this because she'd already been married three times. As she wrote this, in a letter to her brother in 1932, a fourth husband was on the horizon, and a fifth waited down the road. "Five marriages": the words sound comical in themselves, and it's true that parts of Porter's marital history are humorous, if darkly so. But through reading her letters, sifting through her factually challenged interviews, and inspecting the work of her biographers, we understand that Porter took the idea of marriage seriously. She tried, with varying amounts of effort and success, to make her marriages work, and the fact that each ended in divorce caused her a great deal of pain. Her stories give an alternative view of marriage; she portrays one mismatched couple after another, leaving us to wonder whether she thought a good marriage was even possible. To this mixture, add a pair of essays in which an aging Porter reveals her surprising personal thoughts about matrimony, and you have Porter's views on marriage, which, like the woman herself, are a tangle of contradictions.

Growing up in Kyle, Texas, Porter never got the chance to inspect a good marriage from the inside. Her mother died when Porter was two years old, and life with her heartbroken father was always difficult. At the age of sixteen, a headstrong Porter ran off and married John Henry Koontz, a boy of twenty she'd met on his family's ranch in Inez, Texas. They were together for seven years in Lafayette, Louisiana, and Houston, Texas, during which "that filthy J.H.," as Porter later called him, was apparently violent and unfaithful (*Life* 90). Porter reacted to the shame and sorrow of what she called "that preposterous first marriage" (CE 121) as she would to so many painful chapters in her life: she simply changed the facts. Joan Givner tells us that in a wonderful bit of invention, Porter told a friend that she'd been playing the role of Lydia in a traveling theater company performing *Ben Hur* in New Orleans when a member of the audience fell in love with her and convinced her to marry him (*Life* 87). Porter was spin-doctoring the story of her first divorce long before anyone knew what spin was.

Porter got an early education in the horrors a bad marriage could hold, knowledge that was enforced by her intimate look at the marriage of her sister, Gay Porter Holloway. The two girls' married lives had begun on the same day in 1906 in a double wedding ceremony, but when Porter, finally free of Koontz, ended up back in Louisiana, she found her sister in desperate straits. Gay's husband had "run out on her"; she had one small child and was expecting another. Givner says that Porter resolved to see her sister through and that by making a costume and traveling locally as a singer, she was briefly able to scratch out a living for the family. Porter's hatred of Gay's husband was "boundless"; she considered him and Koontz "most ignobly inadequate in mind, or feeling to anything in human life" (*Life* 90). But early in 1915, the husband returned, moved in, and the baby, to Porter's disgust, was renamed "Thomas" in his honor. This was too much; Porter broke for Dallas, and later called

Gay's husband the only person she ever seriously planned to kill.

Eleven years later, at the age of thirty-six, Porter married again, this time to a dashing World War I pilot from England. He was Ernest Stock, a twenty-five-year-old would-be painter with more charm than talent or ambition. The marriage, which lasted all of one Bohemian summer in Connecticut, was so short that Porter often denied that it ever happened. By the end of that summer, Porter was blaming her inability to complete some short stories on the unnerving presence of "Deadly Ernest," as she called him, and soon after, they divorced. Stock was certainly no prize, but Porter's complaints of claustrophobia were to become a recurring theme. She longed for the stability and comfort of domestic life, but the proximity of another person seemed to stifle her creativity.

For years, people assumed that this was Porter's second marriage, but Janis Stout revealed in 1995 that between Koontz and Stock, Porter "had another brief marriage, apparently in name only, that was quickly annulled." Stout goes on to say that in 1929, by which time we have proof of two marriages, Porter apparently told a friend that she had "had *three* mothers-in-law" (172).

By the age of thirty-six, Porter had been in and out of three unsuccessful marriages, and the harsh portrayals of married couples in her early fiction were no doubt tied to her own history. Her characters rush into wedlock expecting the best, but often find the worst, leaving them lost and brokenhearted. In "He," one of her first published stories, most of Mr. and Mrs. Whipple's problems result from their poverty and a simple-minded son, but already we see a wife disappointed by a husband's deficiencies: "Mrs. Whipple kept thinking all the time it was terrible to have a man you couldn't depend on not to get cheated" (*CS* 54). Porter's dissection of marriage in "Rope," published in 1928, is both vicious and funny. Givner says the narrative, in which a short-tempered wife and a confused husband fight over a length of rope, is based on Porter's summer with Ernest Stock (*Life* 174). Long-held resentments about money, clutter, and moodiness boil over until the husband says that the "whole trouble with her was she needed something weaker than she was to heckle and tyrannize over" (*CS* 44). Any amateur psychologists wishing to draw revealing conclusions from that statement, go ahead. Need more? The husband is upset because his wife told him the two weeks they'd spent apart "were the happiest she had known for four years" (*CS* 45).

Marital misery of a different kind shows up in "The Jilting of Granny Weatherall," published in 1929. Granny has spent sixty years lamenting two relationships: one, her apparently successful marriage with "fine children," a "good house," and a dearth of emotional love; the other, an engagement brimming with love and possibilities that ended when she was deserted at the altar. Presented with these two choices, Granny's life has been defined by regret, and the joy of a contented marriage has remained forever out of reach.

In "The Cracked Looking-Glass," a story Porter wrote in 1931, a couple married despite their thirty-year age difference. Dennis, now seventy-five, wants a wife who'll be a quiet companion and a partner on their farm; Rosaleen longs for some excitement and enjoys the attention of younger men. As their mutual resentment grows, Dennis decides that all women are ingrates, while Rosaleen wonders "what had become of her life; every day she had thought something great was going to happen, and it was all just straying from one terrible disappointment to another" (*CS* 134). Porter's characters find that the attraction that lured them into marriage is hard-pressed to withstand the difficulties life presents, and their tortured unions are no guarantee of solace. Love, it seems, does not conquer all.

The effects of her own failed marriages on Porter, a vain and secretive woman, are hard to calculate, but they make for a fascinating puzzle. Nearing the age of forty, traveling to Mexico onboard the SS *Havana*, she wrote to a friend that "love, for me, has been rather more as if I were a bundle of wheat going through the threshing machine than anything else. When I came through, I was clean winnowed" (*Letters* 20). She seems to want to put all that behind her, but a year later, she was in love again, writing to a friend that she had found a "grand person" who "loves me so steadily and infallibly I can hardly believe it" (*Letters* 42). The man was Eugene Pressly, fourteen years younger than Porter and employed by the diplomatic Foreign Service. In the very same letter, Porter laid out good reasons why she should never marry again: "I don't like a domestic life because I have to keep hours and engagements and have always a sense of responsibilities for my moods and my time." She wonders if she might be better off "by myself because that is maybe the only way I can live permanently" (*Letters* 43). She was still on the fence about Pressly a year later when she wrote to her brother, "I'll never marry him nor anybody else unless I go suddenly mad" (*Letters* 76).

But the call of marital bliss was too strong, and Porter and Pressly were married early in 1933. Following his job prospects and her wanderlust, they lived first in Mexico City, then Berlin, Basle, Paris, and New York. Pressly was devoted to Porter, but he turned out to be a passive, indecisive man, and the marriage started to crumble. Porter said later that she and Pressly "could never bear to be sober together" (*Life* 244). Her inner conflict about marriage came into full flower: she claimed she was unable to work with Pressly around, but she wrote long, passionate letters to him when they were apart. She checked herself into a sanitarium, blaming Pressly for a "breakdown" (Stout 100); but she wrote to her friend, Robert Penn Warren, saying, "Myself, I am altogether cheerfully, comfortably and I hope permanently married" (*Letters* 119). This was Porter's fatal duality—her desire for a solid marriage endlessly colliding with her need for space and creative freedom. She appeared to yearn, like many artists, for a super-mate, one who would support her creative aspirations and supply her with love and entertainment, then vanish when it was time for her to work. Pressly couldn't measure up to that standard, and in 1937 Porter wrote to a friend that the marriage was "finished and a good thing . . . I am as done with it as if it had never happened . . . I shall take good care never to see him again" (*Letters* 151).

Early in this marriage, Porter published another bitter portrait of love gone wrong in "That Tree." In this story, a journalist and would-be poet, after three divorces, still has the vague sense that "there was something to be said for living with one person day and night the year round" (*CS* 67–68). He invites his ex-wife Miriam to rejoin him in Mexico. She arrives for her wedding with a trunk full of silk underwear and linen, ready to set up house the same way she would have done back in Minneapolis. But this is Mexico, and her intended has no furniture, no ambition, and no intention of setting up house. What he wants is calm and simplicity, things his earnest new wife cannot provide. Almost all of Porter's unhappy families are alike: they're victims of dashed expectations, of mismatched hopes and dreams. Her women often expect little beyond companionship and a gainfully employed mate; her men want a partner who will share the chores and stay out of the way. For Porter's people, even low expectations for love and marriage often prove disastrously high.

As her marriage to Pressly was falling apart, Porter finished "Noon Wine," a story in which Ellie Thompson finds her efforts wasted on a dim, untalented man: "She wanted to believe in her husband, and there were too many times when she couldn't. She wanted to believe that tomorrow, or at least the day after, life, such a battle at best, was going to be better" (*CS* 226). The defining episode is of course the murder of Mr. Hatch, but throughout the story Mr. Thompson is more concerned with his reputation than providing for his family. Again we see a couple whose original attraction to each other dims as life's anomalies intrude.

As she and Pressly were drawing apart, Porter also finished "Old Mortality," in which Miranda, at the age of eighteen, elopes from school to get married. We also get to know Uncle Gabriel, whose awful marriage has filled his wife with "unquenchable hatred and bitterness" (*CS* 203). Miranda's notions about happiness devolve until the only emotion she can rouse in herself about marriage is "an immense weariness." By the end of the story, she resolves to "have no more bonds that smothered her in love and hatred. She knew now why she had run away to marriage, and she knew that she was going to run away from marriage" (*CS* 220). Miranda, like Porter, had found that what marriage promised and what it delivered were two different things.

Porter wrote the letter describing her marriage to Pressly as "over and a good thing" in August of 1937 from Benfolly, the stately Tennessee home of her friends Allen Tate and Carolyn Gordon. During this same stay, she met Albert Erskine, the man who would become her fifth husband. Erskine was the young business manager of the *Southern Review*, which had published some of Porter's work. Long talks on the verandah led to infatuation, and soon Porter was finalizing her divorce from Pressly (Stout 126). As always, Porter was certain that her latest romance was flush with promise, but when her host Allen Tate discovered the plan, he wrote a bemused letter to their mutual friend, poet Andrew Lytle:

Katherine Anne Porter and Albert Erskine have announced their intention of getting married in April.

Let it sink in.

They already have the Little House in the country, and are setting out I think it is forty trees. A year from this summer we can go down and see forty dead trees around a deserted house. Albert will say nothing. K.A. will say that she couldn't possibly foresee that Albert would develop such sinister qualities. . . . I am convinced that even this isn't the last attempt. There will be others. And they get younger all the time. (quoted in Stout 126)

Eight months after she met Erskine, and ten days after her divorce was final, Porter and Erskine went to the Palais of Justice in New Orleans to be married. It was there that one of the most darkly comic scenes in Porter's checkered marital history took place. Throughout her life, Porter, like a Hollywood actress, routinely shaved four or five years off her age, but as Givner describes, she had overindulged in this practice with the twenty-seven-year-old Erskine, who had no idea of the age of his intended: "He had thought she was approaching forty, and when he found out, during the marriage ceremony, that she was nearly fifty, he was horrified" (*Life* 311). This was deeply humiliating for Porter, whose vanity and self-consciousness were further wounded when people mistook the couple for mother and son. She didn't give up immediately, writing to a friend that she was "living happily ever after" with a man who was charming, amiable and extraordinarily good-looking, adding, "What more could a woman want?" (quoted in *Life* 313) It took a bit longer than Tate predicted, but soon the old antagonisms arose, and Porter was ready to get out. The couple separated in 1940, and the next year she wrote to Erskine that, "Marriage for me has meant pure disaster, and a strange cruel starvation of the heart." Their marriage, she wrote, "ended the day it began, and the rest was just appearance" (*Letters* 186).

During that marriage, Porter published "A Day's Work," a domestic story that ends with a shockingly violent scene of an embittered wife's revenge. Mrs. Halloran expected her husband to earn a living and go to church; instead, he's an unemployed boozer, sick of his "suffering saint" of a wife. When he accepts the one job she can't abide—with the mob— Mrs. Halloran turns the tables on her husband and pounds his drunken face with the knotted end of a wet towel: "Her arm swung down regularly, ending with a heavy thud on the face that was beginning to squirm, gasp, lift itself from the pillow and fall back again" (CS 405–06). As she lists his faults, blow by blow, she extracts her payment in blood. This is new ground for Porter, a place beyond all illusion where souls are broken, and the response to unmitigated despair is rage and violence. She continued raising the stakes in "The Downward Path to Wisdom," one of her harshest indictments of married life. A four-year-old boy catches the brunt of his parents' unhappiness, and he ends the story, angry and confused, chanting, "I hate Papa, I hate Mama. . . ." (CS 387). Married bliss was never even a possibility for these people; marred bliss is more like it.

In 1942, Porter and Erskine got a Reno divorce, and Porter was through with marriage. She followed her pattern of vilifying the men she'd once loved, calling Erskine "that monster" (Life 342), and limited her romantic entanglements to a series of love affairs. As she neared the age of sixty, she wrote a pair of essays about marriage that appeared in Mademoiselle Magazine. The first, called "The Necessary Enemy," was somewhat caustic. Porter admits her views of marriage "have been much modified by painful experience," and calls "a vow to love and honor [a] husband until death" a "very reckless thing, for it is not possible by an act of the will to fulfill such an engagement" (Days 183–84). Unpredictable as ever, she produced an even-handed essay three years later called "Marriage Is Belonging." In words both touching and revealing, Porter calls marriage a "secret alliance" between a husband and wife, a "mystical estate; mystical exactly in the sense that the real experience cannot be communicated to others, nor explained even to oneself on rational grounds" (*Days* 186). She saves her greatest eloquence for the downside of marriage: "The drawback is, it is the merciless revealer, the great white searchlight turned on the darkest places of human nature" (*Days* 187). This was a glare the secretive, mercurial Porter could not endure. She had no interest in the "daily accounting for acts, words, states of feeling and even thoughts" and was hard-pressed to supply "the unbelievable amount of tact, intelligence, flexibility, generosity, and God knows what, it requires for two people to go on growing together . . . instead of cracking up and falling apart" (*Days* 188).

One curiosity of Porter's much-married life is the fact that she claimed, at times, to be a devout Catholic, a religion that prohibits all but a handful of divorces. The strength of Catholicism's hold on Porter was variable. She was not born into it: she grew up around the fundamentalist Presbyterianism of her stern Aunt Cat and other relatives' simple, backwoods Methodism. She converted to the Catholicism of her first husband, Koontz, saying later that she liked the feel of the Mass, the churches, and the saints. She lit candles for friends and enjoyed the company of priests and nuns. Porter, who often treated her life story like a novel-in-progress, asserted at various times that she had grown up Catholic and had even had to flee a New Orleans convent in order to marry, none of which was true. But her faith fluctuated throughout her life, and she attended Mass only sporadically. She drew close to religion at certain points, but whatever her feelings about the church, the strictures of Catholicism had no demonstrable hold over Porter's marital adventures.

Late in life, Porter enjoyed the attentions of interviewers. Her favorites were the ones she could intimidate; she simply rewrote her life for them, weaving fact with fiction. In 1965, when a timid soul from *McCall's Magazine* said, "I vaguely remember the fact that you've been married," the grande dame was in rare form: "I've been married to three very passable men," she said, quietly disposing of two of her husbands. "I suppose the contrary demands of career—my husbands' and mine— got in the way" (*Conversations* 110). We can imagine her questioner searching for a proper response as Porter dreamily insists, "I have no *hidden* marriages. They just sort of escape my mind" (*Conversations* 108). When talk turned to the reasons her unions had failed, Porter exclaimed, "Do you know I attract insane people?" (*Conversations* 110) In 1969, Porter admitted to another questioner that the fact she was so dedicated to her work had caused her "quite a lot of husband trouble. They felt neglected. I don't blame them" (*Conversations* 137). She gave her divorce from Erskine a romantic tint in another interview: "I said to him, 'I guess I'm just no good as a wife.' And he said, 'You just have a permanent engagement with a higher power'" (*Conversations* 153). Did it happen that way? Perhaps we'll never know.

Toward the end, Porter seemed to reach a level of acceptance about what she had once called "my badly-managed but not absolutely wasted life" (*Letters* 367). She said she was "all for marriage and children and all that sort of thing, but quite often you can't have that and do what you were supposed to do, too" (*Conversations* 86). She never conquered the ambivalence that drove her both toward marriage and away from it with equal passion. She captured this struggle herself in a touching letter she wrote to Albert Erskine as their marriage was breaking up. Porter discussed her health, her holidays, her work, and then closed the letter with a shimmering paradox worthy of her muddled marital career: "Darling, I really love you, and oh how glad I am we are separated. Now we can be at ease with each other" (*Letters* 186). ❖

Works Cited

Givner, Joan. *Katherine Anne Porter: A Life.* New York: Simon & Schuster, 1982.

———, ed. *Katherine Anne Porter: Conversations.* Jackson: UP of Mississippi, 1987.

Porter, Katherine Anne. *Collected Essays and Occasional Writings of Katherine Anne Porter.* New York: Delacorte P, 1970.

———. *Collected Stories of Katherine Anne Porter.* 1965. Reprint. New York: Harcourt Brace, A Harvest Book, 1972.

———. *The Days Before.* New York: Harcourt Brace, 1952.

———. *Letters of Katherine Anne Porter.* Ed. Isabel Bayley. New York: Atlantic Monthly P, 1990.

Stout, Janis P. *Katherine Anne Porter: A Sense of the Times.* Charlottesville: UP of Virginia, 1995.

Hosting Miss Porter

Roger Brooks

[Editors' Note: The following is a transcript of a talk that Roger Brooks gave at Southwest Texas State University in April 1999 at the opening of an exhibit of his Katherine Anne Porter archive. The archive contains materials based upon Porter's visit to Howard Payne University in Brownwood, Texas, to receive an honorary degree when Dr. Brooks served as president there.]

I thought I might speak informally about my relationship with Katherine Anne Porter, shortly before her visit to Howard Payne and then afterward up to the point of her death, without encroaching or jeopardizing the integrity of the letters themselves that are now here in the Southwestern Writers Collection. The letters are detailed records that chronicle her coming to Texas again. At the time that she visited Howard Payne University in Brownwood, we didn't know the magnitude or the real meaning of her visit. Since then, others and I have come to realize that this was a major point in her career. Joan Givner in her biography said it was the most important pilgrimage of her career, and I have come to believe that is the true estimate of her visit, as brief as it was, at Howard Payne University. She had been away from Texas and alienated to some extent, from the state, and her coming back meant a reconciliation that brought happiness and peace to what was a really tumultuous career.

Katherine Anne was a person of conflict, as you know; every step of her career was characterized by conflict. To find a place of final peace for her was a great achievement, and it brings me great joy to know that her wish to be buried in Indian Creek beside her mother and brother was finally realized after her remains were brought back to Brownwood.

But my relationship with Katherine Anne Porter was as an appreciator of her work. I read her work for many years as a young man and enjoyed the short stories long before *Ship of Fools* was published. I, as a young man and collector, didn't know that if I wrote a letter to a major author that he or she wasn't supposed to write you back. So I wrote and congratulated her on her birthday. It seemed as if she was in her seventies at that time. I expressed my appreciation of her work, and she wrote back a most interesting letter, to someone she didn't know, to someone who presumed to write to her about something as personal as her birthday. In this lengthy letter she wrote a description of her birthday party about all those people who gathered around her—what one said and the other said. It filled me with great deal of awe to read a letter that she wrote in such detail of such a personal experience. Well, that encouraged me to write to her again on her next birthday.

Eventually I began to feel very comfortable in writing to Katherine Anne Porter. When I moved to Brownwood, as president of Howard Payne, it was one of the greatest coincidences of this relationship that I just moved eleven miles from where she was born—Indian Creek. Others and I went out to the cemetery to see where her mother was buried. Indian Creek is a ghost town now. As I remember, there were remains of an old Masonic lodge and a burned-out schoolhouse, and about the only evidence left out there of some activity is the cemetery where people were occasionally buried. I went into the cemetery where her mother's grave was, an obelisk-like structure and, with great difficulty, read the inscription. It was weathered, and I could make out some but not all of the inscription. In the course of my correspondence with her, she asked about the cemetery and its condition and asked if I would I look at the grave to see what condition it was in, and I did. I made a rubbing of that inscription, and from the rubbing I was able to determine what was inscribed on her tombstone. I then sent the rubbing to Katherine Anne, and I think it was there that a deeper relationship opened up. I had sent her information about her mother that she hadn't had, for she was unable to recall the inscription on her mother's grave. From that point on, the letters became lengthy and very personal about people who lived in the rich, black earth, where things would grow, where a walking stick, if stuck in the ground, would sprout—so we used to say. We discussed those types of things, and it was a wonderful feeling for me to be that close to such an important person.

It occurred to me after being there for a while and after I awarded a few honorary degrees at commencement that Katherine Anne Porter should receive an honorary degree from Howard Payne University. When I approached the subject with the idea, she was delighted and honored. After all, I thought, Howard Payne is a small Baptist institution and to receive an honorary degree cannot be much to a person of that stature, but she wrote me as if she were receiving a degree from Harvard, and so it pleased me. We began to discuss seriously what we might do in terms of a visit to Brownwood and Howard Payne, and she was very receptive to the idea, very agreeable to any arrangements that I would make that would bring her back to her birthplace. The short of it is that we did make arrangements for her to come, but I did so with some trepidation.

Katherine Anne Porter had a reputation at that time of being temperamental. She was also nearing her eighty-fifth birthday and in quite ill health. She didn't move about very much, and finally she was notorious about not showing up at appointments or engagements, which she obligated herself to attend. I think the University of Texas experienced something of that sort. I was fully prepared knowing that in spite of all the preparations we made, she might not actually show up. Our preparations continued, and we eventually had a five-day itinerary, which included the awarding of an honorary degree at the spring commencement exercise in the civic auditorium in Brownwood. It also included a visit with friends in the area, not many she knew personally, but she knew friends of her family and distant relatives. Once people heard she was coming to Brownwood, many wrote and asked to be invited to such occasions as we would permit.

We made a day on which she would visit with her friends; she wanted to visit the cemetery; and, finally, we arranged for an international symposium on her work. I believe it was the first one ever done on Katherine Anne Porter's work, and she was agreeable and receptive to all of these arrangements. We had all the itinerary worked out when two weeks before her arrival, I got the expected telegram saying, "All of our beautiful plans must be set aside. The doctors have advised me that I am too ill to travel." Well, what to do—because the whole town was excited. For that little town of Brownwood, it was a major event, if you could imagine, and for the university of course. What to do? An apology to the community and to the university was simply not sufficient. So I wracked my brain, and I wrote her a letter, and I said something like this: "Dear Katherine Anne, I would not jeopardize your health for anything. That is the last thing I want to do, but I would like to explain to you that the preparations have been made for your coming to Brownwood and Howard Payne University to receive your honorary degree." I went through all the details, and I concluded with this statement, "I asked my personal doctor, Dr. Seal Cutbirth, if he would attend you on every public occasion." Well, I got back a telegram saying because of all of this preparation, "I cannot refuse you." So she did indeed come to Dallas to the amazement of Lon Tinkle and the staff of *The Dallas Morning News.* They had assured me that Katherine Anne Porter would never show up.

I had two professors at that time who were also devotees of Katherine Anne Porter: Dr. Charlotte Loflin and Dr. Alta Ada Schoner, scholars in the English department. I sent those two ladies to DFW to meet Katherine on her arrival. We were going to send them to Washington, but she said, "No, no. That won't be necessary." So they met her at DFW and motored her back to Brownwood to the university, to my office, where I greeted her personally for the first time.

As you look at the pictures, even one of an aged Katherine Anne Porter, you see they represent one of the most beautiful women I've ever seen. Her personality was just as lovely as that even though I say still that she was a very temperamental person, as we learned. But she was a beautiful woman at the age of eighty-five, and we had a wonderful visit. We made arrangements for her to be at the local Holiday Inn, and we made arrangements for Dr. Schoner to be her companion for the entire visit. She lived in an adjoining room. Everything that Katherine Anne Porter wanted, she got.

As I remember the chronology, the day of the commencement exercise came, and we were all fearful because Seal Cutbirth, the doctor, warned me that we had to watch Katherine Anne Porter carefully because she was a nervous person and she could overdo. As we were awarding the honorary degree, I said respectful and proper things about her, at the time expecting her to thank me and sit down. Instead, she moved forward and in front of the platform addressed the county—all six thousand people in attendance at the civic auditorium. And without microphone she spoke at length about her youth, her parents, not much about her works. Had we anticipated it, we could have recorded the talk. Finally, when she did conclude, we began handing out the diplomas, and she wanted to hand one personally to each of the graduates. We got through half of the class. And Seal came up to me and said, "Roger, we have to get her off the stage. I think she is hyperventilating." So as graciously as I could, I said, "Katherine Anne, I think, let's let Dean Jackson finish, let's step away." I took her off the stage and put her into the hands of one of my good friends, who conducted her out of the auditorium and back to the Holiday Inn.

Well, this is the type of person that she was. She loved attention—she loved flattery and this was theatre for her, and she did a good job. She surprised us all.

The next day or two, she was visiting with her friends in the area, and then she went to the cemetery to visit her mother's grave. I wish I had had my tape recorder there because while she was there, the people who were with her said that she carried on a lengthy conversation with her mother, who had died early in Katherine's life. I thought that was one of the most remarkable things that happened during her visit.

Then we had the symposium. All the major Porter scholars of that time were in attendance except George Hendrix, an office-mate of mine in Colorado, who had written that early and first biography of Katherine Anne Porter, skeletal compared to Joan Givner's. So George was not there, but all of the other Porter scholars were there, including Givner. She had in mind to write a biography of Katherine Anne Porter but had not gotten permission, so it was going to be an unauthorized biography. Now, how can I say this? Katherine Anne was very nervous about biographies—she wanted biographies to be written, but she wanted them to reflect her story and her life. She told us that she had married four times and had thirty-seven lovers. She was afraid things like that might have some influence on a proper estimate of her work, and so she worried a great deal about Givner, who was working seriously on the biography of her. She did not want an audience with

Givner at that time. Givner wrote up an account of the Brownwood trip in her biography, but it's very brief and has little substance to it and little scholarship evident. Actually she summarized *The Texas Observer* account of Katherine Anne 's visit to Brownwood and to Howard Payne University. Seymour Lawrence, publisher of *Ship of Fools*, wrote me about Givner's account and asked me to write about what transpired, because he was upset over misleading and unfair accounts by Givner. So I wrote an estimate of the whole affair and sent it to him. It was a great conference, very successful, and Katherine Anne was very pleased.

At the conclusion of the conference, we had a birthday party for Katherine Anne. She was eighty-five. It was well attended, and everyone wished her many happy returns. She was in ecstasy that all the attention was given to her, and as we were concluding, she stepped forward and spoke about thirty minutes again; she couldn't let such an occasion pass. She was a wonderful person. While she was there, she took all the staff who were influential in her visit to the Riverside Lodge, one of the dining places in Brownwood, and had escargot and champagne. Isn't it like Katherine Anne Porter—escargot and champagne? I didn't know how to explain to my board, but by then, I had prepared them for Katherine Anne Porter, and I think they overlooked that and other things, and we had an enjoyable evening. But throughout all, throughout the entire visit, she was concerned about the biography and, at eighty-five years of age, an estimate, a proper estimate of her works. She didn't know how much her life in Paris and in Mexico and her arrest during the Sacco-Vanzetti trial would weigh against the merits of her work. This was a real apprehension of hers. I carried with me from her visit this intense apprehension that she had. When she prepared to leave, we had wonderful farewells and promises to continue the conversations in College Park, where she was living at that time.

At that point in her career, she had already made arrangements for her literary work—manuscripts, letters, these types of things. She was one of these carbonizers. She made a carbon of everything she wrote. All of these, plus letters she would receive, plus any literary memorabilia, went to the University of Maryland, and that is the main research center now for studies on Katherine Anne Porter. While she was at Brownwood, she, of her own will, asked if we would like to have some personal items from her, and of course we said we would like to have them because after all she belonged to the area. We would name a room in the library The Katherine Anne Porter Room and put in there anything she wanted to give us. She made a list of things like her bed, which was a beautifully gilded bed, one fit for a queen, as you can imagine. We wanted to put that there with her desk, her bookcases, many of her books, nothing that would encroach upon the collection in Maryland—she didn't promise any of these things to Maryland. She did give, finally, some foreign translations of her work. Those were shipped shortly after she went back. She made a list of these things she wanted us to have, and she initialed them "K.A.P." and went back to Maryland, and we were expecting that in a reasonable period of time, we would be receiving some of these things to have a Katherine Anne Porter Room in the Moody Library at Howard Payne University. Shortly after she went back, probably about a week, she went to New York to receive a literary recognition and award and returned to College Park to her apartment for rest. But she had a stroke, then a series of strokes. These affected her substantially. She was paralyzed on the right side, so her writing hand didn't function at all, and much of her right side she couldn't move. She sent me a telegram saying come quickly; we must go on with our plans to get these things to Howard Payne.

I flew to Washington and drove to College Park to visit with her. She was surrounded by a large number of people—friends, relatives, doctors, nurses, lawyers—not that she needed all of these people at that particular time. She had talked—she couldn't communicate, but she had sent this telegram to me. When I got there, I was reluctantly received by the nurse and was asked to call a Mrs. Deiterman, a lawyer for Barrett Prettyman. I don't know if you know Barrett Prettyman. He once one of the biggest names in Washington. During the Clinton–Monica Lewinsky episode, the courthouse you saw in the background for interviews with Monica and others on TV was the Barrett Prettyman Courthouse. He sent word that I shouldn't try to take anything from Katherine Anne Porter at that time because she would soon be declared incompetent. I said I would not take anything, but I would like to see her because she had sent a telegram for me to come.

Reluctantly, they permitted me to visit with her. I was shown into the room and she greeted me enthusiastically. The seriousness of the strokes was immediately apparent. She was sitting upright in her bed, which had only the headboard with the hospital bed in front of it, and she greeted me cordially as she did in Brownwood. We had a good two-hour visit. She had difficulty pronouncing certain words but generally her communication was clear. However, she could not do anything with her right hand. While I was there, she gave me several things—this beautiful picture of her youth, which might have been made at Kyle. It is Katherine Anne Porter, at about eight years of age, and about seven or eight of her friends and her teacher. It is one of the most remarkable photographs I've ever seen of Katherine Anne, a lovely, lovely child. She gave me that photograph, and after everyone had left the room and allowed me a little privacy with her, she gave me the book, *The Neverending Wrong*, which was an early venture that she began immediately following the Sacco-Vanzetti trial but never finished. After her stroke, she wanted to be active and her long-time secretary, Bill Wilkinson, encouraged her to write, and so she finished her book. It had been published just a few days before I got there, and she gave me that copy.

Another bit of evidence of the influence of the stroke was that she was very suspicious of all those people who were around her. She thought the nurse at the time had hit her, and that was why she couldn't use her arm. She became suspicious of Bill Wilkinson. She had fired him over a dispute—she thought he was deceiving her—and then rehired him when she found out he was indispensable. Bill was still suspect at that time, but the book was dedicated to him because he had helped her finish it. While she was alone with me, she opened up the pages where the dedication was and with her left hand scratched out the dedication. She wrote, as well as she could, "Is he ready for death?" and signed it "K.A.P," as well as she could and gave the book to me. It is now in the Southwestern Writers Collection. She was as cordial as she could be with me and was still planning to give things to Howard Payne for that room. I saw no change in her toward me or Howard Payne University, but of those around her, she was suspicious. Paul Porter, who was in the vicinity, instigated the incompetency proceedings. I was in Washington at the time, and I thought about going to the hearing and maybe voicing an objection, but when I really thought about it, the evidence was there that perhaps she needed some help in finalizing her life and her affairs. So I didn't go and didn't voice any objections, but I returned to Howard Payne without anything other than the book and the photograph, which were personal gifts to me. Not too long after that, I read that she was declared incompetent and was put into a nursing home with continuous attendance. And not too long after that, I read of her death. Another stroke carried her away. That was one of the saddest days of my life. I keep a journal when I meet important people, and I recorded the day with great sadness. But she was one of the most delightful persons who ever passed through my life, and I am pleased that I could give the remnants of the relationship, that friendship with Katherine Anne Porter, to Southwest Texas State University's Southwestern Writers

Collection.

Question: You wrote to a number of prominent writers and asked them to comment on Katherine Anne, and I wondered, what led you to do that and what were some of the most interesting parts of that response?

Answer: I had on my board, I believe, thirty-seven members, and, of course, giving an honorary degree had to be approved by the board. These were pastors, often in small towns, and I don't mean anything by that except they did not know Katherine Anne Porter, didn't appreciate literature, perhaps as we do. I had a convincing job to do, so I wrote to prominent people, asking them if they would give me their estimate of Katherine Anne Porter's works so that I might use them in persuading my board. Of that list of all the major writers of today, such as Robert Penn Warren, I had only one or two who did not respond, but I think you have a hundred letters from prominent people and writers in the world, who wrote glowingly of Katherine Anne Porter. Now, in all candor, a few said that they never read Katherine Anne, but one of the most interesting letters I got was from John LeCarré. You know John LeCarré—the mystery writer. He said, "You know, I never read anything of Katherine Anne Porter's, but if you'll send me a copy of her work, I'll read it, and I'll write a letter of what I think." And I did. I airmailed a copy of her collected short stories. He read them, and he wrote an estimate that I used and is now in the collection. It was one of the things I used to convince those that didn't know Porter as well as we do of the merits of Texas' greatest writer.

Question: I know of Katherine Anne Porter's many

relationships, often with men younger than herself. I wonder what your wife thought of your time with Katherine Anne Porter.

Answer: When I went to College Park that last time, I bent down to hug Katherine Anne on the hospital bed, and she turned her lips up, and I kissed her on the lips and believe me, it was a kiss. ❖

Katherine Anne Porter (lower left) and schoolmates, probably in Kyle, Texas (Courtesy SWWC).

Katherine Anne Porter at her mother's headstone, Indian Creek Cemetery, Indian Creek, Texas, 1976 (Courtesy SWWC, photo Roger Brooks).

The Prodigal Daughter Comes Home

Lou Rodenberger

When Katherine Anne Porter finally accepted President Roger L. Brooks' invitation in 1976 to come to Howard Payne University in Brownwood, Texas, near her birthplace, and receive an honorary doctorate, she wrote, "I long to return to my homeland just once more before I return as dust." As she presented the banquet speech, the highlight of the symposium that also honored her, she said, "I've never had a real home. I've moved about so much. . . . But this, this is my home. It is a wonderful feeling to be again in my homeland." Dr. Charlotte Laughlin, who with Dr. Alta Ada Schoner and Howard Payne University alumnus Bill Gooding, met Porter at Dallas–Fort Worth Airport on Saturday, May 8, remembers that she emphasized that declaration with "a theatrical sweep of her hands."[1]

Later, after her return to Maryland, Porter wrote Laughlin to thank her and the Howard Payne faculty for the warmth of their welcome to Brownwood, and once again she referred to the region as her home: "I have been a little exhausted since our grand festival in my homeland, but the happiness of those wonderful days will be mine for life—it is a marvel to remember."[2] Early in June of 1976, Laughlin and Schoner visited Porter in her Maryland home, where Porter taught Laughlin how to make her famous "feesh deesh," and the three made plans for publication of a collection of the symposium papers. Porter was excited about the book but insisted that she read the papers because she was not up to attending the symposium sessions during her visit to Brownwood (Laughlin interview).[3] On the day that Laughlin learned of Porter's death, September 18, 1980, she received the galley proofs of the collection, which she had edited for publication. Agreeing with the suggestion of her editor at Pemberton Press, Laughlin titled the book *Return from Homelessness: Katherine Anne Porter in Texas.*

With Porter's references to the region as her homeland during that, her last, visit, a more apt title for the Howard Payne symposium proceedings might have been "Return to Her Homeland." Porter's enthusiastic response to being back in Texas for the first time since her ill-fated trip to Dallas in 1964 was evident at once. Laughlin describes her exuberant storytelling as, "a performance really," as they drove toward Brownwood. In Stephenville, the three stopped at the Ramada Inn dining room for pecan pie, and Porter was delighted. She praised the pie and added that she had not had a good sausage patty since she left Texas.

The lively threesome reached Brownwood late that day where worried faculty members carefully masked their relief. Throughout the long months of organizing the symposium, the planners were aware that their honored guest had a reputation for canceling her appearances at the last minute. To counter their fretting, Laughlin introduced Plan B—a humorous suggestion that because her grandmother had white hair and resembled Katherine Anne, they could just introduce her as KAP if their honoree was a no-show. Fortunately, Plan B was not necessary, and Porter, although frail, displayed considerable energy during her four-day visit (Laughlin interview).

Soon after her arrival, accompanied by Professors Almola James and Elva Dodson and with a school nurse in attendance, Katherine

Anne visited Indian Creek Cemetery, where she placed roses on her mother's grave. Laughlin pointed out that Porter's biographer Joan Givner is mistaken in her report that instead of the blanket of talisman roses that Porter had requested for her mother's grave, "to her chagrin, a bouquet of pink roses had been purchased for her" (Givner 502). Laughlin presented a bouquet of yellow roses to Porter when she arrived in Dallas, which pleased her, particularly when her hosts called them the "yellow roses of Texas." Porter herself purchased the flowers for her mother's grave and was delighted to be able to place them there that day.

Porter and her hosts picnicked in Indian Creek Cemetery, and later Porter became faint from heat and excitement. She was rushed back to her room at the Holiday Inn where she soon recovered with the aid of Dr. Seal Cutbirth, a physician who was also a trustee of HPU. Dr. Cutbirth donned a robe on Sunday to sit beside Porter on the platform during HPU commencement exercises in the Brownwood Coliseum, where she was awarded an honorary doctorate and recognized as "Texas' first writer to receive nation-wide attention" (*Brownwood Bulletin* May 7, 1976). Although the program included the presentation of degrees to 219 graduates, both a choir and band performance, and an address by President Brooks, the eighty-six-year-old honoree kept her poise and received her degree graciously before a capacity crowd.

At 2 P.M. on Monday, Dr. George C. Pittman of the HPU English faculty presided over the first symposium session. First-day participants included Joan Givner, Darlene Unrue, Andy J. Moore, Almola James, and Jack DeBellis (*Brownwood Bulletin* May 2, 1976). That evening, Porter spoke to 120 guests at the banquet honoring her in the Sid Richardson Hall Gold Room, where she read "Anniversary in a Country Cemetery," the poem she had written in 1936 after visiting her mother's grave. The event was not without considerable drama. Laughlin describes KAP's angry reluctance to attend the banquet after seeing that day's newspaper coverage of a book-signing session:

On Monday, May 10, (the day of the banquet) . . . we learned that KAP's aversion to unflattering photos could be serious. [An unflattering] photo appeared in the Monday "Brownwood Bulletin." She saw it just as we were leaving her hotel room to attend the banquet, where she was to speak, and went into a rage. "This is damnable! It's cruel! I can't speak to people after they've seen a horror like this. I won't." With that, she threw to the floor the book containing her poem "Anniversary in a Country Cemetery," which she had planned to read at the banquet. But when we walked in the banquet room, KAP clasped her hands in front of her and exclaimed with a look of rapture on her face, "All these people! They've come to see me! I must speak. Go fetch the book." A gentleman in our group did the lady's bidding and returned with the book in time for her speech, which was spontaneous, fascinating, and a delight.

She announced that evening as well that she would send the university a collection of her works to be featured in a special section of the HPU library. Back home she made an extensive list of furniture she would like the university to have for furnishing a study room at the library. The furniture, however, never arrived. Her nephew, Paul Porter, finally informed the university that the furniture had to be sold to pay expenses after Porter's death. Laughlin says that Porter later sent a number of her books, many in foreign-language editions, but no major library exhibit honored Porter until Brooks, who had become director of the Armstrong Browning Library at Baylor, organized an International Conference in 1992 honoring the writer.

On Tuesday, May 11, 1976, HPU English professors Alta Ada Schoner, Bill Crider, Charlotte Laughlin, and Elva Dobson presided over sessions featuring papers on Porter's works and her role as social critic. Out-of-state scholars represented the University of Regina, University of Nevada at Las Vegas, Lehigh University, Southern Connecticut State College, Brigham Young University, Manhattan College, Clemson University, and the University of Wisconsin at Madison. Others reading papers were from such Texas schools as Baylor, HPU, Tarleton State University, Dallas Community College, and the University of Texas at El Paso.[4]

Brownwood citizens were invited to all sessions, but one of three of Porter's cousins living in the area found the cost too high. Roscoe Jones, son of Katherine Anne's uncle George M. Jones, told Laughlin that "it would cost me and my wife $7.50 apiece to see her. I figured I'd lived 74 years without seeing her, and I wasn't going to pay $15 to see her now." Laughlin asked Roscoe if he had identified himself as Porter's cousin to the HPU receptionist he had contacted. He told her that he really didn't see any reason to "claim kin," but that he was just curious. If Porter was aware that the Jones kin, her first cousins, lived in the area, she failed to mention that familial connection to her hosts (*Brownwood Bulletin* Sept. 21, 1980).[5]

After Katherine Anne returned to Maryland, Givner wrote a warm account of the symposium on May 23, 1976, for *The Dallas Morning News*, which was later published in Givner's *Katherine Anne Porter: Conversations* (189–91). Headlined "A Fine Day of Homage to Porter," the article describes Brownwood as "a little gemstone of a country town and never lovelier than at this time of the year." She praises the Howard Payne faculty for their hospitality and says, "Surely no conference was ever arranged with such good will and such a sure sense of what was fitting to the occasion." She adds finally that "these amiable people entertained, chauffeured, and patiently explained everything from chiggers to bluebonnets. . . . Informality, good humor, and adaptability were the order of the day, and larger institutions with experienced conveners might well envy the success of this group." Porter scholars may be puzzled, as I was, why Givner's tone shifts so obviously from this positive, favorable assessment of Brownwood and the conference to such a dismal, negative portrayal of the town and its citizens six years later when she gives perhaps one of the most dramatic events in Porter's last years a scant two-page coverage in her biography of the writer.

In this version, Givner says that coming back to Howard Payne (which she calls Payne in one reference) was an odd choice for Porter, who had once said that her "bent was to the left," and who had also railed against fundamentalist religious sects. Calling Howard Payne University "a very right-wing institution," Givner cites an essay in *The Texas Observer*, which she says was written by a reporter covering the symposium for the journal, and which describes in great detail the Hall of Civilization in Brownwood, located in the General Douglas McArthur Academy of Freedom. She includes a quote from the essay that warns that the academy's exhibits are "frightening to an egalitarian sensitivity" (501). What Givner fails to point out is that the essay, entitled "Dugout Doug and Drugstore Blitz," was published on December 2, 1977, eighteen months after Porter's visit to Brownwood. Nowhere does the author, James Stanley Walker, described as an Austin-based architect, say he was in Brownwood to attend the Porter symposium. Apparently, Walker came to the area in late 1977, specifically to tour the Academy of Freedom. Walker's main concern in 1977 was that the academy was developing rabid anti-communists. Walker also notes that the architecture and murals were abysmal, but he admits that his well-mannered young guide who took him through the building left a favorable impression.

Givner goes on to say that Porter was spared a tour of the academy and that she did not see enough of the campus to depress her. Laughlin theorizes that this abrupt shift in Givner's tone may have originated in a bedside interview with Porter after her first stroke early in 1977. Givner rushed to Washington, apparently with a proprietary attitude. One of the Howard Payne University faculty who felt she had established an intimacy with Porter and who believed that Porter had given her permission to write a literary biography during the symposium also arrived at the hospital, where a considerable controversy occurred.

Whatever those who were to write about Porter's relationship with her "homeland" came to believe about Porter's last visit to her birthplace, none can dispute that she was greatly moved by the hospitality she found there during those four days in May 1976. A little more than four years later, Porter's ashes were returned to this place she called home as she had requested as early as 1936. Paul Porter, with Laughlin's assistance, arranged for the priest at Brownwood's St. Mary's Catholic Church to preside over the placing of Porter's remains in a grave next to her mother's. Few in Brownwood knew of the event, and perhaps only church officials attended the burial.

Porter's plain but elegant gravestone with the epitaph "In my end is my beginning," is almost in the center of the well-kept Indian Creek Cemetery, and next to the weathered marker at the head of her mother's grave. Not even half-filled with graves, the cemetery is enclosed by a neat cyclone fence. Level and dotted with live oak and mesquite trees, the area is surrounded by low hills that are covered more profusely with these native trees. Located three or four miles west of the ghost town that was once Indian Creek, the cemetery requires a country sense of direction to find off the highway that connects Brownwood with Brady. Several miles out of Brownwood, a sign now points the way east down a narrow, rural road to Indian Creek Cemetery, but that road branches. Bearing right, the persistent seeker winds through hills past signs indicating that several cattle companies occupy the grasslands. Substantial homes, probably of

Brownwood professionals seeking country living, are set back from the quiet road. Indian Creek is located on the stream's bottomlands, the course readily discernable, marked by much undergrowth and tall trees. Several old houses are still occupied, although their vintage appears to be less than that of the original buildings in the little town. Only the ancient Masonic Hall and the ruins of the brick Methodist Church seem likely to have been a part of the early history of the area.

For native Texans and for southerners, it is no mystery why the nationally acclaimed writer chose finally to come to rest near her birthplace. Hard to define but easy to share is that sense of being at home—better known as a sense of place. That emotion "brought the homeless one home again." It seemed highly symbolic on the warm May day I visited KAP's grave that a mockingbird with an extensive repertoire shared his music from a nearby tree until I left. ❖

Notes

[1] "HPU Professor Looks into Life of Author" and "Porter Anticipated Death," a two-part article in the *Brownwood Bulletin* by Dr. Charlotte Laughlin on Sept. 21 and 22, 1980, and a phone conversation with Dr. Laughlin on May 7, 1998, provided much of the information on Porter's Brownwood visit and on her family for this essay.

[2] Laughlin includes this quote from a personal letter in "Porter Anticipated Death."

[3] Unfortunately, Laughlin's editor resigned from her position at Pemberton, a branch of Jenkins Publishing Company, and the book was never published.

[4] Titles of the symposium papers are included in "A Texas

Bibliography," by Sally Dee Wade. In Machann, Clinton, and William Bedford Clark, eds. *Katherine Anne Porter and Texas*. College Station: Texas A&M UP, 1990: 155–57.

[5] In Laughlin's research, however, she spoke with both Brownwood resident Roscoe and his brother Hardin Jones, a resident of nearby Goldthwaite. Their sister, Alice Russell, also lived in Brownwood at the time. Their father, George M. Jones, was brother of Mary Alice Porter, Katherine Anne's mother. It was from these sources that Laughlin learned a different family history from any yet included in KAP's biography.

When Katherine Anne's maternal grandfather, John Newton Jones, came to Brown County in 1883, he settled on 640 acres about seven miles south of Brownwood. In a letter to her sister Gay, according to Givner, Katherine Anne seems to have believed that her Jones grandmother was still living with her family when Mary Alice Porter, Katherine Anne's mother, died in 1892 (39-41). Cousin Alice Russell, however, said that her father George never spoke of his parents' past, but he did know that his mother, Caroline C. Jones (also called Cynthia Frost Jones in Laughlin's essay) was left behind in a mental institution in Seguin when John Newton came to Brown County. She may have been with the family for short periods after that, however. When Katherine Anne was six, her father, acting on his power of attorney as executor for Caroline C. Jones, presented her with papers to sign which would release some of the Jones' farm for sale to provide funds for maintenance and education of his children (*Brownwood Bulletin* Sept. 21, 1980).

John Newton Jones' farm had supported both the family of Harrison Porter, Katherine Anne's father, and the family of George M. Jones. George was married first to Harrison's sister, Louellah, who died at age twenty-seven and was buried in Indian Creek Cemetery near her infant children. According to Laughlin's sources, Mary Alice's mother,

Catherine Anne, never believed the Porter offspring were "good enough" to be spouses of her children and was further embittered by the death of her daughter, Louellah. The tombstone that the grandmother Catherine Anne erected at her daughter's grave in Indian Creek Cemetery omits the information that Louellah was George Jones' wife. Harrison, however, corresponded with his brother-in-law for several years after he left Indian Creek.

Several other contradictions of Givner's version of Katherine Anne's early life are recorded by Laughlin. For example, Katherine Anne was probably not named for an early girlhood friend of her mother's, whom Givner says died young. Laughlin believes that Callie was chosen to honor Callie Hobbs, a close friend of Mary Alice Porter, who later became her brother George's second wife, and Russell was after Harrison's good friend W. H. Russell. It was Russell who would later become the bondsman when Harrison applied for guardianship of the Jones property left to his children. Alice Russell, who told Laughlin her husband Ernest was not related to W. H. Russell, also made clear that she believed that the Jones and Porter families attended the Methodist Church in the small community of Ebony until that church closed. Then they began attending the Indian Creek Church, now a crumbling ruin. Cousin Alice, who says her mother, Callie Hobbs Jones, named her after Porter's mother, insisted to Laughlin that the only Catholic in her entire family connection was the wife of her half-brother Hugh Leon, who died in 1952 in California. Alice said that maybe Katherine Anne "got being a Catholic from Hugh's wife," since cousin Hardin seems to remember that Katherine Anne visited with Hugh and his wife during her California residence. In a 1920s photograph accompanying Laughlin's article, Roscoe, Hardin, and Hugh Leon are pictured. Handsome men, they are dressed fashionably in almost identical suits and ties (*Brownwood Bulletin* Sept. 21, 1980).

Works Cited

Givner, Joan. *Katherine Anne Porter: A Life.* New York: Simon and Schuster, 1982.

———.*Katherine Anne Porter: Conversations.* Jackson: UP of Mississippi, 1987.

Walker, James Stanley. "Dugout Doug and Drugstore Blitz." *The Texas Observer.* Dec. 2, 1977: 20–21.

Katherine Anne Porter and Texas: Ambivalence Deep as the Bone

Mark Busby

Despite its title, the collection of essays titled *Katherine Anne Porter and Texas: An Uneasy Relationship*, edited by Clint Machann and Bedford Clark, muddies the water about Porter's relationship to Texas. Most of the essayists discount the connection. In his essay for that collection titled "A Southern Writer in Texas: Porter and the Texas Literary Tradition," Don Graham, for example, acknowledges that Porter writes about her part of Texas, "pre World War I central Texas," but he finds it "Southern to the core," a place with none of the "ingredients of the Texas myth" (70). And Janis Stout in the same collection reinforces this point: "It is possible for someone who has lived all her life in Texas (myself, for example) and who ought to know Texas when she sees it to read Porter's stories and . . . to imagine them to be set not in Texas but in some Southern region farther east" (86).

Porter, of course, bears the burden for most of the confusion about her regional ties, for throughout much of her early life she consciously created a fictional biography, shaving four years off her birthday and creating a genteel southern heritage. When Willene and George Hendrick went to Indian Creek, Texas, in 1962 and discovered that Porter's mother's tombstone bore as the year of death 1892, part of the fiction began to unravel. For years, Porter had said she was born in 1894—a feat worthy of *Ripley's Believe It or Not* with a mother two years in the grave. With Joan Givner's monumental biography of Porter in 1982, revised in 1991, most of the other fictions were laid to rest, and the picture of the real Katherine Anne Porter comes more clearly into focus.

James T. F. Tanner's *The Texas Legacy of Katherine Anne Porter* takes us closer toward the truth of Porter and Texas, as he points out the Texas ties and then provides concise analyses of Porter's work. Tanner makes it clear that we must remember that Porter was indeed a Texas writer, and he finds five consistent motifs in her work that stem from her Texas childhood:

> Repeatedly we find in her narratives: (1) a passive, ineffectual male unable to cope with domestic responsibilities . . . ; (2) a dominant, take-charge female imposing order in domestic chaos . . . ; (3) a defective child or helpless individual in a hostile environment . . . ; (4) the passive advancement and encouragement of evil by ostensibly "innocent" or "respectable" people . . . ; and [5] betrayal of trust in many forms. . . . (41)

Although Tanner correctly attributes these themes to Porter's Texas experiences, he does not demonstrate what it is about Texas that led her to some of her most profound and recurring feelings and themes in her most significant stories.

In his early book on southwestern literature, *My Blood's Country*, Tom Pilkington points out that Texas' geography makes it a land of borders. Both borders and the frontier suggest a line where two differing factions meet. In fact, one of the major features of Texas fiction is ambivalence. Early settlers who both conquered nature and felt simultaneously at one with it began the feelings of ambivalence that Larry McMurtry admits still cut him "as deep as the bone" in his luminous essay "Take My Saddle From the Wall: A Valediction" from *In a Narrow Grave*. McMurtry's epigraph for *Lonesome Dove* is the following quote from T. K. Whipple's *Study Out the Land*:

> All America lies at the end of the wilderness road, and our past is not a dead past, but still lives in us. Our forefathers had civilization inside themselves, the wild outside. We live in the civilization they created, but within us the wilderness still lingers. What they dreamed, we live, and what they lived, we dream.

The Texas frontier experience produced these deep feelings of ambivalence as Louise Cowan notes,

> Texans from the beginning were confronted with a dual consciousness: were they transplanted Americans or a new breed? Should they look to the aristocratic landed gentry for their ideals or to Rousseau's noble savage? Should their allegiance be with the Anglo-Saxon or the Spanish culture? Should they be cultivated or primitive? Should they hold to the idea of progress or to pastoralism? Were they pious or iconoclastic? barbarian or civilized? isolated or communal? materialistic or ascetic? Was the new territory they settled garden or desert? Caucasian, Christian, Yankee, Southerner, Westerner—Texans found themselves to be all of these. (*Texas Myths* 20)

Ambivalence, being drawn at the same time toward two almost opposing forces such as civilization and wilderness, is central to the southwestern legend, and it appears forcefully in many Texas writers' works. J. Frank Dobie's *A Vaquero of the Brush Country*, for example, laments the end of open country and at the same time acknowledges that human greed made barbed wire necessary. And ambivalence is central to McMurtry's *Horseman, Pass By* with its combined feelings of sadness and good-riddance at the end of the old world's ways. And more recently Stephen Harrigan in *A Natural State: Essays on Texas* acknowledged that "Texas is an imperfect place to write about nature. . . . The Texas landscape is not always beautiful, and in some places, at some moments, it is hardly bearable. But it is resonant and full of secrets" and that he was writing as "a tribute to the power with which those secrets are guarded" (xi).

Katherine Anne Porter's ambivalence also cut deep as she struggled to get away from Texas and returned to it again and again in stories that some think appear to be about somewhere else. As Givner makes clear, much of Porter's early feelings for Texas resulted from her family's poverty, her failed first marriage, and perhaps her desire, like Miranda in "Old Mortality," to leave "any place . . . that threatened to forbid her making her own decisions" (222).

Later as she became an established author, other events estranged her again from Texas. The first event concerned the Texas Institute of Letters. Givner explains:

> In 1939, the Texas Institute of Letters, founded in 1936 for the "Promotion and Recognition of Literature in Texas," announced its first award for the best book by a Texas writer. *Pale Horse, Pale Rider* had been in the running and seemed a certain winner, since no other author had achieved Porter's national stature. When she learned that the prize had gone to J. Frank Dobie for *Apache Gold and Yaqui Silver* because of the "indigenous nature" of his subject matter and because he was not only a native but had remained in Texas, she was convinced once again that Texas was no place for her. (Givner, *A Life* 315)

Her anger at Texas was still hot in 1946 when she wrote to her favorite nephew, Paul Porter, and advised him how to approach his future. In this letter in the Southwestern Writers Collection at Southwest Texas State University, she wrote:

> Darling what would you do in Mexico? Go to the University there? Don't run away anywhere, from anything. Don't go anywhere unless you have a real reason. . . . I wanted for years to go to Europe, but I kept getting little jobs that took me back to Mexico. And finally came the Guggenheim which took me to Europe, and once there, I managed to stay for six years. Never go back to Texas—I mean, not for years. Stay where you are until you take some decisive step, make some plan, find your balance. . . . You know perfectly well you are going to be an artist, that is a life time occupation, full time. One begins slowly and must be full of strategy.

The second major estranging event occurred after Porter was invited to lecture at the University of Texas at Austin in the fall of 1958. The visit, as Givner makes clear, seemed on the surface to be perfect. She was interviewed by Winston Bode for *The Texas Observer*, met several old friends who had gone to school with her, and best of all from Porter's perspective, became convinced that Harry Ransom planned to name a large new section in the library for her. Delighted, Porter began planning to settle in Austin and to give her papers to the university, which was then amassing the fortune of works that would become the Ransom Humanities Research Center. Additionally, she was nicely treated by an English faculty member, William Handy, and also his wife, Diedre, who had written a master's thesis about Porter. As she left Texas, the Handys gave her a copy of the thesis, and the euphoria began turning to dust first as she read the thesis on her return home:

I gave up in despair, seeing that it would take another essay of the same length to refute this. . . . I want to ask only one question: Does the rejection and denial of a Christian and moral idea of life by the lowest elements of the population (which began taking over some time ago, and has now got our society debased beyond recognition) prove that system to have been evil and corrupt, or has it been simply cast aside by the evil and corrupt powers of our society. This is, I think, pragmatism in a very dangerous form . . . good is not turned to evil merely because it has, apparently at least, lost the battle. Things are not per se good simply because they are in power. (quoted in Givner, *A Life* 427)

Her anger at this thesis was compounded, for as the months went by, she heard nothing from Harry Ransom about the library wing to be named in her honor. Before long, she realized that she had either been misled or had misunderstood, and she decided in anger to leave her things to the McKeldin Library at the University of Maryland.

In her recent book, *Katherine Anne Porter: A Sense of the Times*, Janis Stout takes another look at the relationship between Porter and Texas and points to the conflicted feelings Porter had toward her native area, noting that even before the ill-fated library experience, Porter had written to her nephew Paul in 1948: "[T]he library of Texas recently asked me please to contribute another manuscript to their collection. Pore lil ole thaings. But I haven't got one handy. Filthy little bastards, the lot of them." And then finding herself listed as a writer of the "Lone Star mystique" in Louis Rubin's and C. Hugh Holman's *Southern Literary Study: Problems and Possibilities* (1975), she wrote in the margin, "Include me out, please." And Stout concludes:

Her feelings toward her native place are curiously conflicted—

almost as conflicted, perhaps, as her feelings toward her family. Indeed, the two are inexplicably intertwined. They emerge in her continual search for a home and loving relationships and her continual inability to settle into either. (35)

Her unhappy experiences explain much of her ambivalence, but R. G. Vliet, another Texas writer who grew up in Kyle, Texas, attributes Porter's contradictory feelings to a more deep-seated source: the geography of her home countryside.

As you drive toward Austin through, for instance, Kyle, the town where Katherine Anne Porter was raised by an archetypal grand-mother and where much of her early fiction is set, the boundary is palpable. On your right is the rich, black, softly rolling cotton-farmland of the South, on your left the leading edge of the rocky, cedar and post-oak, ranch-section Hill Country. There is very nearly a clean division in idiom there too: toward the right the soft, drawling pronunciation general to the South, to the left the brusque consonantal harshness understood as "western" that so reflects the harsher landscape. This accounts for the difficulty we sometimes have in deciding whether Katherine Anne Porter in her early fiction is in fact writing about the South or the Southwest. In her great short novel, "Noon Wine," she is writing about the Southwest. In "Old Mortality" and in the series of sketches in *The Old Order*, she is writing about the South. South and Southwest ran simultaneously through her childhood, right there in Kyle. (19)

In a 1928 letter to her friend Josephine Herbst, Porter seems to find ambivalence as a human condition produced by the conflicted feelings of memory:

I believe we exist on half a dozen planes in at least six dimensions and inhabit all periods of time at once, by way of memory, racial experience, dreams that are another channel of memory, fantasy that is also reality, and I believe that a first rate work of art somehow succeeds in pulling all these things together and reconciling them. When we deliberately ignore too much we make a fatal mistake. (quoted in Givner, *A Life* 72)

Givner's biography documents clearly how Porter lived a life being drawn in different directions. She admired her grandmother so much that she was incensed at criticism of the character based on her, Sophia Jane Rhea, but Porter rejected much of her grandmother's precepts. Porter's Aunt Cat, Givner writes, "rarely indulged in full immersion in a bathtub, preferring instead a discreet pitcher of water in the bedroom. Similarly, she considered it shameful for the children to be naked at any time and they were hastily bundled in towels when they bathed" (54). But Porter later had nude photographs taken of herself for her lovers and sent copies home to family members perhaps in raw defiance of Aunt Cat, and at age forty, she bragged to Robert Penn Warren that she had had four husbands and thirty-seven lovers.

This ambivalence cut across her life. Politically, Porter aligned herself with the left, but as Givner notes in her introduction to *Katherine Anne Porter: Conversations*, Porter's interviews show her to be "confused on political matters." Givner notes: "She is torn between her wish to identify with the 'guilt ridden white pillar crowd' on the one hand and with the rebels of the radical left on the other. Sometimes she tries to get the best of both worlds by depicting herself as someone of aristocratic origins who has turned her back on those origins" (xiii). In an interview with Robert Van Gelder her political ambivalence seems clear when she stated that her three major interests were "friends, revolution, and cooking" (quoted in *Conversations*, xiii). By 1958 she moved from the left to the conservative right and spoke out against school desegregation.

And as Givner's revised edition of the biography points out, Porter seems to have been conflicted about one of her major literary themes as well: betrayal. Elinor Langer's 1984 biography of Porter's friend Josephine Herbst indicates that in 1942 Porter became an FBI informant and gave the FBI information suggesting that Herbst was a Soviet courier, a supporter of Stalin, and an opponent of the American system of government. Givner continues:

> Such serious charges had the potential of destroying completely Herbst's career and chances of finding work. But the enormity of the betrayal was compounded by the fact that Porter's version of Herbst's activities was false. (Givner, *A Life* 3)

Reading Givner's traditional biography or Stout's intellectual one, it is clear that ambivalence, contradiction, duality, confliction, antithesis—call it what one wishes—the feelings cut across her life: she decried feminists and lived feminism; she disparaged blacks and Jews and wrote about freedom; she deplored homosexuals and consistently sought relationships with homosexual or bisexual men. This extreme changeability, Stout suggests, might have resulted in her noted inability to complete a long work, perhaps because of what Givner supposes was a short attention span. Stout comments:

> One day she was wanting to buy a mountain in California and live there forever, another day she was deciding that Pennsylvania felt more like home than any place she had ever been, and almost the next, it seems, she was declaring Virginia the most perfect place in the world for her. (202)

The ambivalence Porter displayed in her life—an especially clear Southwestern trait—appears in her work as well, perhaps most explicitly in her presentation of the grandmother, Sophia Jane Rhea. In most of the stories in which she appears, Porter draws her in both positive and negative terms. In "The Source," the first story of *The Old Order*, for example, Porter's ambivalence toward the character of Sophia Jane Rhea is apparent. The story concerns how Miss Sophia feels the need to return to the farm early every summer as a method of relaxation. Thus on one level the title refers to the farm as a primitive source of Miss Sophia's power. This is the positive side of the character—a woman who is the source of order in a natural world where entropy prevails without a counter force. When Miss Sophia returns to the farm, she is a returning general, a martinet who becomes a "tireless and efficient slave driver of every creature on the place" (324).

In "The Journey" the grandmother and Aunt Nannie sit as old women and reminisce about their lives as representatives of the old order anticipating the new. It seems clear that the two women whose lives are intertwined suggest duality with the two combining to make a whole person. As they sit quilting—a metaphor for the fragmentation and wholeness that the story dramatizes—the grandmother represents the time-bound character of authority: "Grandmother's role was authority, she knew that; it was her duty to portion out activities, to urge or restrain where necessary, to teach morals, manners, and religion, to punish and reward her own household according to a fixed code" (328). For her dates are important: "Grandmother had masses of dates in her mind, and no memories attached to them."

Nannie, on the other hand, represents pure feeling: "Old Nannie had no ideas at all as to her place in the world. It had been assigned to her before birth, and for her daily rule she had all her life obeyed the authority nearest to her" (328). Instead of recalling dates, she remembers names, people's dress and looks, and the weather and food of special occasions, but no dates. The two together represent feeling and form, but even so it is a passing order—one to be replaced partially by the new western woman who becomes her third daughter-in-law, a woman Grandmother finds "altogether too Western, too modern, something like the 'new' woman who was beginning to run wild asking for the vote, leaving her home and going out in the world to earn her own living. . . ." (333), in short, the kind of woman Porter herself became, in fact, the kind of strong, pioneer woman the grandmother herself had been forced because of geography and circumstance to become.

Ambivalence enters throughout these stories of *The Old Order*, because almost all of them are built on dualities. "The Grave," for example, turns on the dualities of youth and age, birth and death, innocence and experience, past and present, fertility and infertility, male and female, guilt and innocence, all intertwined through the power of memory.

Darlene Unrue, in *Understanding Katherine Anne Porter*, identifies a similar searching for truth as Porter's overriding theme:

In 1940, looking back on twenty years of writing, Porter commented that her stories were "fragments of a much larger plan," which she was "still engaged in carrying out." Later she praised Caroline Gordon's perspicacity in seeing a unity in all her stories. What Porter called her "larger plan" is the motif of a journey toward truth about oneself and the universe. The progress toward truth is hard won, and relatively few of her stories contain illuminations. Although many stories contain representative trips, voyages, and excursions, Porter often subsumes the journey in a surface story that illustrates the obstacles in that movement toward enlightenment. She identified as obstacles civilized men's and women's ingrained distaste for the primitive that coexists with the intellectual in the human psyche, their grasping at systems, rituals, or romantic ideas as a substitute for truth, and their failure to acknowledge that at the heart of the universe stands a mystery, the answer to which, Porter says, may be God, or love. (7–8)

Porter made her peace with Texas at age eighty-five when she returned to her home state to receive an honorary degree from Howard Payne University, a small, fundamentalist Baptist school in Brownwood, near her place of birth and her mother's grave in Indian Creek. After a visit to the grave, Porter decided that on her death her remains would return to Texas. As she made the preparations for the trip, she wrote to Roger Brooks, then president of Howard Payne:

> I happened to be the first native of Texas in its whole history to be a professional writer. That is to say, one who had the vocation and practiced only that and lived by and for it all my life. We have had a good many lately in the last quarter of the century perhaps and we have had many people who wrote memoirs and saved many valuable stories and have written immensely interesting and valuable things about Texas: and they are to be valued and understood. But I am very pleased that I am the first who ever was born to the practice of literature. (quoted in Givner, "Southwest" 564–65)

The ambivalence Porter felt during her life extends through her death, as Givner notes in her essay "Katherine Anne Porter and the Southwest":

> After her own death, three years later, Porter's physical remains were brought back, according to her wishes, and placed in her mother's grave. It seemed that she had really come home at last. Her large and

144

important literary archive, however, was willed to the Katherine Anne Porter Room at the University of Maryland's McKeldin Library, and it is there that Porter scholars must do their research. This two-fold disposition of her remains correctly indicates that the ambivalences of a lifetime were never finally resolved. (559)

If she reconciled herself to her home state during her life, the question remains: did Katherine Anne Porter reconcile her own personal ambivalence? It was through her art—a process of shaping conflicting, disparate pieces into a whole—that she achieved wholeness. She told Winston Bode:

> I think everyone lives a story three times over. . . . The first time is when the events occur . . . then when you remember them . . . and the third time is when you begin to put them into art. . . . And there is a fourth time when people ask how it happened when they ask artists to explain themselves. . . . Tracing the art through the labyrinth of experience . . . childhood memory . . . is really an impossible undertaking, a little like tapping one's own spinal fluid. (Bode 36; his ellipses)

And in "Noon Wine: The Sources," she wrote:

> By the time I wrote "Noon Wine" it had become real to me almost in the sense that I felt not as if I had made that story out of my own memory of real events and imagined consequences, but as if I were quite simply reporting events I had heard or witnessed. This is not in the least true: the story is fiction; but it is made up of thousands of things that did happen to living human beings in a certain part of the country at a certain time of my life; things that are still remembered by others as single incidents; not as I

remembered them, floating and moving with their separate life and reality, meeting and parting and mingling in my thoughts until they established their relationship and meaning to me. So I feel that this story is "true" in the way that a work of fiction should be true, created out of all the scattered particles of life I was able to absorb and combine and shape into new being. . . . (Porter, *CE*)

Porter once said that her life was a work of art and that she didn't believe a word of it. But throughout that life she remained fiercely committed to the unifying power of her art. Perhaps, then, one can say about Katherine Anne Porter's life what Chief Bromden in Ken Kesey's *One Flew Over the Cuckoo's Nest* does about the story he is telling: "All of this is true even if it didn't happen." ❖

Works Cited

Bode, Winston. "Miss Porter on Writers and Writing." *Katherine Anne Porter: Conversations*. Ed. Joan Givner. Jackson: UP of Mississippi, 1987.

Cowan, Louise. "Myth in the Modern World." *Texas Myths*. College Station: Texas A&M UP, 1986.

Dobie, J. Frank. *A Vaquero of the Brush Country*. Boston: Little, Brown, and Company, 1929, 1943.

Givner, Joan. *Katherine Anne Porter: A Life*. Rev. ed. Athens: U of Georgia P, 1991.

———, ed. *Katherine Anne Porter: Conversations*. Jackson: UP of Mississippi, 1987.

———. *Katherine Anne Porter: A Life*. New York: Simon and Schuster, 1982: U of Georgia P, 1991.

————. "Katherine Anne Porter and the Southwest." *A Literary History of the American West*. Ed. J. Golden Taylor, et al. Fort Worth: Texas Christian UP, 1987.

————. "Katherine Anne Porter: The Old Order and the New." *The Texas Literary Tradition: Fiction, Folklore, History*. Ed. Don Graham, et al. Austin: U of Texas P, 1983.

Harrigan, Stephen. *A Natural State: Essays on Texas*. Austin: U of Texas P, 1988.

Hendrick, George. *Katherine Anne Porter*. New York: Twayne, 1965.

Machann, Clinton, and William Bedford Clark, eds. *Katherine Anne Porter and Texas: An Uneasy Relationship*. College Station: Texas A&M UP, 1990.

McMurtry, Larry. *Horseman, Pass By*. New York: Simon and Schuster, 1961, 1990.

Porter, Katherine Anne. "The Circus." *Southern Review* 1 (July 1935): 36–41.

————. *The Collected Stories*. New York: Harcourt Brace, 1965.

————. *Katherine Anne Porter's Poetry*. Ed. Darlene Harbour Unrue. Columbia: U of South Carolina P, 1996.

————. "Notes on the Texas I Remember." *Atlantic Monthly* 235:3 (1975): 102.

————. *Ship of Fools*. New York: Atlantic–Little, Brown, 1962.

————. *Uncollected Early Prose of Katherine Anne Porter*. Ed. Ruth M. Alvarez and Thomas F. Walsh. Austin: U of Texas P, 1993.

Stout, Janis P. *Katherine Anne Porter: A Sense of the Times*. Charlottesville: U of Virginia P, 1995.

Tanner, James T. F. *The Texas Legacy of Katherine Anne Porter*. Denton: U of North Texas P, 1990.

Unrue, Darlene Harbour. *Truth and Vision in Katherine Anne Porter's Fiction*. Athens: U of Georgia P, 1985.

———. *Understanding Katherine Anne Porter.* Columbia: U of South Carolina P, 1988.

Vliet, R. G. "On a Literature of the Southwest: An Address." *The Texas Observer*, Apr. 28, 1978: 19.

Walsh, Thomas F. *Katherine Anne Porter and Mexico: The Illusion of Eden.* Austin: U of Texas P, 1992.

———. "Braggioni's Jockey Club in 'Flowering Judas.'" *Studies in Short Fiction* 20 (spring/summer 1983): 136–38.

Knowing Nature in Katherine Anne Porter's Short Fiction

Terrell F. Dixon

Like the accomplishments of many American writers whose work is imprinted on a definite, recognizable landscape in the West or Southwest, Katherine Anne Porter's fiction is frequently described as providing "a sense of place." As critical attention to her work expanded from an early focus on her stylistic accomplishments to encompass a variety of topics including her views of the South, her explorations into the psychology of family relationships, her renditions of the complexities inherent in coming of age, her conflicted considerations of women's role in a patriarchal society, and her often contradictory attitudes about the intellectual and social history of her times, the underlying assumption that the work conveys "a sense of place" has remained a constant.

But for all of the frequency and confidence with which we use "a sense of place" in discussing Porter's fiction (as well as the accomplishments of other writers whose work has a strong regional component), it has largely remained without any precise and widely agreed upon definition. When we apply it to Porter's short stories, what we often seem to mean is the ability to embody compellingly realistic observations about family, gender, class, and ethnic attitudes set in those places—Texas, the South, and Mexico—where much of her fiction takes place. An ecocritical reading of her fiction, however, suggests that her own sense of place ultimately involves more than an ability to sketch regional settings and to depict regional culture. In some of her most interesting and important stories, Katherine Anne Porter looks closely at our human relationship to the rest of the natural world, firmly grounding her own highly developed sense of place in the importance of knowing nature.

For Porter the emphasis on knowing nature has a specific local focus. She is not writing the John Muir/John Burroughs/Enos Mills type of non-fiction literary natural history, that is, work which features a naturalist's adventures in the remote wild and/or which works for the preservation of pure wilderness territory. Her interest is, instead, in nearby nature. Her subject matter thus is closer to that found in the major work of another important American woman writer with a strong bioregional interest: Susan Fenimore Cooper's *Rural Hours*.[1] Porter's Southwest shares with Cooper's Northeast in Cooperstown, New York, an interest in the interactions with the natural world that take place on farms and in accessible rural areas nearby. When the character called Grandmother in Porter's story "The Old Order" looks forward "with an indefinable sense of homecoming" to "the black, rich soft land and the human beings living on it,"[2] she expresses a sense of the human-nature connection that Porter's fiction has in common with Cooper's nature writing.

Porter's way of writing nature does, of course, differ greatly in form from Cooper's major work and also from what we have traditionally included under the rubric of American nature writing, and this may well be one of the reasons that literary criticism has been somewhat slow in paying much attention to Katherine Anne Porter's interest in nature. As ecocriticism is beginning to acknowledge, however, the familiar form of a non-fiction nature journal organized around the four seasons of a rural year and presenting the writer's direct observations of nature is not the only prose genre that provides serious explorations of nature and the environment. Ecocriticism's expansion of the boundaries of what is considered to be nature literature is starting to include not only the study of such contemporary fiction as Charles Frazier's *Cold Mountain* or Jane Smiley's *A Thousand Acres* but also of significant earlier American fiction about nature.[3] From this perspective, it is clear that Porter's nature stories form part of a significant tradition of American ecofiction, a heritage that includes, among others, such important predecessors of her work in place-based short fiction as Sarah Orne Jewett and Mary Wilkins Freeman.

Once we begin to consider her fiction from an ecocritical viewpoint, it is abundantly clear that Porter's literary imagination is deeply involved in the natural world. The short stories are filled with passages where she uses a nature metaphor or simile to sketch a place, to define a relationship, or—most frequently—to present a character with vividness and efficiency. In "María Concepción," for example, the sense of security in the title character's home is conveyed by its placement with a "clump of pepper trees" above and a "wall of organ cactus enclosing it" (3) on the side. The whippoorwill calling "clear out of season" (42) at the end of "Rope" echoes the situation of its main characters and underlines that story's fascination with the magical unpredictability of male-female relationships. "The Leaning Tower" describes the seductive Lutte's mouth as "like a ripe peach" (490), and "Pale Horse, Pale Rider" conveys Bill's sexual energy through eyes that are "soft and lambent but wild, like a stag's" (287). Amy of "Old Mortality" is seen in her white dress as "glimmering like a moth in the lamplight" (177) and Bragionni, boasting of his fondness for luxury in "Flowering Judas," has "eyes that are the true tawny yellow cat's eyes" (93).

Accompanying this veritable bestiary of character depiction in

151

Porter's fiction are several stories that embody a more sustained consideration of our human relationship to the rest of nature. In "Noon Wine" and "That Tree," for example, the theme of work is central and how one works with nature, or views nature in relationship to one's work, comes to signify the character's moral worth. Mr. Thompson's failure to do the farm work makes him the subject of mockery in "Noon Wine." Thompson has ridiculous and rigid notions of what constitutes "woman's work," what constitutes "hired man's work," and what very few kinds of work might conceivably be important enough and "manly enough" for him, as the boss, to consider actually doing with his own hands. Even after all this contemplation, however, Thompson is still lazy; he thinks and pontificates about work rather than doing any of it. The would-be-writer turned journalist featured in the biting portrait of "That Tree" is a more educated version of the same type. He always talks about writing serious literature when in reality he is quite content to be a well-paid journalist, living a lie and talking, but only talking, about real writing. His fantasy about writing someday always locates him lolling in the shade under "That Tree" of the title. His indolence curtails his relationship with the natural world as well as his writing.

The other central character of "Noon Wine" is in striking contrast to these two. Mr. Helton's quiet and efficient work is not hindered by any such laziness or by any foolish gender or status considerations. It is rooted in a solid knowledge of the farm's natural world and manifest in the husbandry of his continuous and responsible work on the farm. As the knowledgeable steward of nature's bounty on the farm, Helton does so well with the cows, hogs, horses, and chickens that without him the small farm would be in financial difficulty.

This emphasis on engagement with the natural world takes on additional significance and complexity in two of Porter's most intriguing stories—"The Fig Tree" and "Holiday."[4] In them, the natural world becomes central, and knowing nature clearly emerges as a primary and complex theme in Porter's fiction. Even as she chooses not to "allegorize the landscape," to "mythicize it into a Virgilian pastoral mode," or "to politicize it" (Graham 65), Porter's fiction embeds its accurate renditions of Texas nature as central sections of stories that explore both the importance of knowing nature and how such knowledge can be attained.

Miranda, the protagonist of "The Fig Tree," delights in the natural world, and her first excursion in this story takes her into nearby nature on a path that she knows well:

> [D]own the crooked flat-stone walk hopping zigzag between the grass tufts. First there were pomegranate and cape jessamine bushes mixed together; then it got very dark and shady and that was the fig grove. She went to her favorite fig tree where the deep branches bowed down level with her chin, and she could gather figs without having to climb and skin her knees. (354–55)

What she thinks she finds in this known part of her world, however, is unsettling. In the wake of her mother's death, Miranda has sought solace in nature, not simply in tasting the sweet air and fruit of the fig grove but also in noting the rhythms of life and death in nature and in repeating the rituals that we use to mark that transition.

Miranda remembers the long string of carriages and the tolling bell of her mother's funeral, and whenever she found any creature that didn't move, "she always buried it in a little grave with flowers on top and a smooth stone at the head." This time, however, the ritual burial elicits anxiety and anguish. After she buries the one little chicken that didn't move, Miranda hears a cry that seems to come from the grave. Those cries mix with those of the grown-ups commanding her to come right away to the carriage and depart on the family outing to her Great-Aunt

Eliza's place at Cedar Grove. The adults won't listen, so she must go along, burdened with the fear that she has mistakenly taken the life of a baby chicken and that the solace she has found in knowing the great cycle of life and death in the natural world was illusory.

Although Cedar Grove, too, has always offered her its own pleasure-giving natural bounties—"watermelons and grasshoppers and the long rows of blooming chinaberry trees where the hounds flattened themselves out and slept" (353), those natural features are not prominent on the first part of this visit. During this day, Miranda only observes her family members, noting differences and the tension between them and especially the fascinating behavior of Great-Aunt Eliza. This mountainous woman continually uses her scientific instruments to search the natural world, going to the roof with her telescope and even—in a scene that shows the humorous side of her dedication to scientific work—bringing her microscope to the dinner table where she dissects a scrap of potato peeling.

The natural world finally starts to come alive again for Miranda in the two scenes that end this story. This process begins when Aunt Eliza invites the children to view the skies through her telescope:

> . . . . [T]hey were so awed they looked at each other like strangers, and did not exchange a word. Miranda saw only a great pale flaring disk of cold light, but she knew it was the moon and called out in pure rapture, "Oh, it's like another world!"
>
> "Why, of course, child," said Great-Aunt Eliza, in her growling voice, but kindly, "other worlds, a million other worlds." . . ."Like this one?" asked Miranda, timidly. "Nobody knows, nobody knows," Miranda sang to a tune in her head, and when the others walkedon, she was so dazzled with joy she fell back by herself, walking a little distance behind Great-Aunt Eliza's

swinging lantern and her wide-swinging skirts. (361)[5]

Great-Aunt Eliza briefly becomes the kindly mentor concerned with what she can teach her young family members, and her telescope works on Miranda not to enlist her adherence to a codified, scientific mastery of nature but to re-awaken her sense of wonder.

The view Great-Aunt Eliza provides, one directed outward to the awe-inspiring scope of the universe, is complemented by a second climactic event that immediately follows it, and that forms a companion, concluding scene for "The Fig Tree." In this scene, the focus of the story shifts back to nearby nature as Great-Aunt Eliza walks Miranda through the other fig grove, the one at Cedar Grove. Here Miranda once again hears the "terrible, faint, troubled cry" that haunts her from the earlier incident: "'Weep weep, weep weep. . . . ' murmured a little crying voice from the smothering earth, the grave." She reacts in such a strong way that her aunt asks, "What on earth's the matter child?"

When Miranda starts to tell her, Great-Aunt Eliza stoops, puts her arm around Miranda, and offers this explanation: "'They're not in the ground at all. They are the first tree frogs, means it's going to rain,' she said, 'weep, weep—hear them?'" (361). The moment is a crucial one for Miranda and for the story. Great-Aunt Eliza acts as a naturalist passing on important information about local nature gained through first-hand observation, and it is that knowledge that frees Miranda from her fear.

This moment disappears quickly. Great-Aunt Eliza moves out of her local naturalist mode and back into her unintentionally humorous scientific mode with a mini-disquisition on how tree frogs shed their skins, delivered—as the narrative voice emphasizes—in "her most scientific voice" and with a promise to show Miranda "one some time under a microscope" (361). But the change in Miranda is substantial. She listens to the tree frogs sing, and she is able to abandon the anxiety that has plagued her since the morning. Knowing nature in "The Fig Tree" stems from a sense of wonder about the beauty and vastness of the natural world and includes an everyday attentiveness to nearby nature.

In "Holiday," the ways of knowing nature unfold in a very different context. The story features an unnamed first-person narrator providing a retrospective account of what happened on her rural retreat, and the whole journey is initiated and framed by conversations with her friend Louise. When the sensitive young narrator, deeply enmeshed in her own personal, albeit unspecified, troubles, tells Louise that she wants "to go somewhere for a spring holiday, by myself, to the country," Louise tells her that she knows the perfect place. It is a Texas farm, twelve miles from the Louisiana border, inhabited, in Louise's words, by "a family of real old-fashioned German peasants, in the deep blackland Texas farm country, a household in real patriarchal style—the kind of thing you'd hate but is very nice to visit" (408). Although she realizes that her friend is something of an unreliable narrator, that she possesses "something near to genius for making improbable persons, places, and situations sound attractive. She told amusing stories that did not turn grim on you till a little while later. . . ."(408) The narrator nonetheless sets out to visit the countryside.

From the start, however, the storyteller's perceptions tend to parallel those of Louise; like her, she persists in approaching the land with a sense of ironic detachment. Even as she accuses Louise of being overly literary, of indulging in a novelist's imagination as she describes the place, she wants to maintain her own ironic distance from "this paradise" and to make what she sees on this journey fit her own preconceived patterns. She describes, for example, her first human encounter in humorous terms: the boy in hand-me-down clothes that don't quite fit drives a spring wagon where the wheels have a precarious relationship to the wagon and where what holds the harness together is a mystery. This narrator also comes into the country with a preconceived notion of what constitutes landscape beauty. The land is very much like the boy driver whom she says has beautiful eyes, but the rest of his face is "not to be taken seriously." She cannot find beauty in what she chooses to see as this "moribund coma" of a winter landscape, one that has "the forlorn look of all unloved things."

She does gradually begin to move away from the detached brittleness that marks this beginning, but the rewards from her journey to the countryside are not automatic or easy. To realize them, she finally has to accept assistance from an unexpected source. At first, however, she chooses to critique what she sees while sitting at the farmhouse window, carefully situated on the margins both of the farm family's life and of the land. She views the blue-eyed German Müller family as one animalistic body characterized by "the almost mystical inertia of their minds in the midst of this muscular life." Only the crippled Ottilie, whom the narrator assumes must be a servant, stands apart from this group; her slavish role, working inside the house, cleaning and serving food, appears to the narrator as a sure sign that she is the only other outsider in the family's midst.

The gradual change begins when the narrator begins to help cover the seeds in the kitchen garden plot, an engagement with nature that lessens her tortured self-absorption: "I forgot to count the days, they were one like the other except as the colors of the air changed, deepening and warming . . . and the earth grew firmer underfoot with the swelling tangle of crowding roots" (418).

Soon after, she begins to walk the nearby land, an activity that signals the possibility of further growth. Not only is she now out in the landscape, rather than distancing herself from it, but she also finds and chooses to walk a narrow, "less travelled"(419) lane along an aisle of mulberry trees. This evocation of the Frost poem works in several ways. That poem is, among other things, a paean to nature walking and one that helps to emphasize one of Porter's main points in her nature stories: where and how we choose to walk does shape who we are and what we will become. It does make, in the poet's words, "all the difference."

In the context of "Holiday," this choice of the less-traveled walkway, set apart from the working farm with all of the strenuous striving for productivity, also extends Porter's concern with what constitutes a desirable, productive human relationship with the rest of nature. We have already noted how Porter values the hard-working stewardship of farm work over an idle living on the land—Mr. Helton over Mr. Thompson. This story, however, uses another contrast to supplement, complement, and refine that valorization of work and nature. Mr. Müller, the hard-working and successful patriarch of this farm clan, does work hard, but he does so in ways that display his own limitations. He sees the land only in economic terms, and there is sharply dismissive commentary implicit in how his delight in the money and the power that stem from his successful transformation of the land into a commodity contrasts with his diligent nightly reading of Karl Marx.

The real center of what "Holiday" adds to the land ethic of Porter's nature stories, however, occurs in the story's contrast between his family's economically driven work and the narrator's walks in nature. If it is clearly better to engage in a knowledgeable working of the land than to live idly on it, this story also makes the point that it is better to be a wise steward of a small farm's productivity than to become obsessed with expanding at the expense of any other ways of knowing the land. It is the nature walk, a way to encounter the land marked by respectful attention and personal regard that holds the highest place among all the nature activities in these nature stories.

The narrator's nature walking thus suggests that she is moving closer to the natural world. But the tone of her observations suggests that she is not yet able to approach it from the distorting filter of her own preconceptions. Her aesthetic evaluation of the landscape has moved away from disparagement and into its opposite, a kind of purple praise, but the very extravagance of her descriptions suggests that there is still some detachment from the land:

> I had never seen anything that was more beautiful to me. The trees were freshly budded out with pale bloom, the branches were immobile in the thin darkness, but the flower clusters shivered in a soundless dance of delicately woven light, whirling as airily as leaves in a breeze, as rhythmically as water in a fountain. Every tree was budded out with this living, pulsing fire as fragile and cool as bubbles. (420)

The final stages of change come through her acquaintance with Ottilie. Ottilie insists that the narrator examine the family picture and, finally, really look at her and acknowledge her place in the family. Thus, the narrator is made to see what is actually before her eyes, rather than what she has expected to see. It is important, too, that this key change occurs despite the fact that Ottilie—in direct contrast to the verbal facility and detachment of both Louise and the narrator—is unable to speak. As she starts to see how her aesthetically based preconceptions about looks have restricted her vision, the narrator begins also to make the crucial connection between Ottilie's physical disability and her own emotional handicaps, to see that "her life and mine were kin, even a part of each other" (426).

The final stage in her learning to see the land comes after the huge storm and Mother Müller's sudden death. The narrator at first misreads Ottilie's agitation; she assumes that Ottilie is upset because she wants to follow the others and join the long funeral procession. When she hitches up the only vehicle left—the same spring wagon that originally brought her to the farm—she again learns from Ottilie. As the outing unfolds it is once again Ottilie, the woman who cannot speak, who manages to communicate with the highly verbal narrator, the woman who uses words to wall herself off from the world. The narrator grabs Ottilie so she will not fall, and when they look at each other, the narrator gains a deepened awareness of their kinship.[6]

By clapping her hands and then waving one hand in a circle to indicate "what wonders she saw," Ottilie conveys her pleasure in "the hot sun on her back, the bright air," and "the peacock green of the heavens" (434). What she wants, the narrator now knows, is not to follow the funeral party but simply to enjoy the outdoors—to have a holiday respite from her slavish indoor duties. Hers is an unmitigated joy—neither aesthetically nor verbally detached from the world.

Just as she has misread Ottilie, our storyteller has also been slow in learning how best to know the natural world. However, when she does allow herself to see Ottilie and to share her sense of wonder and her direct joy in the pleasures of nature, she begins to change. She starts by recognizing that they share a joy in nature. The narrator's altered tone, her own more modest and descriptive language at the story's end also indicate that she is changing.[7] So do her plans for a joint "stolen holiday," a vacation presumably not only from Ottilie's housework but from her own isolation. She will take Ottilie with her down the less traveled road to the land of mulberries and the river, and the act of taking another to share that place where she loves to walk indicates that she has begun to see the world anew. She has moved away from seeing nature as the occasion for detached aesthetic contemplation and verbal display, and she is now beginning to view nature in ways that are direct and sensual rather than abstract or detached, and shared rather than isolated.

By the end of her story, the narrator knows more about herself and about how she can know nature. From a superficial observer caught up in brittle irony, stereotypes, and misreadings of people and the land, she grows into a trustworthy observer, one who looks back with deeper insight into what and how she learned from her spring holiday.[8] In a reversal of her friend Louise's own holiday story, the "Holiday" narrator's narrative turns hopeful, wise, and insightful—not grim—at the end.

It is worth noting in conclusion that both "Holiday" and "The Fig Tree" have some central elements in common with non-fiction nature narratives. In these stories, what sets in motion the crucial act of knowing nature is also the element that consistently drives traditional non-fiction nature writing: the nature walk. From Thoreau's classic final essay "Walking" to the work of such contemporaries as Annie Dillard, John Hanson Mitchell, and Robert Michael Pyle, it is most often the nature walk, carried out with appropriate attention and respect, that forms the heart of the narrative. And in both the nature essays and these nature stories, choosing such walks come about more easily with example and instruction. The role models provided by the characters of Great-Aunt Eliza, the unnamed narrator, and Ottilie have a function similar to that of the heuristic Thoreauvian narratives of Dillard, Mitchell, and Pyle: all seek to help us learn how best to walk in the world. And in both the essays and the stories, the yield of such nature walks is both joy and knowledge. For Thoreau and Dillard, Miranda and the "Holiday" narrator, such walks help celebrate the wonders of nature, and they also help anchor that wonder in the kind of local knowledge that can come from careful, caring attention to the local flora and fauna.

⌒

Katherine Anne Porter's nature stories sustain and help to expand an important segment of American literature. These stories, like those of

Sarah Orne Jewett, Mary Wilkins Freeman, and other nineteenth-century predecessors, encourage us to re-examine how we relate to the natural world, reminding us how important it is that we humans know and honor the rest of nature. Her stories, along with those of such figures as Eudora Welty and Mary Austin, also help extend the range of ecofiction into the South and the Southwest.

These nature stories also suggest how we might begin a reconsideration of what we mean by the phrase "a sense of place." By foregrounding specific natural features of the region—blackland farms, catalpa trees, lanes of mulberry trees, and tree frogs—and by emphasizing how important it is to know these features, the stories help make an important point: a truly viable sense of place, in criticism and in literature, needs to be firmly grounded in knowing local nature. ❖

Notes

[1] Soon available in a new edition from the University of Georgia Press.

[2] *The Collected Stories of Katherine Anne Porter* 320. Subsequent references noted in the text.

[3] Attention to ecofiction or to ecological themes in other fiction is beginning to emerge as a more important part of ecocriticism. As a result of the attention to fiction in such studies as Louise Westling's *The Green Breast of the New World* (Georgia, 1996) and the criticism in such journals as *ISLE: Interdisciplinary Studies in Literature and the Environment*, the canon is expanding to include ecofiction.

[4] These are not the only short stories of hers that feature nature, but they do illustrate some key features of her nature stories. Among the other important stories are "The Grave" and "Pale Horse, Pale Rider."

[5] Stout's "Miranda's Guarded Speech: Porter and the Problem of Truth-Telling" explores how Miranda's speech relates to that of her namesake in *The Tempest*.

[6] See Hinze for a general discussion of Ottilie and her role in educating the narrator about reality.

[7] Stout explores the moral values attached to volubility and reserve in "Noon Wine." See "Mr. Hatch's Volubility and Miss Porter's Reserve."

[8] Brinkmeyer provides a larger discussion of the role that memory played in Porter's artistic creation.

Works Cited

Brinkmeyer, Robert H. "Endless Remembering: The Artistic Vision of Katherine Anne Porter." *The Mississippi Quarterly* 40 (1986–87): 5–20.

Graham, Don. "A Southern Writer in Texas." *Katherine Anne Porter and Texas: An Uneasy Relationship*. Eds. Clinton Machann and William Bedford Clark. College Station: Texas A&M UP, 1990.

Hinze, Diana. "Texas and Berlin: Images of Germany in Katherine Anne Porter's Prose." *The Southern Literary Journal* 34 (1991): 79–81.

Porter, Katherine Anne. *The Collected Stories of Katherine Anne Porter*. New York: Harcourt, Brace and World, 1965.

Stout, Janis P. "Mr. Hatch's Volubility and Miss Porter's Reserve." *Critical Essays on Katherine Anne Porter*. Ed. Darlene Harbour Unrue. New York: G. K. Hall, 1997.

———. "Miranda's Guarded Speech: Porter and the Problem of Truth-Telling. *Philological Quarterly* 66.2 (1987): 259–75.

Katherine Anne Porter and William Humphrey: A Mentorship Reconsidered

Bert Almon

Katherine Anne Porter was the major influence on her fellow Texan, William Humphrey. The relationship went virtually unnoticed for many years, while reviewers were eager to trace Faulkner's impact on Humphrey's themes and style. Frank Kappler, reviewing *The Ordways for Life*, was an exception, noting that the book "has a perception approaching the Faulknerian but has the advantage of reading more like Katherine Anne Porter" (17). Joan Givner's biography of Porter changed the situation: Givner had access to the lengthy correspondence of Porter and Humphrey, which included some of their best letters, letters which do not appear in Isabel Bayley's selection from the correspondence. In fact, Humphrey is mentioned only once in Bayley's lengthy edition. Givner devoted a chapter in her biography to the influence of Porter on Humphrey and another young Texan, William Goyen, and she went over the subject again in an article, "Katherine Anne Porter, The Old Order and the New," included in *The Texas Literary Tradition*, published in 1983, the year after the first edition of her biography appeared. The relationship with Porter was indeed important to Humphrey, though Givner slants it in a way that needs correction.[1]

Humphrey began reading Porter on the recommendation of Randall Jarrell. A copy of *Flowering Judas and Other Stories*, purchased in a secondhand bookstore, made an immediate convert of him, and he told her later in a letter that he always wrote with "copies of 'Old Mortality' and 'Noon Wine' and 'The Cracked Looking Glass' and 'The Old Order' open on my table at favorite paragraphs" (September 28, 1950). He was able to invite her to read at Bard College in Hudson, New York, where he was teaching, and so he wrote his first letter to her, a short one, on September 20, 1950. He must have been overwhelmed by her lengthy response: she had heard much of him from Eudora Welty already and had discussed his progress as a writer of short stories with publishers and magazine editors. In fact, she asked if she could help him obtain a Guggenheim Fellowship. Clearly they were going to be close friends if their meeting in person turned out to be as friendly as their opening exchanges by mail.

They met at a dinner she held at her apartment in New York in October 1950. It had a comic touch: she made one of her celebrated Mexican dinners for Humphrey and his wife, Dorothy, without realizing that the younger writer had a stomach ulcer. The food was also a little scorched. She had invited another young writer, William Goyen, on the assumption that they would like one another. Both were from East Texas, and both were superb stylists. Porter learned only years later that Humphrey did not like Goyen at all. As for Goyen, he wrote to Porter within a day or two of the dinner, making Humphrey appear to be a kind of southern "Man Without a Country":

> William Humphrey worries me—some kind of rancour simmers inside him. Was it me, do you think? Anyway, I'll tell you what I think—I believe he is fighting himself. Once he said to me, "I hate all Southerners; I never want to see the 'South' again." And I said, "Even Faulkner and Katherine Anne Porter?" What I know for myself, and maybe Humphrey will know, is that until one writes

from himself, from that tiny center of light in him he goes a bit wrong and shadowy. (Goyen 163).

Humphrey reacted angrily to Goyen's statement almost thirty years later. Givner had put the gist of Goyen's letter into circulation in her article of 1983, and L. Dwight Chaney repeated the story in "William Humphrey, Regionalist: Southern or Southwestern?" Humphrey must have felt that he would be spoken of as a hater of the South forever after. In one of his journals at the Harry Ransom Humanities Research Center, he observed in November or December 1988 that he had met Goyen only twice, thirty-five years apart. And on that occasion in Katherine Anne Porter's New York apartment, he did not have a real conversation with Goyen: "I reckon I must have exchanged a dozen words with him, because as anyone knows who knew her, in her presence nobody could get a word in edgewise. Not that she was not worth listening to—she was!—but talk was a disease with her."

What Givner does not explain in her article is that Goyen was a well-established disciple of Porter's—indeed he was on the verge of an affair with her—and his rather condescending comments were perhaps meant to deflate a rival. He presented himself as a rather wise person in comparison with the rancorous Humphrey.

Givner's comments on Humphrey and Goyen have a particular slant, shown by the chapter title on them in her biography of Porter: "Disciples Must Be Very Hard for a Mere Human Being to Endure." Her subject is Porter, not Goyen or Humphrey. She presents the younger writers as dependents, as they were when Porter first met them, and they don't quite escape from that role. Humphrey in particular suffers from this treatment. He was indeed Porter's disciple at the start of his career, but as his work developed, he followed a number of directions quite on his own.

Perhaps the most damaging comment in Givner's biography is a brief summary of a letter Porter wrote to Humphrey on January 6, 1951. Porter's comments are summarized this way: "She was shocked when she learned that he was rewriting rejected stories, slanting them to appeal to the editorial preferences of certain journals, rather than simply writing as best he could" (375). The summary gives as fact a misunderstanding of Porter's and omits Humphrey's long and eloquent response to it.

Porter's misunderstanding resulted from her complicated relationship to the academic world. It was often the hand that fed her, but she could bite it, especially in her letters. She was an outsider, brought in for her celebrity to adorn a program briefly, and she often felt isolated in traditionalist English departments. Givner describes, for example, Porter's alienation at Stanford in 1948–49 (362). When Humphrey told her that he had rewritten one of his stories ("Report Cards") many times, she reacted with a long denunciation of the academic world, having concluded that Humphrey lived in a terrifying publish-or-perish situation in which he was overworked and would do anything to survive, including tailor his stories to fit the biases of editors. Much of her letter was devoted to criticizing the flaws of the American academic system: Humphrey seems to have been the trigger for a diatribe that she had been brooding on for a long time.

Sometime in 1951, Humphrey responded with an unusually long letter, now preserved in the McKeldin Room. He assured her that academic life did not constrain his writing and that he was not required to publish or perish at Bard. Indeed, nothing in the many letters that he exchanged with his fellow teacher at Bard, the poet Theodore Weiss, suggests there was a publish-or-perish atmosphere in this liberal arts college. What Bard hoped for, Humphrey told Porter, was that when he published a story, the name of the college would appear in the contributor's note. He assured her that he didn't know enough about the biases of any editor to tailor a story to fit them; indeed, he said that he generally didn't read other writers' stories in magazines (something true of many writers, certainly). He declared that he was too stubborn to take advice from editors:

> Moreover, if anything, I sin in the direction of refusing to take any constructive suggestions for my work, being the most bull-headed person I know, so much so that when I've been contemplating a certain change in one of my stories I refuse to make it for the longest time if someone else suggests it. Myself, my wife, and you are the only three people in the world I will listen to for criticism.

Humphrey's archives make it quite clear that he was indeed bull-headed, to use his own cliché. A year after his exchange with Porter, he was extremely condescending and difficult with the fiction editor of *The New Yorker*, William Maxwell, and with the august chief editor himself, Harold Ross. Many years later Humphrey boasted to José Yglesias about his clashes with Maxwell and Ross. The galley proofs of a story had arrived with many unauthorized changes. Yglesias reports:

> There ensued much argument with [William Maxwell] about the changes. At one point the editor said, "Mr. Ross is in the hospital and he is very unhappy about the stubbornness you are showing— he would like to make you one of our stable." "I am not a horse," Humphrey replied; now he whinnies at his remembered effrontery. He was pleased to see in the final galley that a sentence was circled and a comment in the margin said: "This sticks out like a sore thumb." He recalls that he had the satisfaction of writing: "That's what I said when you put it in there." (65)

In his career as a novelist he would be tactless and obstinate with

Herbert Weinstock at Knopf and with Alfred A. Knopf himself. Knopf was the most eminent American publisher, but in 1961 Humphrey wrote him a letter so supercilious that it seems to have destroyed his relationship with the publisher and his firm. He was hard on Jackie Farber at Delacorte when she proposed changes in *Hostages to Fortune*. He ended his relationship with Harold Hayes at *Esquire* in 1972 by writing a belligerent letter over a special issue of the magazine that printed fifty outstanding pieces from the past. Nothing by William Humphrey was included, but, as the angry novelist said, the issue included Nora Ephron's well-known article "about the size of her tits."

Some residual belief that Humphrey was a commercial sellout lingered in Porter's mind, and she expressed that feeling at a symposium in 1960. Contrasting *Home from the Hill* with his early stories, she said:

> He is an extremely good short story writer. He preceded that book with a number of very short stories, I think, but he did want to write a successful book if he could, you know, and he got the idea of what is success mixed up with what would be good sales and so he spoiled his book by trying to make it popular. (Givner, *Conversations* 50)

When Louis Rubin responded, "He succeeded in that," Porter said, "He did and good luck to him. He was my student for years and I thought he was going to turn out better than that, I must say."

When *Home from the Hill* appeared in 1958, Humphrey sent a copy, now in the McKeldin Room, to Porter. It had a warm inscription: "To Katherine Anne Porter, whose stories fixed my standards, whose life gave me courage, and who taught me the great thing a writer can teach another: that the place and the life and the speech to which he was born is his place and his subject and his speech." Whether or not she had reservations then about the popularity of the book, she responded warmly. She noted, as many critics have not, that Humphrey satirizes the macho myth of the hunter, observing that his Captain Hunnicutt was a "murderous hedonist" and his wife an abject bitch. She also said that the boar hunt in the novel was pure Faulkner. Early in their friendship Humphrey had expressed irritation over Faulkner's winning the Nobel Prize, claiming (out of the anxiety of influence, surely) that Faulkner was his "pet hatred" (undated letter of 1950). Now he confessed immediately that the boar hunt was imitated from the Mississippian.

Humphrey's inscription to Porter makes it clear that his principal influence as he created a style was Porter, not Faulkner. Thematic influences of Faulkner are easy to spot in his work: both men deal with race, hunting, and class attitudes. But in the matter of style (one of Humphrey's obsessions), Porter was his chief influence. The influence was hardly noticed because Porter's style does not have the mannerisms that make Faulkner so recognizable. Givner's description of Porter's style is excellent:

> [S]he forged out of the soft rhythms of southern speech and the racy idioms of her native Texas a unique style, at once elegant and tough, lyrical and vigorous, formal and witty, truly a classic style for all seasons. That accomplishment is not, as she seemed to think, to be scorned as a minor achievement. She has quite simply done what every significant artist does, left her medium the richer for her having used it. All coming after her who use the English language artfully must be indebted to her, as everyone must who uses the genre that was truly hers, the short story. (Givner, *A Life* 511)

One problem with such a contribution to the medium is that it may be overlooked: Hemingway and Faulkner have mannerisms that are easily recognized, even quantifiable without much effort. Porter, like F. Scott Fitzgerald, has a style that is eloquent without eccentricities.

Humphrey also aimed for a classic style. Writing in 1985 to one of his admirers, Frederick Stout, he said: "I resort to this kitchen simile: I would like it to be like Saran wrap: it should conform to the shape of the object and be transparent. It should be so memorable as to make the reader feel there is not and had never been any other way for it to be said but that." Humphrey wanted a style flexible enough to deal with the demotic—the many illiterate or barely literate characters in his fiction— and yet capable of expressing the tragic reaches of human experience. Porter was an excellent model.

In his "Irony with a Center," Robert Penn Warren deals with Porter's style not by listing its characteristics but by the close reading of passages. The style, he suggests, succeeds through its texture. He called it "a kind of indicative poetry"(144) and referred to it with terms like precision and transparency. He is careful to distinguish it from fine writing, the kind of purple or exquisite prose that Warren terms "the fallacy of agreeable style" (139): "Miss Porter's imagination . . . is best appreciated if we appreciate its essential austerity, its devotion to the fact drenched in God's direct daylight, its concern with the inwardness of character, and its delight in the rigorous and discriminating deployment of a theme."

Humphrey admired such qualities, and in writing to Frederick Stout quoted Virginia Woolf: "What's wrong with a purple patch is not that it's purple but that it's a patch." Humphrey strove to create a texture and a deployment of theme through style comparable to Porter's. His style avoids sameness of tone and diction within his books and among them. He writes a sensuous but melancholy prose in *Home from the Hill*, while in *The Ordways* he begins in tragic mode in the first third of the book, then switches to the picaresque. Probably no reader familiar with

Home from the Hill would recognize Humphrey as the author of the intricate psychodrama of *Hostages to Fortune*. In his notebooks Humphrey liked to cite James Joyce's dictum that "a writer has only one book which he writes again and again." "It's not true of me," Humphrey said (Almon 140). He wrote with notorious slowness because he worked sentence by sentence, fitting the style to the subject rather than the subject to the style.

After Humphrey's departure for Europe in 1958, his correspondence with his mentor seems to have lapsed. In 1963–64, Humphrey was teaching at Washington and Lee College in Lexington, Virginia. Porter had taught there herself, and the coincidence was a good enough reason to write her when he learned her address from Robert Penn Warren. He wrote on January 11, 1964, and mentioned that he had been living abroad but had heard about the great success of *Ship of Fools*. He received a quick and friendly answer. In April 1965, she wrote to him during one of his stays in Alassio, Italy, and suggested that he and his wife come for a visit immediately after their return to the United States. And a few weeks later, she suggested that Humphrey might serve as her literary executor, now that her previous choice, Glenway Westcott, was getting old himself. (Her nephew, Paul Porter, was the ultimate choice.) Friendly relations are the tone in the letters, and over the next eight years they exchanged visits as well as letters. Humphrey no longer sounded like the worshipful disciple. Rather, his letters are humorous and frank. He had become a fellow author rather than a neophyte, happy to recommend writers like Thomas Berger and Ben Robertson (*Red Hills and Cotton*)—to his friend.

They would eventually have Seymour Lawrence in common. Lawrence, an editor who later became a publisher, lured Porter away from Harcourt, Brace and World to Little, Brown and Company. He later established his own imprint and persuaded her—with a huge advance—to publish her *Collected Essays* with him. He also courted

Humphrey as an author, a campaign that began in 1966. Knowing that Humphrey felt neglected at Alfred A. Knopf, Lawrence, a good friend, would invite Humphrey for drinks and discuss leaving the company. He also pursued the subject in their correspondence. Humphrey finally switched after the failure of his memoir, *Farther Off from Heaven*. He came back from a holiday to find that Knopf had done nothing to promote the book in spite of the fine reviews it had received. It soon turned up on remainder shelves. Seymour Lawrence brought the book out in paperback under his imprint with Laurel, which certainly ingratiated him with Humphrey, who broke formally with Knopf in 1981 and signed with Lawrence. Humphrey's subsequent books were all published with Lawrence, who issued them in conjunction with Delacorte and Houghton Mifflin.

Among the subjects that Lawrence and Humphrey discussed over the years was their friendship with Porter. In 1970, Humphrey, as an eminent writer of sporting stories, was asked to write the text for a photo article on the environmental impact of the Soil Conservation Service. On his way back from Alabama he visited Porter in a Washington hospital in May 1970. She had broken her hip. He describes the visit this way in a letter preserved in Lawrence's archive at the University of Mississippi:

> Saw Katherine Anne in the hospital about a month ago. I was on my way back from Alabama where I had gone to do an article on an aspect of conservation for *Life*. We had a great couple of hours together. I smuggled in a pint of Virginia Gentleman in the pocket of my raincoat (the sun was shining bright) and she and I and Stan Wayman, the *Life* photographer I had been down south with, just about did that bottle in. She then revealed that she had a whole case of the same medicine under her bed. (June 20, 1970)

Porter and Humphrey were both fond of drink, and he discussed his problems with alcohol in letters to her.

Lawrence endangered Humphrey's friendship with Porter in that same year when her *Collected Essays* appeared. The book had a publisher's note in which Lawrence thanked a number of writers, including Humphrey, for assisting in the completion of the book during one of Porter's illnesses. She was angered by what she took to be an imputation of incompetence to her, and she was antagonistic toward members of what she referred to as the "committee." Humphrey too would become ambivalent about Lawrence. He began to feel neglected, a view in which his agent, Toby Eady, concurred: in several letters now in the Harry Ransom Humanities Research Center Eady wonders why Lawrence is paying so little attention to a distinguished novelist.

In January 1973, Dorothy Humphrey visited Porter, who was seriously ill again, and she wrote a long letter to her husband about Porter's condition, a letter preserved in Humphrey's archive at the Ransom Center. Porter had convinced herself that she couldn't eat solid food, and Dorothy had to entice her to try it. Dorothy, who was from Brooklyn, recounts with some amazement listening to Porter playing the southern belle, talking about fashion and ways to preserve her white skin from the sun. She noted that Porter used an egg treatment on her face and would receive a gentleman caller like Rhea Johnson in a Christian Dior nightgown. Dorothy was surprised at her ability to remember details of clothes and dressmakers. The two women would sit up late drinking bourbon and wine together, which Dorothy admitted was not the best treatment for an invalid. Porter gave Dorothy two versions of her latest (perhaps imaginary) "liaison": one for Dorothy herself, another to tell to William. In fact, Dorothy felt that Porter always concealed things, different things from different persons, so that every person constructed a version of her. There was some recovery: one morning when Dorothy was downstairs fixing a southern dish, corn pone, to Porter's recipe, the hostess slipped into the guest's room and changed the sheets for her. But by October 1977, Porter was declared mentally incompetent.

Seymour Lawrence had a kind of reconciliation with Porter before her death, and one of his letters to Humphrey in the Harry Ransom Center gives a sad glimpse of her delusions near the end when she had turned on Paul Porter and Barrett Prettyman:

> But KATHERINE ANNE PORTER treated both of us shabbily over her COLLECTED ESSAYS. She turned on me in a vicious manner because we only sold 8000 copies of the ESSAYS as opposed to 150,000 of SHIP OF FOOLS. She was my daughter's godmother and a year before she died she asked me to visit her. She was paralyzed by a stroke and blinded in one eye, barely coherent, railing against her nephew Paul Porter and Barrett Prettyman and their treachery, and repeating from time to time: "Angel, give me work. I still have another book to write." It was very sad. She died lonely and miserable.[2]

While she did in fact outlive her own mental faculties, she did leave the legacy of a distinguished body of work and a powerful prose style. One of the inheritors of that legacy was William Humphrey. ❖

Notes

[1] I have dealt briefly with the Porter-Humphrey relationship in my book, *William Humphrey, Destroyer of Myths.*

[2] Prettyman has communicated his distress to me over Porter's allegations of treachery. He had in fact gone to great trouble to protect her possessions at a time when they were being taken from her rooms. Mr. Lawrence's letter was not intended to denigrate Barrett Prettyman and Paul Porter. Barrett Prettyman's integrity is quite clear in the major biographies (Givner 506 and Stout 279). Mr. Lawrence's letter certainly was not meant to endorse Porter's deluded accusation.

Works Cited

Almon, Bert. *William Humphrey, Destroyer of Myths.* Denton:
    U of North Texas P, 1998.
Chaney, L. Dwight. "William Humphrey, Regionalist: Southern or
    Southwestern?" *Journal of the American Studies Association of
    Texas* 19 (1988): 91–98.
Givner, Joan, ed. *Katherine Anne Porter: Conversations.* Jackson:
    U P of Mississippi, 1987.
———. *Katherine Anne Porter: A Life.* New York: Simon and Schuster,
    1982; U of Georgia P, 1991.
———. "Katherine Anne Porter: The Old Order and the New." *The
    Texas Literary Tradition: Fiction, Folklore, History.* Ed. Don
    Graham, et al. Austin: U of Texas P, 1983. 58–68.
Goyen, William. *Selected Letters from a Writer's Life.* Ed. Robert
    Phillips. Austin: U of Texas P, 1995.
Humphrey, Dorothy. Letter to William Humphrey. January 1973.
    Harry Ransom Humanities Research Center, U of Texas at Austin.

Humphrey, William. Letter to Frederick Stout. (1985). Harry Ransom
    Humanities Research Center, U of Texas at Austin.
———. Letters to Seymour Lawrence. Mississippi Room,
    U of Mississippi Library.
———. Letters to Katherine Anne Porter. McKeldin Room,
    U of Maryland.
———. September Song Diaries, 1988–89. Harry Ransom Humanities
    Research Center, U of Texas at Austin.
Kappler, Frank. "Texas with Another Accent." *Life* Feb. 5, 1965: 17.
Lawrence, Seymour. Letter to William Humphrey. June 19, 1985. Harry
    Ransom Humanities Research Center, U of Texas at Austin.
Stout, Janis P. *Katherine Anne Porter: A Sense of the Times.*
    Charlottesville: U of Virginia P, 1995.
Warren, Robert Penn. "Katherine Anne Porter: Irony with a Center."
    Selected Essays. New York: Random House, 1958. 136–55.
Yglesias, José. "William Humphrey." *Publishers Weekly* 235.22
    (June 1989): 64–65.

A "taste for the exotic": Revolutionary Mexico and the Short Stories of Katherine Anne Porter and María Cristina Mena

Rob Johnson

In a 1923 essay addressed to the editors of *The Century Magazine* entitled "Why I Write About Mexico," Katherine Anne Porter said, "I write about Mexico because that is my familiar country. . . . I have been accused by Americans of a taste for the exotic, for foreign flavors. . . . All the things I write of I have first known, and they are real to me" (*CE* 355-56). In this same essay written in defense of the veracity of her work, she boldly fabricates, as we now know, her famous story about an Indian woman and the revolution:[1]

> During the Madero Revolution I watched a street battle between the Maderistas and Federal troops from the window of a cathedral; a grape-vine heavy with tiny black grapes formed a screen, and a very old Indian woman stood near me, perfectly silent, holding my sleeve. Later she said to me, when the dead were being piled for burning in the public square, "It is all a great trouble now, but it is for the sake of happiness to come." She crossed herself and I mistook her meaning. "In heaven?" I asked. Her scorn

was splendid. "No, on earth. Happiness for men, not for angels!" She seemed to me then to have caught the whole meaning of revolution, and to have said it in a phrase. (*CE* 355)

In essence, while making up a story about the Indians to suit her own socialist politics and anticlerical beliefs, Porter defends herself against charges of pandering to the magazine-reading public's love for romance set in "exotic" places by replacing the term "foreign" with "familiar."

I do not intend to argue here with Porter's statement that her stories are "real to her," but I am interested in Porter's defensiveness about having her "familiar" stories called "exotic." There is, I believe, a specific context for her bristling response to this characterization of her fiction. Porter was publishing her stories and essays about Mexico in *The Century Magazine,* and she must have been aware of another woman writing for the same magazine a few years earlier who had been dubbed "the foremost interpreter of Mexican life" (Doherty xii). This was the Mexican-born María Cristina Mena, and her stories have recently been collected by Amy Doherty. Mena, as Doherty says, was expected to "entertain a privileged, conservative, Anglo audience with a passion for travel and the exotic" (xi)—the very characterization Porter resented. Although recent criticism of Mena's work shows that she was not simply reinscribing Anglo stereotypes about Mexicans, for Porter to be called an "exotic" writer was to have her stories looked at the same way Mena's were.

The fact that both women writers—one Mexican, one American— published stories about Revolution-era Mexico in the same magazine during the same time period (Mena in the teens, Porter in the early twenties) allows us to make an exceptionally meaningful comparison of their work. Mena's works are not a simple foil for better-known writers such as Porter, and excellent stories by Mena such as "John of God, the

Water-Carrier" (1913), "The Gold Vanity Set" (1913), and "The Sorcerer and General Bisco" (1915) will undoubtedly start to appear in the standard anthologies. Still, I have to admit these stories—uncollected during her lifetime and little commented on even by scholars of Latina literature—surprised me by being better than I thought they would be. I was also surprised to find that it was apparent Porter had read Mena's work. I say surprised because none of the biographical material indicates she knew anything about Mena or her Mexico stories.[2] But Porter evidently did read Mena, and more: a comparison of Mena's "The Sorcerer and General Bisco" (1915) and Porter's unpublished story "The Dove of Chapacalco" (1922) shows that Porter consciously adapted the plot and details of Mena's story for her own purposes. In this process of revision she has left us an understanding of her view of contemporary literature about the Revolution written by Mexican writers. Porter's own "exotic" fiction, as her critics call it, was in part written in reaction to such literature.

About Mena we know little, most of it from Amy Doherty. She was the child of Mexican aristocrats who moved to New York City in 1907 just before the Revolution. At the time, she was fourteen, three years younger than Katherine Anne Porter. Educated in New York, she evidently developed literary aspirations, and she found herself filling a demand for stories about her native land and the Revolution of 1910. In 1913, when she was only twenty-one years old, she published "John of God, the Water-Carrier" in the popular *Century Magazine.* Over the next three years, she published seven more Mexico stories in *Century.* There was a price for her success, though. Doherty shows how Mena struggled against the editors of *Century* to write stories that went beyond stereotypes about Mexican life and Mexican women. By 1916, that struggle must have become too difficult, for Mena was dropped as a contributor; or, as Amy Doherty speculated in a letter to me, when the politics of the journal diverged too far from Mena's, she stopped writing for it.[3]

Chronology is important here: Mena stopped publishing for *Century* in 1916; Porter started writing fiction and essays about Mexico for *Century* in 1923. Porter thus fairly directly inherited Mena's role of "official interpreter of Mexican life." In 1923-24, Porter would contribute a total of three Mexican stories and one essay about Mexico to *Century*.

After 1916, Mena would only write one more short story about the revolution, "A Son of the Tropics" (1931), which was published just a few months after Porter's "Flowering Judas." That these two stories bear important resemblances to one another is emblematic of a general similarity in content that can be found when comparing Mena's and Porter's stories. In "Flowering Judas," Laura inadvertently aids in the suicide of a young revolutionary. In "A Son of the Tropics," the *soldadera* Tula assembles the explosive with which the Revolutionary kills himself. Both stories are complex portrayals of the competing personal, political, and religious forces embodying revolutionary Mexico, and both stories depend upon self-deception in a key character. But the differences, even minor ones, distinguish the two writers' views. In Porter's story, for example, it is the revolutionary who wears "Jockey Club" cologne; in Mena's story, it is the *hacendado* come to re-claim his land from the Indians, who, after being captured, is so "disordered" that "the habitués of the Jockey Club"—a center of Porfirian decadence in Mexico City[4] —"would not have recognized their fastidious friend" (146). In her stories, Mena frequently and somewhat guiltily portrays the aristocracy as villains, while Porter in this story and others focuses on failed revolutionaries, rapacious foreign capitalists, and corrupt church officials. In Mena's case, her own family represents the wealthy upper class she attacks; in Porter's case, her disillusionment with the socialist revolution determines her view of Mexico. Both stories are a final development in each author's portrayal of the Revolution. Mena's stories were initially framed as romances ("The Emotions of María Concepción," "The Gold Vanity Set") but developed into unromantic, ideological critiques (as in "A Son of the Tropics"), and Porter moved from portraying an *indita*—"María Concepción"—to finding herself more comfortable speaking not for the Indians but for the outsider's view of Mexico, such as Laura exhibits in "Flowering Judas."

The list of similarities between the Mexican fiction of these two writers is lengthy. Both wrote stories in which women take on the powers of the men who dominate them and avenge themselves (Porter's "María Concepción," Mena's "The Sorcerer and General Bisco"). Even more specifically, both wrote stories of artists whose female models revenge themselves upon the men who objectify them (Mena's "The Vine Leaf," Porter's "The Martyr"). For whatever reason, both women tended to tell the same story. But they tell it very differently. Nowhere is this more apparent than in a comparison of Porter's unfinished "The Dove of Chapacalco" (1922) and Mena's "The Sorcerer and General Bisco" (1915). In many ways, they are the same story, and Porter—perhaps picking up a copy of *Century Magazine* in 1916 during her convalescence in a Fort Worth hospital—evidently read Mena's story sometime before she wrote her own. Clearly, as Thomas F. Walsh discovered, Porter's story is also based on the political events of mid-1921 involving the Archbishop of Chiapas, but Walsh and others seem to have been unaware that the plot of Porter's story as well as key details come from Mena.[5] Both stories can be accurately summarized as having the following unmistakably parallel elements: a young girl is taken into bondage by a rich and powerful man and kept as his mistress/wife in a palace, where she learns the secrets of his power over the peons; against the background of the Revolution, and aided by a lover, she uses her knowledge of her master's weakness to overthrow him.

Anyone reading these two stories would be struck by their similarities and by key differences—most prominently that in Porter's story the villain is an archbishop, not a *hacendado*, and that the lovers in Porter's story, unlike those in Mena's tale, do not re-unite in love following their common victory. In fact, characteristic of many Porter women, the heroine rejects the hero's proposal of marriage. Porter, particularly in regard to her reversal of the ending of Mena's story, has not so much based her story on Mena's as she has co-opted it, even colonized it, turning Mena's story against itself while simultaneously advancing her (Porter's) agenda—one in line less with the Victorian-era *Century* of the teens than with Carl Van Doren's "modernist" *Century* a few years later. Porter evidently saw Mena's story in much the same light as did first-wave Chicano critics such as Raymund A. Paredes, who criticized Mena for "sentimentality and gentility" (49). Paredes wrote in 1982:

> [Mena] knew what Americans liked to read about Mexico, so she gave it to them: quaint and humble inditos, passionate señoritas with eyes that "were wonderful, even in a land of wonderful eyes," dashing caballeros "with music in their fingers"—all these characters in a country Mena described as "the land of resignation." Mena's portrayals are ultimately obsequious, and if one can appreciate the weight of popular attitudes on Mena's consciousness, one can also say that a braver, more perceptive writer would have confronted the life of her culture more forcefully. (50)

Only recent critics such as López and Doherty are able to separate the subversive content of Mena's stories from their magazine-made form. Porter, like Paredes, saw the surface sentimentality of Mena's "The Sorcerer and General Bisco." Through formal revision and by reversing the significance of Mena's story, Porter would be Paredes' "braver, more perceptive writer."

Implicit here is an unstated belief on Porter's part that she could tell this story better and more truthfully than the Mexican-born Mena could. It was, after all, Porter's "familiar" country, too. In order to understand Porter's careful revision of this story, then, it is necessary to know something about her views on Mexican literature written *by Mexicans* about the Revolution. When Mexicans themselves created literature about the Revolution in prose and poetry, what did they say? In an essay entitled "The Mexican Trinity," published in 1921, Porter contrasted the Russian Revolution and the Mexican Revolution in terms of the role literature played in the two societies. "The Revolution," she writes,

> has not yet entered into the *souls* of the Mexican people. There can be no doubt of that. What is going on here is not the resistless upheaval of a great mass leavened by teaching and thinking and suffering. The Russian writers made the Revolution, I verily believe, through a period of seventy-five years' preoccupation with the wrongs of the peasant, and the cruelties of life under the heel of the Tsar. Here in Mexico there is *no conscience* crying through the literature of the country. A small group of intellectuals still writes about romance and the stars, and roses and shadowy eyes of ladies, touching no sorrow of the human heart other than the pain of unrequited love. But then, the Indians cannot read. What good would a literature of revolt do them? (*CE* 401; italics mine)

Porter here is critical of the failure of the intellectual class in Mexico to create a true literature of revolution; instead, like the poets in "Flowering Judas" and in the unpublished story of Mexico, "The Lovely

184

Legend" (in which the poet realizes he loves the woman who inspires his poetry better dead than alive), they write romantic and sentimental works. Her description of Mexican literature from this time—"romance and the stars, and roses and shadowy eyes of ladies"—is remarkably similar to Raymund A. Paredes' description of Mena's stories, quoted earlier.

Even the *corridos*, folk songs that tell the people's side of history, are criticized by Porter for being unrealistic and overly romantic. In an essay entitled "Corridos" (1924) she says, "A collection of these corridos . . . has a curious *sub-historical* value. Revolution after revolution has risen, broken and passed over the heads of these singers, and there is not a single revolutionary *corrido*. With the true temperament of the minor poet, the folk singer concerns himself with personalities, with intimate emotions, with deeds of heroism and crime" (*UEP* 197; italics mine). She says of the many *corridos* about Emiliano Zapata that all concern his personal "sub-historical" qualities; "not one of them," she says, "mentions that he revolutionized the agrarian system of Morelos, or was one of the first Mexicans to apprehend the principles of soviet government. Such things are ephemerae to the maker of ballads. He is concerned with eternal verities" (*UEP* 197). Today, of course, the corridos are seen as subversive counter-truths to the dominant Anglo histories, but Porter sees no true revolutionary spirit in the *corridos*, only romance.

By contrast, Porter's Mexico stories are self-consciously anti-romantic, and I believe this fundamental quality of her stories has to do with her attempt to distinguish her fiction about Mexico from Mexicans' literature about themselves. Porter's "María Concepción" certainly fits this description of an anti-romance about the Revolution. In the story, the Revolution is simply an excuse for María Concepción's husband to leave her for love and adventure with a *soldadera* named María Rosa, who bears his child. María Concepción, of course, gets her revenge by killing María Rosa and taking the child for her own; her

185

husband, on the other hand, switches places with María Concepción, the powerful now powerless, and feels his "veins fill up with bitterness, with black unendurable melancholy" (*CS* 20). Even more harshly anti-romantic is Porter's *Century*-published "Virgin Violeta," a story that reveals romantic love as self-destructive, a false mixture of passion and piety. In the story, Carlos, ostensibly wooing an older cousin, forces a kiss upon his younger cousin: "Ah, you're so young, like a little new-born calf," he says to Violeta (*CS* 29). When she rejects him and wants to run away and "kill herself," he says to her, "What did you expect when you came out here alone with me" (*CS* 29). Later, in front of her mother and sister, he requests the familial kiss at his departure, and Violeta "wavered for a moment, then slid up and back against the wall. She heard herself screaming uncontrollably" (*CS* 31). In "That Tree," a story which in title and theme is a precursor to "Flowering Judas," Miriam, an American living in Mexico, says disparagingly of the dewy-eyed Mexican girls, "She hadn't the faintest interest in what Mexican girls were born for, but she had no intention of wasting her life flattering male vanity" (*CS* 71). In "Flowering Judas," revolution is corrupted by love, leading Laura to choose an ascetic life. As in other Mexico stories by Porter, the Revolutionists are also poets—such as the leader of the typographers union who stalks Laura—but their poetry is all "stars, and roses and shadowy eyes of ladies," as Porter says of Mexico's Revolution-era literature.

Porter's criticism of the excessive sentimentality in Mexican literature helps us understand why she kept the plot of Mena's "The Sorcerer and General Bisco" (1915) but changed key details as she transformed it into "The Dove of Chapacalco," Porter's first Mexico story, written in 1922. Mena's "The Sorcerer and General Bisco" certainly is framed by a romance storyline written in a style that would have offended Porter. The two lovers—Carmelita, wife of the evil *hacendado* Don Balthazar Rascón, and Aquiles, brother of Rascón's first wife, whom Rascón murdered—run off together into the woods, fearful that Rascón has sensed their love for one another. For one night they claim ethereal love, even comparing themselves to Paolo and Francesca and other celebrated lovers. Their experience on the run hardens them, particularly Carmelita, who, in a remarkable scene, becomes a *soldadera*:

> Even when a large serpent reared at them obliquely with a strategic hiss as it spurted into the rustling mystery of a marsh, Carmelita laughed with sympathy, and then laughed again at the transformation of her own once fearful and fastidious self. Scratched and sunburned, soaked to the knees in black swamp-ooze, her dress torn, her bosom laboring from the exertion of the march, she wove a wreath of narcissus for her loosened hair; and when Aquiles showed fatigue she enticed him on with snatches of song. (98)

Later, she slips into a clairvoyant trance as they rest in the woods (one of several examples of Carmelita's mystical powers), and in this trance she foretells the arrival of the revolutionary General "El Bisco," the "cross-eyed one." As predicted, General Bisco does occupy the hacienda in a bloodless coup and captures Don Balthazar. Carmelita and Aquiles, too, are brought to the confiscated house. There Don Balthazar uses his knowledge of mesmerism to hypnotize El Bisco; Carmelita, however, who knows Don Balthazar's powers, manages to expose his trickery: "While you looked into the crystal he made himself your master, as he is master of many others, as he was of me until I freed myself and learned to use his own arts to spy upon him—I, little and weak as you see me, with *no power but love*" (109; italics mine). El Bisco, realizing that his true allies are Carmelita and Aquiles, shoots Don Balthazar, saying, "Dios, I think I am El Bisco once more, yes?" (Mena,

CS 111). The two lovers are reunited by Carmelita's power of love: "Then came the trembling voices of Aquiles and Carmelita as they groped toward each other through the smoke" (Mena, *CS* 111).

Written seven years after Mena's story appeared in *Century*, Porter's "The Dove of Chapacalco" maintains this basic plot—a powerful man forces his love upon a girl and takes her to his stronghold, where, aided by a revolutionary, she uses her knowledge of his "secrets" to overpower him—while stripping it of all of its romantic elements: the lovers' ecstasy, Carmelita's magic powers, the union of the two lovers as it is linked to the revolutionary cause. The story is also harshly anti-Catholic (whereas Mena's does not even mention religion) and is clearly based in history (Mena's story is historical, as Tiffany Ana López has shown, but in fairness it does read much more like political allegory than fact-based fiction).[6]

Significantly, Porter changes the *hacendado* (favorite target of the guilty aristocrat Mena) to an archbishop, who is even more villainous and lecherous than Mena's Rascón. He first sees Vicenta in a convent when she is only fourteen years old: "Soft and warmly colored as a ripe mango," he thinks. The Indian girl will be his new maid, the archbishop tells the suspicious sisters, and while taking her back to his palace in his coach, he rapes her: "Poor little dove! Here, put up your mouth. Learn to kiss me!" (*UEP* 113). Vicenta, however, like Carmelita, uses a "secret" knowledge to overpower her master:

> She had come into the palace a pitiable, bewildered child afraid even to weep, and within a year she had cleared the rooms of priests who disliked her; she had brought in new servants who had no privileges except those she allowed them. The entire palace was in her hands, emptied of everyone except her allies. . . . She did not know why she possessed this power. She was sure only of one

thing: the Archbishop loved her, and so long as he loved her, she would be powerful. And she was careful to nourish the secret sources of her influences. To the Archbishop she was Youth, the clean fire at which he warmed his failing, chilling body. (*UEP* 121)

Her power, too, is love, but in this instance love used against those who love her, not love that conquers all adversity, as is the case in Mena's story. Vicenta's love is El Bisco's loaded gun.

As love is reduced to power, so, too (in comparison to Mena's story) is magic shown to be merely religion's hoax. The church encourages superstitious beliefs and keeps the peons in submission by playing on those superstitions: "[Vicenta] cared nothing for María La Soledad. She knew by what agency those hands lowered themselves in benediction on the first day of May. She knew what miracle brought those tears of blood to those agate eyes at three o'clock every Good Friday" (*UEP* 128). In a reference to Marxist doctrine (explicitly absent in Mexican literature and the *corridos*), Porter has Vicenta inhale the incense of the Church "into her nostrils like suave opiates" (*UEP* 128).

Love, religion, and now revolution are debunked in Porter's story. The revolutionary who will save her, Porter's real-life acquaintance Angel Gómez, is characterized as an unbalanced man whose obsession is destruction, accomplished with dynamite. He is also one of Porter's characteristic revolutionaries who confuses love with revolution. Gómez reads Rubén Darío's "Sonatina" (1896) but misses the way in which the poem's refrain ("The Princess is sad") anticipates modernist poetics; instead, Gómez is in *love* with Darío's "blonde princess."[7]

Gómez becomes involved in a scheme to overthrow the archbishop, whose despotic rule is threatening the peace between the government and the church. And here Porter's story becomes shrewd political analysis—a *corrido* that is not "sub-historical." In fact, her description of the president's cabinet and its complicated machinations comes mostly from her journalistic essay of the previous year, "The Mexico Trinity."

Much of the rest of the story is described in Porter's summary of the unfinished tale: Angel Gómez falls madly in love with Vicenta (who also "falls in love with him, a *little*" [*UEP* 108], as Porter says), and Vicenta helps Gómez overthrow the archbishop and destroy his palace. A fragment of a scene following this destruction suggests the revolutionary moral of this story is similar to the message of Porter's "Letter to the Editor" in *Century*: "The fields will be open to any man who sows his grain, and every man shall make his house with his own hands, and every woman shall have milk enough for her children" (*UEP* 130). Still, there is no happy ending here: "Gómez, in patio of wrecked palace tells her to follow him—he will marry her. The judge will marry them. She says she is free, too, and she does not want marriage or children. This freedom is only for men, then? It is, he tells her, for she must be a slave to his love. . . . She goes" (*UEP* 109). Evidently, not with him. The story reverses the ending of Mena's story in several obvious ways. Unlike Carmelita, Vicenta uses "love" to get what she wants from men until she can either escape from him (the archbishop) or no longer needs him (Angel Gómez). Earlier in the story, when she tells the old servant Antonia of her longing for love and for adventure (she wants to become a *soldadera*, like María Rosa in "María Concepción"), Antonia warns her, "You dream, Niña. Pretty words. You read those things in your books, maybe, and that is not good for anybody. Hunger is not happiness, and a *soldadera* carries her pack on her back and her cub inside of her, and is beaten by whatever man she belongs to, and eats what is left after the man and sleeps when he is done with her, and life is a long trouble" (*UEP* 123). By rejecting both the revolution—which, as Porter shows in "Flowering Judas," is one for men but not for women—and love, Vicenta resembles a characteristic Porter heroine

190

much more than Mena's Carmelita does.

Accordingly, although Porter never finished nor published this story,[8] Ruth M. Alvarez and Thomas F. Walsh argue, "'The Dove of Chapacalco' could be considered a dress rehearsal for 'María Concepción,' whose setting is also borrowed from Teotihuacán and whose heroine is also an Indian woman who subjugates her husband to her will. The triumph of María Concepción is less spectacular than that of Vicenta but a triumph nonetheless" (*UEP* 108). If Porter's "Dove" is in part defined by its revision of Mena's "sub-historical" romantic fiction, then we can see how Porter's art as it developed in Mexico did so not only in relation to historical events and her personal experiences but also in relation to how those events were "fictionalized" and "poeticized" by Mexican poets, folksingers, and, most importantly, by María Cristina Mena.

Reading Mena through Porter provides insight into Mena's work; reversing the angle offers new understanding of Porter. Mena's is a fully realized art, if a different art from Porter's. Tiffany Ana López has defended Mena against unsympathetic critics such as Charles Tatum and Raymund A. Paredes by explicating the subtle interplay of cultures at work in her stories. Amy Doherty points to Mena's complex and prescient handling of issues of gender and class in Mexican society, and through an analysis of the numerous mirror images in Mena's tales, relates her work to Gloria Anzaldúa's critical observations on border fictions, thus convincingly placing Mena in the position of Latina literary foremother (xlvi-l). When I first compared Porter's Mexico stories to Mena's, what struck me was Mena's powerful understanding of the colonial gaze—the ways in which colonizer and colonized view each other. In "The Gold Vanity Set," for example, Mena first establishes the story of Petra, who marries a prosperous young musician; then, abruptly, Mena shifts to a scene where we encounter a group of American tourists

191

invading the inn where Petra's husband works: Says one of the American women, "catching sight" of Petra, "'Oh, what a beautiful girl! I must get her picture'" (3). The effect is crude and powerful. The character Mena has made us care about becomes a commodity, a subject for a thoughtless tourist snapshot. I have read all of Porter's Mexico works—and she can be outright colonial in an essay such as "Xochimilco" or harshly critical of outsiders pretending to be insiders, as in her review of D. H. Lawrence's *The Plumed Serpent*—but nothing by Porter captures as well this sense of Mexicans as Others in their own land.[9]

Porter and Mena are two "interpreters of Mexican life" writing for the same magazine but from different positions. *The Century Magazine* Mena wrote for was still quite Victorian in its sensibility, and Mena was expected to write stories portraying Mexico and Mexicans in a manner that did not conflict with the colonial point of view. That she managed to write stories that subtly undermine this point of view is remarkable. Porter, on the other hand, was, only a few years later, contributing to *Century* under Carl Van Doren's editorship, and Van Doren had turned it into, as he says in a memoir, "almost an anthology of . . . the new literature" (196). Porter, too, wrote for a particular audience, a "modernist" one that was suddenly disdainful of gentility, sentimentality, and romance. For that reason, it is easy to understand how Porter and others could miss the subtlety we can now find in Mena's tales. Porter's vision was one of revision. In their own way, her *Century* tales on Mexico, such as "María Concepción" and "Virgin Violeta," are just as tied to the politics and aesthetics of *The Century Magazine* as Mena's were.

There is a key difference, though, in their positions as writers, one Mexican, one Anglo. Mena's fiction for *Century* abruptly ceases in 1916. Porter's Mexico essays and fiction continued to evolve artistically throughout her career, according to her shifting views on Mexico,

192

ultimately leading her to write stories that reflect her sense of alienation in a land she had once described as her "familiar" country. Well ahead of the post-colonialists, Porter "knew better than to give advice to Mexicans" (*UEP* 255). María Cristina Mena did not have the opportunity to work her way through these issues as Porter did. As Amy Doherty wrote to me, "One could speculate that Porter was in a more powerful position as a writer, and that may have made her more outspoken than Mena. . . . It seems she [Mena] was in constant negotiations with her [*Century*] editors, defending the integrity of her work. I imagine that her work met her editors' needs at a certain time in the publication's history, and that at a point their agendas no longer coincided." [10] That was 1916. Katherine Anne Porter's first Mexican story would appear in the pages of that same magazine just seven years later. ❖

Notes

[1] Robert H. Brinkmeyer, Jr., confirms Porter's fabrication of this story: "Porter later admitted that the conversation was invented" (32).

[2] Although I am convinced—by the close similarity of these stories and because both Porter and Mena published stories in *Century*—that Porter knew and adapted Mena's work, it is not necessary for this to be true for my argument to have merits beyond this "discovery." The important point is that Porter consciously created her early fiction against what she felt was "sub-historical," romantic, and sentimentalized literature written by Mexicans about Mexico. This would also include Mena's works, of course.

[3] Amy Doherty's "Introduction" to *The Collected Stories of María Cristina Mena* is the single-best source of information on Mena's life and work. Tiffany Ana López also includes biographical

information in her essay on Mena and tricksterism. See also Leticia Garza-Falcón's " 'A Tolerance for Contradictions': The Short Stories of María Cristina Mena."

[4] Doherty (146) cites Camín and Meyer as her source for this characterization of the Jockey Club. See also Walsh ("Braggioni's").

[5] Thomas F. Walsh's discussion of "The Dove of Chapacalco" in his essential work *Katherine Anne Porter and Mexico* (1992) is the best extended study of this story. My own conclusions dovetail with his, particularly in regard to the character of Angel Gómez. Walsh's fine history of the parallels between Porter's fictional characters and real-life ones obviates the parts of the story I argue Porter borrowed from Mena—the character of Vicenta, her sexual bondage, her romance with the revolutionary, and her overthrow of the archbishop. Walsh has no explanation for the creation of these elements and assumes that this is an example of how she "fictionalizes" reality. As for why Porter never finished the story, Walsh speculates, "Not allowing herself enough time to digest the raw experiences of a few months before, she may have felt the story too melodramatic, the anticlericalism too explicit, and the motivation of the three principal characters too simplistic." See 49–57.

[6] See Tiffany Ana López 45, note 28: "This story could be and probably was read as a metaphor for political struggles in Mexico. Bisco would represent Pancho Villa, the Mexican revolutionary who joined the rebels and fought vigorously for President Madero [against Porfirio Diaz]. . . . In this reading, Rascón would represent Diaz." The full note describes many other parallels with historical persons.

[7] Gómez is reading "Sonatina," from Darío's collection *Profane Hymns and Other Poems* (1896), which Octavio Paz has called "the book that best defines [Darío's] earlier Modernism" (13). Porter presents the "princess" in contrast to "the women who reeked of

grease and milk and sweat" (*UEP* 119).

[8] I found no biographical information on why Porter left the story unfinished and unpublished, but my own research here indicates that she was probably self-conscious of its indebtedness to Mena's story—even though she reverses Mena's emphasis. Ultimately she saw "The Dove of Chapacalco" as unoriginal. Certainly, "María Concepción" is a much more original tale and one completely in keeping with Porter's mature style.

[9] This is not to say that Porter is, even in her early work, insensitive to her own outsider's view (see, for example her review of Blasco Ibanez's *Mexico in Revolution* [*UEP* 28–31]); however, she still succumbs to portraying the "inditos" in a Rousseau-like fashion. The key words in early essays such as "The Fiesta of Guadalupe" (*CE*) are "strange-looking" and "fantastic." An essay such as "Xochimilco" (*UEP*) is almost unreadable in the wake of post-colonial theory: Being taken for a guided ride in a canoe through the canals of Xochimilco, Porter makes thoughtless anthropological comments such as, "These Xochimilco Indians are a splendid remnant of the Aztecs." In unself-conscious prose, she projects upon the "primitive" every admirable quality lacking in civilization—they are not guilty about sex, they have no anxieties, suffer no sleeplessness, etc. Later, from their boat, they observe a "child . . . bathing her feet, standing on a wet stone. We pass almost near enough to touch her. Mary throws her a few pansies. . . . She is too amazed at the sight of us to pick up the pansies" (*UEP* 73–78). After a while, you feel as if you are on the Mexico Ride at Disneyland.

These are, of course, examples chosen for effect, and I could find similarly unflattering generalizations made by Mena, for there is some evidence in her work that she does, as Paredes says, reinforce stereotypes held by her Anglo readers. In contrast, I found in my reading of Porter's published and recently collected unpublished Mexico pieces that Porter anticipates our now almost modish use of post-colonial theory. Her famous tomahawking of D. H. Lawrence's *The Plumed Serpent* is a case in point: "Altogether, Lawrence cannot be freed from the charge of pretentiousness . . . in having set down his own personal reactions to a whole race as if they were inspired truth. His Indians are merely what Indians might be if they were all D. H. Lawrences" (*CE* 425). In a little-read catalog description of an exhibit of Mexican folk art, I find Porter coming as close as any description I know to capturing a people's right and authority to their own view of themselves. Describing folk art depictions of the conquistadors, she writes, "This accounts for the objective precision of that pictured account the Mexican left us, of the first Spaniards: there they are, seen by implacably honest eyes, those helmeted conquerors on horseback, those wide skirted stiff-waisted ladies with monstrous coiffures, those imported dogs and incredible household furnishings. Painted chests and wooden trays of that period silently point to the ugliness of our kind of civilization as beheld by the civilized of another race and ethical code" (*UEP* 165–66).

A good example of an analysis of Porter's Mexico stories from a post-colonial viewpoint is Robert H. Brinkmeyer, Jr.'s "Mexico, Memory, and Betrayal: Katherine Anne Porter's 'Flowering Judas,'" in Carr. Jeri R. Kraver's essay in this collection is another strong post-colonial reading of Porter.

[10] Amy Doherty made the first part of this statement to me in regard to Porter's fearlessness at attacking D. H. Lawrence versus Mena's silence on Lawrence's novel. Mena and Lawrence were friends, although his comments on her writing are backhanded compliments at best. See Doherty, xiv, xv. The rest of the quotation here deals specifically with Mena's struggles within the power structure of *The Century*. ❖

Works Cited

Ammons, Elizabeth, and Annette White-Parks, eds. *Tricksterism in Turn-of-the-Century American Literature: A Multicultural Perspective*. Hanover: UP of New England, 1994.

Baker, Houston A., Jr., ed. *Three American Literatures*. New York: MLA, 1982.

Brinkmeyer, Robert H., Jr. *Katherine Anne Porter's Artistic Development*. Baton Rouge: Louisiana State UP, 1993.

Camín, Héctor Aguilar, and Lorenzo Meyer. *In the Shadow of the Mexican Revolution: Contemporary Mexican History, 1910–1989*. Trans. Luis Alberto Fierro. Austin: U of Texas P, 1993.

Carr, Virginia Spencer, ed. *"Flowering Judas": Women Writers, Texts and Contexts*. New Brunswick: Rutgers UP, 1993.

Darío, Rubén. *Selected Poems of Rubén Darío*. Trans. Lysander Kemp. Austin: U of Texas P, 1983.

Doherty, Amy. "Introduction." In *María Cristina Mena*.

———. Letter to Rob Johnson, May 1998.

Garza-Falcón, Leticia M. " 'A Tolerance for Contradictions': The Short Stories of María Cristina Mena." In Kilcup.

Kilcup, Karen L., ed. *Nineteenth-Century American Women Writers: A Critical Reader*. Malden, MA: Blackwell Publishers, 1998.

López, Tiffany Ana. "María Cristina Mena: Turn-of-the-Century La Malinche, and Other Tales of Cultural (Re)Construction." In Ammons and White-Parks 21-45.

Mena, María Cristina. *The Collected Stories of María Cristina Mena*. Ed. Amy Doherty. Houston: Arte Público P, 1997.

Paredes, Raymund A. "The Evolution of Chicano Literature." In Baker, Jr.

Paz, Octavio. "Preface." In Darío.

Porter, Katherine Anne. *The Collected Essays and Occasional Writings of*

Katherine Anne Porter. New York: Delacorte P, 1970.

———. *The Collected Stories of Katherine Anne Porter*. New York: Harcourt, Brace, and World, Inc., 1965.

———. *Uncollected Early Prose of Katherine Anne Porter*. Ed. Ruth M. Alvarez and Thomas F. Walsh. Austin: U of Texas P, 1993.

Rebolledo, Diana Tey, and Eliano S. Rivero, eds. *Infinite Divisions: An Anthology of Chicana Literature*. Tucson: U of Arizona P, 1993.

Tatum, Charles. *Chicano Literature*. Boston: Twayne, 1982.

Van Doren, Carl. *Three Worlds*. New York: Harper and Brothers, 1936.

Walsh, Thomas F. *Katherine Anne Porter and Mexico*. Austin: U of Texas P, 1992.

———. "Braggioni's Jockey Club in 'Flowering Judas.'" *Studies in Short Fiction* 20 (spring-summer 1983): 136–38.

Gender and Creativity in Katherine Anne Porter's "The Princess"

Christine H. Hait

"The Princess," an unfinished story recently published in *Uncollected Early Prose of Katherine Anne Porter*, provides further evidence of Katherine Anne Porter's interest in the relationship between gender and creativity. "The Princess" joins other works by Porter that reflect this interest by highlighting in some way women's creativity or the male artist's relationship to women. "The Princess" not only has important connections to various Porter works but also provides further support for viewing Porter's writing—its imagery, plots, and themes—within the context of female modernism. It is not surprising to find Porter confronting issues of gender and creativity in 1927–28, the period, according to the editors of *Uncollected Early Prose*, of the story's composition. Porter's interests in feminist thought and aesthetics were particularly acute in the 1920s. Additionally, her personal connections to other modernist women writers were stronger during this decade than during any other period in her life. These interests and connections make themselves felt in this fable of a woman's struggle against the forces that would limit her freedom to express herself creatively.

The setting of "The Princess" is a kingdom whose citizens, with the exception of children and women beyond childbearing age, wear no clothing. Girls give up their virginity at the age of fifteen. The Princess of the kingdom, however, refuses at thirteen to take off her shift and at eighteen remains a virgin and unmarried. Instead of obeying her country's custom and law, from the age of thirteen, she begins to devise increasingly elaborate ways to clothe and decorate her body. She agrees to marry a young man who agrees to share her "dream" and who loves her despite her strange ways, which have created an uproar in the kingdom. Her betrothal and her lover's requests to touch her inspire new ways for her to conceal herself and armor herself against touch, and she begins to wear gloves set with thorny jewels and a mask with amethyst eyes. Finally, her actions bring down upon her the punishment of the sacred tribunal. Scheduled to die by drowning the next day, she agrees to escape with her betrothed but drowns when she refuses to take off her heavy clothes and jewelry in order to cross a lake safely. The young man, now a poet, writes poetry inspired by her, and from this poetry the narrator learns of the legend of the Princess.

Porter's fable of female creativity brings into play a variety of issues of significance to Porter and to modernist women writers in general: it reflects upon the relationship between creation and procreation, between the woman artist and her body, and between the woman artist and her culture; it explores images of masking, costuming, armoring, and petrifaction; and it reflects upon the role of woman as artistic object and subject of male-produced myth and legend. Particularly in its concluding section, "The Princess" suggests important questions concerning the validity of cultural narratives about creative women.

As one scholar has noted, "To wield a pen is a masculine act that puts the woman writer at war with her body and culture" (Friedman 49). In "The Princess," Porter creates a corollary to the woman writer's war against the physical and social forces that discourage her art. She presents a kingdom "dedicated to the love and worship of nature" (230).

The residents of the kingdom consider heretical any desire to embellish nature. The young princess of the kingdom, however, plans on "rejecting utterly the banal sufferings imposed by nature" (235). When she claims that nature is "abhorrent, a vulgarity perpetually to be denied by the soul of man" (234), she is accused of heresy and of speaking in riddles. By suggesting that she will not bear children, she brings upon herself "the canonical curse" (235). According to the High Priestess, "if [the Princess] scorns and rejects the natural office of motherhood it is written that she will never rule over this kingdom. For the fruitless woman may not inherit the throne, no, not even if she is the sole child of her father" (235).

Porter's kingdom is a fanciful construct, which she portrays humorously. It is ruled by a hapless king and a silly queen, both dominated by the High Priestess, whom they refer to in private as a "cross old maid" (236). For all its humor, though, Porter's fable is a serious commentary on the intersection of social law and natural law and the plight of a woman caught in the crossing point. Through exaggeration, she satirizes her own culture's control of the female body and its indictment of women who resist "the natural office of motherhood." Additionally, Porter reveals in this fable a concern with the loss of women's birthright. Here, the woman born to be a queen loses access to her proper station when she defies the laws of society and nature. A child born with a gift, she "read the magic runes on her father's sword at the age of five and without instruction" (229), an act that the High Priestess calls a "certain sign of holy madness" and a demonstration of "too great wisdom for a natural infant" (229). The "unnatural" wisdom with which she was born must be replaced by an understanding of the social customs that dictate female development. Here, as in so much of her fiction, Porter places her heroine in a society that enforces femininity, punishes women who consider self-fulfillment a birthright, and declares mad women who claim truth and language for themselves—who "read the magic runes."

It is significant that Porter would imagine a woman artist who defies nature, who demands control over her body, and who substitutes creation for procreation. At one point in "The Princess," an old lawgiver declares that the Princess is mad and another lawgiver adds, "[a]nd a heretic besides. . . . Since when has she become a god, to create with her hands?" (237) The Princess uses her art to create for her body a new form. As a creator, she shapes an image and brings to life a vision. To the citizens of her society, she seems a heretic or a madwoman because she usurps the divine powers of creation. But to herself, Porter suggests, the Princess is in her creative powers not like a god but like a natural procreative woman, pregnant with her own kind of child. She tells the townspeople,

> This is the beauty I have dreamed and made, and that is the only beauty. . . . If you should strip me, you will find nothing but that beauty I have made . . . and if you kill me, you cannot destroy my dream. . . . If I am heavy with it, it is because the love of beauty is a heavy sorrow, and the making of beauty a task too great for the soul to endure for long. (237)

Like the High Priestess, whose religious responsibilities include taking a potion each month in order to experience labor pains, the Princess experiences the exercise of her artistic responsibilities as a reenactment of the process of giving birth. Adorning herself through time with more jewels and adding layers of fabric, she becomes, like a woman going through the stages of a pregnancy, heavier and heavier. She is "heavy" with her love of beauty, as if it were a child in her womb. Having vowed to "devise [her] own cruelties and [reject] utterly the banal sufferings imposed by nature" (235), she has made herself "pregnant" through her own devices, not nature's. Just as a woman's body can endure the carrying of a child for only so long, the Princess' soul cannot endure the weight of its burden indefinitely. The Princess suggests that her "child" will kill her, while it will live on. Porter's concept of the child murdering its mother and her fears of reproduction and sexuality infiltrate her story of the dangers of outlawed female creativity. She links creation with procreation, both by comparison and contrast. In her fable, the creative woman is not the procreative woman, yet at the same time she, too, carries a burden and risks death for the sake of that which she carries within her.

In its exploration of the relationship of the woman artist to nature and to motherhood, "The Princess" has ties to "Holiday," a story Porter began in 1923 and completed in 1960. As Mary Titus points out, "In 'Holiday' Katherine Anne Porter depicts the alienation of the woman artist in a culture that advocates motherhood, not authorhood, as a woman's natural and ideal achievement" ("'A little stolen holiday'" 73). The culture that "Holiday" portrays, a Texas farming community of German immigrants, like the kingdom in "The Princess," is bound to the cycles of nature, and the women of the culture are bound to the rituals of early marriage and motherhood. The narrator of "Holiday" finds herself outside of the cycles and rituals that mark the lives of the women she encounters in the Müller household that she visits on a "holiday." Clearly a narrative of the woman artist, "Holiday," as Titus points out, explores the narrator's anxiety about the relationship to nature and to "the natural" in which her vocation places her. However, the narrator's ability at the end of the story to feel connection with and comfort from the natural world around her makes "Holiday," according to Titus, "Porter's most positive fictional resolution of the conflicts between being a woman and being an artist" ("'A little stolen holiday'" 90). In this regard, the two stories, both begun in the 1920s, serve as contrasting examples of narratives of the woman artist, for the

Princess—who dies for her art—finds no satisfactory means by which to resolve her conflict with nature.

The Princess not only makes declarations against nature but embraces artifice as well, making herself the object upon which she practices her creativity. Porter, like many of her contemporaries in the 1920s, understood well the feminine impulse to make one's self the object of one's art. "Many female modernists have studied the deflection of female creativity from the production of art to the re-creation of the body" (Gubar 250). They used metaphors of mask and costume to explore issues of female identity and to express ambivalence toward their bodies and their cultural roles. They also creatively imagined in texts the re-formation of their physical selves, confronting the duality that Alicia Ostriker describes as the duality between vulnerable nature and invulnerable art (86). In reference to twentieth-century women's poetry, Ostriker writes: "[I]mages of self as stone, or armor, or metal, are extremely common. . . . Often the precise point is that the self was once soft but has become self-protectively hard" (85). The female body and a male culture are often the enemies the woman artist struggles against and protects herself from; as she refigures one, she challenges the other.

Through images of masking, armoring, and petrifaction in "The Princess," Porter explores the extremes to which a woman artist might take her efforts to assume control over her body and to express herself through an art that is intricately connected to her physical nature. Commanded to take off her white linen shift at the age of thirteen, the Princess refuses and stubbornly puts on a second shift. Later she rebels further by designing and wearing multi-colored clothing. In a reversal of the Lady Godiva legend, "[w]hen she went in to the streets of the city even her maidens blushed for shame of her strangeness" (231). Soon she is "directing her maids in the art of beating heated metal into diverse shapes, and fashioning splendid ornaments of brightly colored stones" (231). Continuing to meet resistance to her art, she appears in public, "an image in stiff woven robes of gold, with corselet and girdle of jewels, and a tall crown of pointed crystals, and the face of the image was a golden mask, with eyes of amethyst" (234). Making herself the object of her art, she also makes herself invulnerable, untouchable. The young man who courts her cuts his hands on the stones in her hair and on the sharp edges of her gloves when he tries to touch her. Porter relays the gradual process by which the obsessive practice of her art dehumanizes the Princess and distances her from others. The Princess' costume and jewelry remove her from sexuality: she conceals her body and, finally, even her face from view, and her jewels serve as weapons against human touch. Visionary, self-destructive, defensive—the woman artist in Porter's fable, caught in a rigid society that loves nature excessively, takes her attraction to artifice to disturbing extremes.

Human hands may not touch the Princess, referred to in the last half of the narrative as "the Mask," but the law can. Strange and cruel and wondrous, the Princess becomes in the public's eye "the enchantress, the stone image, the heretic" (238). At her hearing, the public witnesses another wonder: while the Princess laughs at the tribunal's charges, tears flow from the emerald eyes of her mask. She has protected her body from touch and hidden it from view. She has fashioned her face and her eyes to reveal no emotion, for she has substituted for them a mask with jeweled eyes. Yet she is still the object of sexual longing: "[T]he men searched the folds of her robes with cautious stares, wishing their eyes were hands"; "[m]any a youth tossed and sweated at night with the thought of her" (231). And she still feels emotion, as the tears from her mask attest.

The Princess reshapes her identity through her art in increasingly dramatic ways as the pressures to conform to society's demands strengthen as she moves toward womanhood. "The Princess" anticipates "Old Mortality," "Pale Horse, Pale Rider," and "The Old Order" stories that recreate cultures with clearly delineated gender roles and feature a character, "Miranda," who struggles to establish her identity in the face of societal expectations. Porter's interest in clothing and the domestic arts as means of creative expression for women makes its way into these fictional works as well. The Princess' decision to act out her rebellion against society through clothing anticipates Miranda's reflections on clothing and femininity in "Old Mortality" and "The Old Order." The descriptions of the Princess' and her maidens' work with fabric and jewelry may remind readers of Porter's loving reenactment of the patchwork of the grandmother and Nannie in "The Journey." The armoring and costuming images of "The Princess" are found again at the end of "Pale Horse, Pale Rider," when Miranda requests makeup, perfume, "gray suede gauntlets," and a "walking stick of silvery wood with a silver knob" (Porter, *CS* 316) as she prepares to leave the hospital and re-enter society after a near-death experience. "The Princess" reinforces the significance of the traditional female arts of costuming and handiwork to Porter's plots and characterization. It suggests also Porter's recognition of the allure—and danger—of art and artifice as means by which women achieve both power and protection, participate in both display and concealment.

"The Princess" also reveals Porter's outrage at the denial of power to women that results from their traditional roles as artistic objects and subjects of male-produced myth. One more peril awaits the Princess after death: the peril of male appropriation of her art. Avoiding the romance plot during her life, she is absorbed into it after death through the songs that the man who loved her, the Poet, sings about her. She has predicted this outcome. At the brink of the water, pleading with her to shed her robes and jewels, the Poet asks, "It was you I loved, oh,

Princess, I loved your eyelashes and your nostrils and your thin rosy fingernails, and your naked heels . . . and now these things are gone, and I cannot see them any more—and what good is it to me to love a stone, an image wearing a mask?" (238) The Princess answers calmly, "But you will make songs about me until your last day," and with these words leans into the water (239). The Poet does make use of her, but the narrator, who for the first time speaks in the first person, reveals that the Poet's song is really not about the Princess at all. It is about the Poet, about "what a faithful lover he was, and how fine a poet" (240).

Nevertheless, it is from his song that the narrator learns about the Princess. The narrative reveals itself at the end as a revision of this song. From the Poet's song about himself, his faithful love and fine poetry, the narrator has created a story of the woman artist, and thus the Princess is rescued from the romance plot in which she has been imprisoned in legend and returned to her own plot of self-fulfillment. The Poet in his song emphasizes how cruel the Princess was in love and, thus, how much he suffered as her lover; the narrator emphasizes how creative the Princess was in her efforts to make beauty out of a vision and how much she suffered for her art. The message is clear: the songs of the poets must be reinterpreted. The narrator participates in what Adrienne Rich calls "writing as re-vision" (33–49).

"The Princess" gives further evidence of the significance of myth and legend to Porter's imagination from the beginning of her writing career. Editors Ruth Alvarez and Thomas Walsh in their introduction to "The Princess" point out the similarities between this fable and the three stories from legend that Porter crafted for publication in the children's magazine *Everyland* in 1920, also included in *Uncollected Early Prose*. They also point to the poem "Requiescat," written in 1924 and included in *Collected Essays* under the title "Little Requiem," as a kind of companion piece to the story, for it shares the story's mythic elements, imagery of armor and royalty, and theme of a lost birthright (this theme is also found in "Holiday"). "The Princess" is one of the strongest examples of what Darlene Harbour Unrue calls "the mythic feminism that pervades much of Porter's canon" (*Katherine Anne Porter's Poetry* 39), matched only perhaps by "In Defense of Circe," which shares its atmosphere of magic and aestheticism. Porter's mythic feminism unites her with other modernist women writers—Edna St. Vincent Millay, H. D., Elinor Wylie, and Louise Bogan, to name a few—who found the making and revising of myth a powerful creative outlet.

Like much of Porter's writing from the 1920s, "The Princess" reveals Porter's interest in the intersections of love, art, and power and her willingness to employ violent imagery to convey the complex, often unsettling, relationship between love and art. Unrue in *Katherine Anne Porter's Poetry*, notes the imagery that connects "The Princess" to Porter's poem "Ordeal by Ploughshare" (Porter 23), written in the early 1920s, in which a first-person persona speaks of unworldly dreams of the death of a "lost changeling creature" in the dark of night. This poem, with its description of sharp points (ploughshares) that cut, shares the masochistic imagery of "The Princess," imagery also found in "Virgin Violeta." Porter's Mexican fiction of the 1920s, Mary Titus argues, explores "sadomasochism and romantic fantasy" ("Booby Trap" 621) in terms of male artists and models. "The Princess," of course, in part reverses the pattern of this fiction, offering as it does a woman artist who dominates and hurts, through her sharp jewelry, a passive lover. Yet the Princess, like the women in Porter's Mexican fiction, is the object of male fantasy, made more erotic by the concealment of her body, and she is ultimately the muse for her lover who makes a legend of her cruelty and loveliness. Although not as predatory or malevolent in intent as male characters from the Mexican fiction, such as Carlos in "Virgin Violeta" or Braggioni in "Flowering Judas," and in some ways more closely connected to Rubén in "The Martyr," the Poet, by making her a legend and making her story his own, deprives the Princess of her human features, in much the same way, ironically, that her masking and making a stone image of herself had previously done.

It seems that Porter inscribed in her fable all her own fears (of reproduction, of sexuality, of community, of male appropriation of her art, but also of sterility, rejection, and isolation) and desires (beauty "after [her] own secret thought," vision, and self-fulfillment). Her sympathy for her heroine remains strong throughout the narrative: her descriptions of the Princess' extravagant behavior hold little hint of mockery or disapproval. And her description of the Princess' death is lyrical: the Princess trails into the water "like a falling star" (239); the waters cradle and caress her; her hair streams out "like a soft flame" (239).

The question remains, then, whether this is an enabling fable of creativity for the woman artist who wrote it. It was enabling in that it allowed Porter to indulge in pure fantasy. In it she gave free rein to her fancy and imagined a fairy tale kingdom full of strange customs and odd rituals, complete with a royal family, sacred tribunal, and a fanatical priestess. She indulged her humor and love of irony by exaggerating certain tendencies in her own culture toward Puritanism and reversing the traditional story (think of Amy shocking her father with her revealing shepherdess costume in "Old Mortality") of the rebellious daughter who flaunts her sexuality. She indulged her well-known love of clothing and jewelry by composing beautiful descriptions of the Princess' creations. She certainly indulged some of her own bitterness toward the objectification of women in art by men in her depiction of the Poet's song. Most important, she voiced her own passionate commitment to her art through the character of the Princess. She must have taken great pleasure in creating a woman artist who broke the laws of her society with such proud defiance and fearless contempt.

At the same time, the fable allows her as an artist to confront real and serious issues concerning both her position in society and her attitude toward nature as a woman artist. Her fable makes it clear that she knew the consequences of taking to extremes her own tendency to value the soul and the mind over the body, art over nature, vision over reality, freedom and autonomy over community. Her Princess may have reconciled herself to the knowledge that "the making of beauty" was "a task too great for the soul to endure for long," but Porter's long career points to nothing if not her stubborn will to survive. The representative conclusion of her fiction is the moment at which a character resists the temptation to renounce her body and to escape fully into the spirit. Both "Pale Horse, Pale Rider" and "Flowering Judas," for example, conclude with the main characters returning to their bodies after a dream or illness takes them to the edge of a precipice where they are tempted to leave their bodies behind and let their spirits take flight. It is to this temptation that her heroines state their most fierce and commanding "No!" That "No!" is a resounding, if bitter, "Yes!" to life that characterizations of Porter's fiction as renunciatory gloss over. "The Princess" is an exception in this regard and is, thus, one of the most truly renunciatory of Porter's stories. Its exceptional nature may be a clue to why Porter failed to complete and publish the story.

However, the actions of the narrator at the end provide the fable with some affirmation. The narrator listens to the song of the Poet and his charges against the Princess and subtly reveals them for what they are: a misreading of the character of the Princess. The narrator also reveals that the secret tribunal charged the Princess with "corrupting the youths and maidens of her court," "conspiring against the power of the High Priest and especially the High Priestess," and "wantonness with her favorite courtier, who was of low birth" (238). Yet the sacred tribunal does not articulate all its charges against the outlawed woman artist, for she is sentenced to death for the crimes named and also for "other crimes . . . not to be named, but written in the state secret parchments, and preserved sealed in the archives of state" (238). The story the narrator tells of the Princess contests both the Poet's song and the charges of the state. What might those unnamed crimes be, known and recorded by the sacred tribunal yet too unspeakable to announce in the public proceedings? The narrator never says. But the narrative poses the questions: "What are the women's stories lurking underneath the poets' songs? What are the secret charges of the state against the woman who practices an art?" The questions it asks and the issues it explores make "The Princess" a provocative new narrative for readers of Porter's work and for students of modernist women's writing. ❖

Works Cited

Alvarez, Ruth M. and Thomas F. Walsh, Eds. *Uncollected Early Prose of Katherine Anne Porter*. Austin: U of Texas P, 1993.

Friedman, Susan Stanford. "Creativity and the Childbirth Metaphor: Gender Difference in Literary Discourse." *Feminist Studies* 13.1 (1987): 49–82.

Gubar, Susan. "'The Blank Page' and the Issues of Female Creativity." *Critical Inquiry* 8 (winter 1981): 243–63.

Ostriker, Alicia. *Stealing the Language: The Emergence of Women's Poetry in America*. Boston: Beacon, 1986.

Porter, Katherine Anne. *The Collected Essays and Occasional Writings of Katherine Anne Porter*. New York: Delacorte P, 1970.

———. *The Collected Stories of Katherine Anne Porter*. New York: Harcourt, Brace and World, 1965.

Rich, Adrienne. *On Lies, Secrets, and Silence: Selected Prose 1966–1978*. New York: Norton, 1979.

Titus, Mary. "The 'Booby Trap' of Love: Artist and Sadist in Katherine Anne Porter's Mexico Fiction." *Journal of Modern Literature* 26 (1990): 617–34.

———. "'A little stolen holiday': Katherine Anne Porter's Narrative of the Woman Artist." *Women's Studies* 25 (1993): 73–93.

Unrue, Darlene Harbour. *Katherine Anne Porter's Poetry.* Columbia: U of South Carolina P, 1996.

Cover-Ups: Katherine Anne Porter and The Economics of Concealment

Robert K. Miller

Informed by Porter's experience in Berlin during the winter of 1931–32 and completed nearly ten years later (Givner 319), "The Leaning Tower" describes a nation in political and economic turmoil as seen through the eyes of a young American artist living in a stifling pension. The political aspects of this story led Robert Penn Warren to consider it a failure because of excessive "topicality" (Stout 113–14). But like Janis Stout, I believe "The Leaning Tower" is a "major work" (Stout 114) and I am struck by how it has received relatively little attention from scholars— perhaps because it has traditionally been read as a "piece of political commentary" (Stout 114). This richly textured work shows how political and economic concerns cannot be divorced from the dramas of domestic life and, in particular, from the decoration of houses. As the most cosmopolitan character in the story explains, "The whole art of self-importance is to raise your personal likes and dislikes to the plane of moral or aesthetic principle and to apply on an international scale your smallest personal experience" (484).

Worn out by his search for a room in Berlin, Charles Upton, the young American protagonist of this story, eventually rents space that seems to offend his eye and oppress his spirit. His initial impression is worth quoting at length:

The room. Well, the room. He had seen it several times before in his search. It was not what he would choose if he had a choice, but it was the least tiresome example of what he recognized now as a fixed style, with its somber rich oriental carpet, the lace curtains under looped-back velvet hangings, the large round table covered with another silky oriental rug in sweet, refined colors. One corner was occupied by deep couches heaped with silk and velvet cushions, the wall above it adorned with a glass-doored cabinet filled with minute curiosities mostly in silver filigree and fine porcelain, and upon the table stood a huge lamp with an ornate pink silk shade, fluted and fringed and draped with silken tassels. The bed was massive with feather quilt and shot-silk cover, the giant wardrobe of dark polished wood was carved all out of shape.

A hell of a place, really, but he would take it. (445–46)

What is it, we might well ask, that makes this space a "hell of a place"—a hell into which Charles chooses to consign himself. The answer, at first, would seem to be the oppressive number of coverings that either conceal objects or distort their form.

The table is covered, the lamp is overwhelmed by its elaborate pink shade, the couches buried under heaps of silk and velvet cushions. And as for the windows—which he later finds to be "closed tightly" (447)—they are covered with two layers: velvet hangings looped over lace curtains. Later, when attempting to sleep in this space, Charles "found that he was wallowing in the airless deeps of the feather quilt, hot and half smothered" (460). The multiple layers of covering that fill his room make it a perfect site for home burial.

The room reveals much about the landlady, Rosa Reichl. A middle-aged woman who had been a member of the upper middle class until she was impoverished by war and the hyperinflation through which

Germany suffered during the 1920s, Rosa could easily be transported to the south of Porter's childhood: a genteel figure scrambling hard to preserve family memories—symbolized by a plaster reproduction of the Leaning Tower purchased on her wedding journey—and seizing every occasion to talk about how well she lived *before the war*. The furnishings of her home become the principal means through which she can signal that she has a past that is grander than her present. Fashions have changed, and the elaborate furnishing of her home seems oppressively old-fashioned to the modernist sensibility of 1931—the year in which the story is set. The house is, in fact, a kind of museum that could eventually be featured on a home tour if preserved long enough for out-of-date fashion to become perceived as romantically old-fashioned (*historic,* rather than *old*). Rosa is the curator of this space, a curator without a sufficient budget.

Much of the tension in the story can be traced to her inability to refurnish or *re-cover* her space. When Charles accidentally breaks the replica of the Leaning Tower, she tells him, "It cannot be replaced" (447). All she can manage is a clumsy repair job, after which the object seems grotesque. Behind this small drama of breaking and repairing an object of sentimental value loom larger questions involving the economics of interior decoration. The story suggests that Rosa will never again be able to afford furniture or even window treatments of the quality to which she had grown accustomed. Consider, for example, the description of the chair in which Charles tries to work. It was "a delicate affair with curved spindle legs and old mended tapestry in seat and back: a museum piece beyond a doubt" (453). When Charles begins to work, he momentarily forgets that he is sitting on a museum piece that his landlady cannot afford to replace. Trying to make himself comfortable, he lights a cigarette and leans back in the chair, "balanced on the back legs for a split second and came down with a thump, his heart seeming to turn over as the thin joints complained in a human voice" (454). God forbid the chair should break; having already broken the Leaning Tower, Charles is in enough trouble already. And the close association between Rosa and her possessions is conveyed by how the joints complain "in a human voice."

Wherever Charles turns within this space, he is oppressed by what appears to be excessive ornamentation—details that distract attention and seem ridiculous to his modernist eye. When he peers through the layers which conceal his window, he is distressed to find "a dozen infant-sized pottery cupids, gross, squat limbed, wanton in posture and vulgarly pink" (447) decorating the roof of a neighboring house. Charles, it seems, would prefer a simpler setting in which he wouldn't have to look at pink cupids or pink lampshades. But when we look closely at Charles, we find that he has secrets that he wishes to conceal— secrets that make him ill-suited for a glass house by Philip Johnson.

Consider, for example, the scene in which he opens the wardrobe that has been carved all out of shape. Upon doing so, he is horrified to discover that Rosa has unpacked and arranged his belongings while he was out of the room, an "invasion" (453) that has exposed all their weaknesses of quality and condition:

> His meager toilet articles, his frayed hair brushes and his flabby leather cases were in array on the middle shelf. Conspicuous among them, looking somehow disreputable, was his quart bottle of brandy, a third empty, and he realized that he had in effect taken to secret drinking during his search for a room. He peered into the lumpy laundry bag hanging on a hook, and shuddered with masculine shame. Its snowy sweet-smelling whiteness concealed his socks that needed darning, his soiled shirts worn too long for economy's sake, and his stringy underwear. On the pillow of his bed,

half concealing the long effeminate lace pillow ruffles, lay a pair of neatly folded clean pajamas. (453)

Whatever secrets that laundry bag had contained are secret no more. Rosa has, in a manner of speaking, stripped Charles of his belief that he could conceal both his underwear and his underself—and further challenged his fragile sense of masculinity by placing his nightclothes on top of "effeminate lace pillow ruffles."

Small wonder then that Charles yearns to break free. When he ventures onto the streets of a city in which he feels deeply alien, he feels "trapped" and unable to communicate with people who "could not hear him" (458) which leads him to return resentfully to his home with Rosa, where he imagines breaking his lease and possibly trashing the room he finds so disturbing: "No more chairs with tapestry on them and legs that broke if you leaned back in them. No more of those table rugs with their nasty sweet colors. If the corner whatnot should be knocked over, just once, there would be no more of that silly bric-a-brac and a good thing too, thought Charles, hardening his heart" (458).

But forty pages later, Charles is still living under Rosa's roof—unable to tear himself away. In the final paragraph of the story, he breaks into "a cold sweat" and goes to bed where he "rolled himself into a knot" (495). It is New Year's Eve, and he has had too much to drink—but something deeper than inebriation is going on here. It is in this same paragraph that he notices, with shame, that Rosa has returned the plaster Leaning Tower to its place in his room. Studying it, he finds that "it was mended pretty obviously . . . [and] would never be the same" (494). He then comes to realize that for Rosa it "stood for something she had, or thought she had"—a recognition that almost leads him to violence: "It stood there in its bold little frailness, as if daring him to come on; how well he knew that a thumb and forefinger would smash the thin ribs, the mended spots would fall at a breath" (495). This thought, in turn, prompts him to remember how the pottery cupids outside his window also irritate him. Porter tells us that these objects "had some kind of meaning in Charles's mind" and concludes the story by inviting readers to make the connection that Charles is unable to make for himself. "Well what?" he asks himself as he looks upon the mended souvenir:

> What had the silly thing reminded him of before? There was an answer if he could think what it was, but this was not the time. But just the same, there was something terribly urgent at work in him or around him, he could not tell which. There was something per- ishable but threatening, uneasy, hanging over his head or stirring angrily, dangerously, at his back. If he couldn't find out now what it was that troubled him so in the place, maybe he would never know. He stood there feeling his drunkenness as a pain and a weight on him, unable to think clearly but feeling what he had never known before, an internal desolation of the spirit, the chill and the knowledge of death in him. (495)

Charles is clearly having a crisis, and Porter is challenging us to figure out what this crisis is about. Why is Charles living in Rosa's house, and why is he suffering there? Why has a young male artist chosen to spend the winter in an overfurnished room in which there is too little light for him to draw when, as we know, there are other kinds of space available to him if he is willing to pay the price—including "bare expanses of glass brick and chrome-steel sparsely set out with white leather couches and mirror-topped tables" (444)—the aesthetic opposite of the room in which he tries vainly to closet himself.

The answer, I believe, is deeply rooted in the anxiety of belonging to an uncertain social class in an age when class is determined by income. Charles rejects modern rooms on the grounds that they can be rented only "at frightening expense" (444). The expense in question cannot be measured by dollars and marks alone, for underlying the price of things is the issue of what a culture values. As a boy back home in Texas, Charles had been frequently in conflict with his best friend Kuno, the son of prosperous German immigrants who embrace mercantile values that Charles scorns, priding himself on a lineage traced back to old Kentucky:

> Though Kuno's mother was said to be a Baroness in Germany, in Texas she was the wife of a prosperous merchant, a furniture dealer. The Kentuckians, who were gradually starving on the land, thought the land the only honorable means to a living, unless one entered a profession; and Charles, whose family made their living, such as it was, from a blackland farm, wondered at the pride with which Kuno would lead him past his father's shop windows to show him the latest display of fashionable, highly polished and stuffed furniture. Looking through the broad clear window into the depths of the shop, Mr. Hillentafel, Kuno's father, could be seen dimly, pencil behind his ear, in his black alpaca coat, his head inclined attentively before a customer. Charles, used to seeing his father on horseback . . . felt he would have been ashamed to see his father in a store, following someone about trying to sell him something. (437-438)

Kuno, however, is proud of his father and infuriates Charles by telling him, "In Germany only low-down people work on farms" (438). Unlike Mr. Upton, Mr. Hillentafel is rich enough to take his family abroad "for a few months every two years" (438). Charles is fascinated by Kuno's stories about Germany and yearns to see Berlin, where, he is told, "there are marble houses carved all over with [. . .] loops of roses" (439).

A decade later, and many years after his friend's death, Charles realizes his dream of visiting the city with richly ornamented houses. Like the boy who looked with anxiety and confusion through shop windows back home in Texas, Charles looks through the shop windows on Kurfürstendamm and tries to decipher the value of the goods he sees as well as to figure out who has the money to purchase such goods. And in one of the story's most memorable scenes, Rosa lectures Charles about what happens to currency based on inflated values. She rebukes his failure to understand what drives her need to economize and shows him millions of worthless marks, including a five-million-mark note that will no longer buy even a loaf of bread. "I know it is all a horrible business—but, what can I do?" asks Charles. To this "dull question," Rosa responds, "You can do nothing" (477)—thus echoing their earlier exchange about how Charles could make amends for breaking the Leaning Tower.

Despite what Charles perceives to be a "high-faluting manner" (445) and an obsession with maintaining the semblance of a haut-bourgeois lifestyle after the collapse of the German economy, Rosa, like Kuno, is ultimately more realistic than Charles, who is sentimentally attached to the values of a landed gentry that is "gradually starving" just like the beggars he sees on the streets of Berlin. At the same time, he is struggling to make sense of commercial values that his southern heritage has scorned as ignoble. Porter is showing that Americans—or at least southerners—can be naïve about money, more naïve than Europeans. Stubbornly insisting that he is not rich while surrounded by people with far fewer resources, Charles expresses an economic naïveté which contributes to the political naïveté noted by Thomas Austenfeld (30). By taking a room with Rosa Reichl, he has found a mentor to replace Kuno. It is true that he finds Rosa infuriating, but his friend had gotten under his skin as well. This tendency to be irritated by people with values different from his own helps account for the difficulty Charles has in understanding what he sees and hears.

Despite their differences, Rosa and Charles have much in common even if he is unable to recognize the tie that binds them. They are both associated with an old order that is "gradually starving"; they are both fiercely proud; and they are both obsessed with concealment. There is even a link between their names. Rosa Reichl's last name carries within it a claim to empire. *Upton* carries a similar, if more modest claim to grandeur. If Rosa protects her furniture and strives for a kind of outdated elegance by using layers of fabric as part of her decorating scheme, Charles, for his part, is obsessed with preserving the privacy of his papers and troubled when strangers get a glimpse of his underwear. Shortly before the scene in which he is mortified to find that Rosa had unpacked his baggage, Charles had suffered through a parallel scene: When he checked out of the disagreeable hotel where he had been staying temporarily, he was asked to produce papers packed in his luggage. He opened the larger of his two suitcases, "exposing a huddle of untidy clothing" at which point the proprietors of the hotel "leaned forward to gaze at his belongings, and the woman said, 'So,' in a contemptuous voice" (449). What is it about this man, I find myself asking, who seems to have a genius for exposing untidy clothing and then bitterly resenting the people who catch a glimpse of his underpants? Surely there is some sexual anxiety in play here. Among other things, "The Leaning Tower" is the story of an inexperienced and uncertain male who is apparently incapable of finding a girlfriend. In this respect, a critic inclined to psychoanalytic readings might make much of the story's title—that vulnerable tower that Charles likes to touch, getting himself in trouble for putting his hands where they are not supposed to be.

I leave that reading to others, but I will note that a fear of letting people see what one has can signal an inability to be intimate. Although

Charles scorns Rosa for being affected, he is most distressed when she allows herself to break down before him in a genuine display of emotion. Charles would prefer that Rosa keep her inner life safely closeted and his own belongings safely hidden in his baggage.

It is important, however, that we avoid reading the story as a simple conflict between a nosey woman and a man who wants to avoid intimacy. There are, to be sure, elements of the story that would support such a reading, but the story as a whole suggests that men and women alike are committed to "cover-ups." Both Charles and Rosa want to conceal their relative poverty by keeping up appearances and casting themselves as heirs to a noble past. Rosa may be more practiced at concealment, better able to keep strangers from peeking into untidy closets or suitcases. She is older, after all, and more experienced. Given time and effort, Charles may learn to keep his belongings carefully locked up. He is already ahead of Rosa when it comes to keeping his feelings hidden. Indeed, the principal difference between these two characters is that Rosa is willing to disclose her feelings while Charles firmly believes that feelings—like underwear—should be concealed at all cost. Charles loses control of his underclothing, and Rosa loses control of her emotions. Nevertheless, Charles has intuitively found a home with a kindred spirit.

In focusing upon the relationship between Rosa and Charles and discussing how "The Leaning Tower" foregrounds an interest in cover-ups, I do not mean to discount other dimensions of a rich story that addresses the role of the artist in trouble times (Givner 321–22) and in which "sorry emotional circumstances" help Porter to portray "political *aporia*" (Austenfeld 32). Moreover, much can be said about the gender politics of male tenants conspiring against their landlady while also seeking to accommodate her. But interior decoration, like politics, involves controlling what others are allowed to know and how they are allowed to know it. The economics of concealment—or the struggle to pay for how one wants to be seen in the world—contributes to the strong sense of oppression conveyed by Porter on every level of this well-crafted work.

"The Leaning Tower" is ultimately concerned with power—a subject that has a political dimension to be sure, but which nevertheless reaches deep into what is traditionally seen as private life. Power, according to this story, goes to those who either have money or can, at least, manage to appear as if they have money. Rosa is desperately holding on to her furniture not because she is a fussy old woman who is absurdly attached to her possessions, but because she has the intelligence to perceive that the trappings of her home give her whatever is left of her status as a person of consequence. Her personal power is directly tied to her ability to keep those lace curtains hanging in her windows. Similarly, Charles' own power within this social world is determined by the way other characters perceive him as a rich American—or, more accurately, rich because he is an American. Hence his own desperate need to keep Europeans from seeing his stringy underwear. Charles would not have been exposed if he had enough money to frequent better places. "With his limited money, he was frightened to go any place where things were for sale," Porter writes. "Because he was poor, he went to poor places, and felt trapped. . . ." (458). Had be been able to afford staying in a better hotel, he might not have been cheated on the bill, and he almost certainly would have been spared the humiliation of opening his luggage in the lobby. Then again, if he had more money, the untidy clothing within his suitcase—and later his laundry bag—would probably be in better condition. Porter is demonstrating that the *need* to conceal springs principally from poverty while the *ability* to conceal springs principally from wealth.

In the economics of concealment, the greatest success thus goes to those who least need it. People without money—like poor Mrs. Whipple in "He"—lack the wherewithal to conceal what they desperately wish to hide. Those who are prosperous—like the grandmother in "The Old Order"—can successfully conceal a family portrait in an "envelope of cut velvet and violet satin" (326). In "The Leaning Tower," Porter explores the anxiety of occupying the shifting middle ground between wealth and poverty, where we might be able to keep up appearances but face the ever-present risk of dirty laundry spilling out from wherever we have hidden it. Although the setting of this story happens to be Berlin—the drama played out in Rosa's home can be found wherever people use fabric and fabricating to assert social position. ❖

Works Cited

Austenfeld, Thomas. "Katherine Anne Porter Abroad: The Politics of Emotion." *Literature in Wissenschaft und Unterricht* 27 (1994): 27–33.

Givner, Joan. *Katherine Anne Porter: A Life.* New York: Simon & Schuster, 1982.

Porter, Katherine Anne. *Collected Stories of Katherine Anne Porter.* 1965. Reprint. New York: Harcourt Brace & Co., 1979.

Stout, Janis P. *Katherine Anne Porter: A Sense of the Times.* Charlottesville: UP of Virginia, 1995.

Memories That Never Were: Katherine Anne Porter and the Family Saga

Sylvia Grider

With her photograph on the poster for the 1998 Texas Writers Month and with the purchase and restoration of her childhood home,[1] Texas at last welcomes home this native daughter who has been shunned for so long by the literary establishment of her beloved state. Taking into account also her tombstone and marker at the Indian Creek cemetery and the marker in Kyle, it can truly be said that the name of Katherine Anne Porter is "carved in stone and cast in bronze" on the Texas landscape.

The tombstone, the historical markers, and the childhood home all fall into a broad category that folklorists, cultural geographers, and anthropologists designate as "material culture," but it is the house that holds the most interest. Just as the world has gazed in awe at the incredible photographs of the sunken *Titanic,* and souvenir hunters have paid enormous sums for otherwise useless and trivial lumps of *Titanic* coal recovered from the floor of the Atlantic Ocean, we are likewise intrigued by the homes and possessions of the famous, and literary figures are no exception. One need think only of the well-preserved home of Charles Dickens in London or Shakespeare's birthplace at Stratford-on-Avon. Closer to home, Texans have turned J. Frank Dobie's beloved ranch into a writer's retreat administered by the Texas Institute of Letters and the University of Texas at Austin.

But what of Porter's childhood home in Kyle? Why do we find value in a small frame house that, according to oral tradition, cost only $75 to build at the turn of the century? Porter herself described the house in an *Atlantic Monthly* memoir:

> My grandmother lived on a corner of the stony, crooked little road called Main Street, in a six-room house of a style known as Queen Anne, who knows why? It had no features at all except for the two long galleries, front and back galleries . . . and these galleries were shuttered in green lattice and then covered again with honeysuckle and roses, adding two delightful long summer rooms to the house, the front a dining room, the back furnished with swings and chairs for conversation and repose, iced tea, limeade . . . sangria— and always, tall frosted beakers of mint julep, for the gentlemen, of course. (102)

As I have remarked elsewhere, "This house has an existence of its own. Who are we to know what it has to say? If we can save it, one day it will speak."[2] What did I mean by that seemingly enigmatic remark? As a folklorist and material culture specialist, let me deconstruct my own statement. The house itself is less significant than the creative energy it inspires us to bring to it. The association of a house with its occupant is almost mystical; the house stands for the person who lived in it. When the person is gone, the house remains, a messenger from the past, a witness to a world we can no longer see or touch or inhabit. By entering that house, we enter the realm of memory, and it causes us to reflect upon what transpired there. We can share the same space with the person we wish to venerate when we can no longer share the same time with her. It is infinitely appropriate, therefore, that young Callie's child-hood home become a creative writing center because of the ideas that will be formed there, the inspiration for new generations of writers-yet-to-be. These intangibles can be made manifest because of the continued reality in the present of this artifact from the past, "this place of memory," this house where Katherine Anne Porter spent her childhood. It is through those that it can inspire that the house will find its voice.

If this house, therefore, is a memory made manifest, what else can be said about the *mentifacts*, or memories, associated with Porter, especially her memories of Texas? Much has been made by literary critics about the fabrication and unreliability of Porter's faulty memories of growing up in and around Kyle. As a folklorist and one who is also chided for having a "creative" memory, let me come to the defense of Porter's memories. How can anyone question that we all remember what we want to remember about our childhoods? Some have said that this selective memory is deliberate, a conscious attempt to conceal that which is unpleasant or controversial, but I think much more is involved.

Folklorists have long studied a common narrative genre known as the "family saga," described by Porter's fellow Texan and contemporary, Mody Boatright, in a celebrated essay first published in 1958. Boatright defined this narrative genre as follows: "I use the term mainly to denote a lore that tends to cluster around families, which is preserved and modified by oral transmission, and which is believed to be true" (124); any episode related in these narratives has a "relation to a social context and reflects a social value" (125). He goes on to say that "[t]his does not mean . . . that the event is invariably in harmony with the actual social conditions of the region where it is believed to have happened." In other words, these stories are not empirically and literally *true*. They relate the deeper family values of what *might have been* or what *ought to have been* rather than what *really was*. These narratives are a form of oral literature; they are not oral history, and they are not genealogy. Furthermore, they flourish best in oral tradition; they are rarely written down because then they lose their intimacy and become vulnerable to the prying eyes of historians, biographers, and other fact-checkers. Porter's use of family saga is therefore the exception rather than the rule because she committed her stories to print.

Most of us tell and believe in our own family sagas without ever questioning whether or not they are empirically true by a professional historian's standards. These elaborate narratives, seldom told outside of the intimate family circle, describe fanciful aspects of the family's history so as to reflect attitudes and values as opposed to empirical reality. I contend that Porter's lyrical descriptions of a pampered and aristocratic Old South upbringing, complete with devoted family retainers who never existed, are engaging in this sort of folk wish fulfillment. She is often describing the past as it *might have been* if her family had not fallen on hard times or the past as it *should have been* in order to provide a plausible explanation for the genteel, great southern lady that she really did become and the image of which she carefully cultivated. Other Texas women writers have done the same in order to associate themselves, for whatever reason, more with the Old South than with raw, frontier Texas, among them Mollie E. Moore Davis and Dorothy Scarborough.[3]

Such *fabulation*, or creative reshaping of the past, is not limited to Texas women writers. Larry McMurtry, by all accounts the most widely read of all Texas authors, skillfully invoked the family saga in an essay first published in 1968. According to McMurtry:

Of all the hardship stories I heard, the one which remains most resonant in my mind is the story of the molasses barrel. It was, for all witnesses, a traumatic event. Late one fall, not long after the turn of the century, William Jefferson had gone to the small town of Archer City to purchase the winter's provisions. Archer City was eighteen miles from the ranch, a tedious trip by wagon. He returned late in the afternoon, and among the supplies he brought back was an eighty-pound barrel of good sorghum molasses, in those days the nearest thing to sugar that could be procured. Such sweetening as the family would have for the whole winter was in the barrel, and all gathered around to watch it being unloaded. Two of the boys rolled the barrel to the back of the wagon and two more reached to lift it down, but in the exchange of responsibilities someone failed to secure a hold and the barrel fell to the ground and burst. Eighty pounds of sweetness quivered, spread out, and began to seep unrecoverably into the earth. Grace, the oldest girl, unable to accept the loss, held her breath and made three desperate circles of the house before anyone could recover himself sufficiently to catch her and pound her on the back. Indeed, the story was usually told as a story on Grace, for most of them had suppressed the calamity so effectively that they could not remember how anyone else had responded. They could speak with less emotion of death and dismemberment than of that moment when they stood and watched the winter's sweetness soak into the chicken yard. (159–60)

As presented, this is a poignant and believable episode in the life of this turn-of-the-century Texas family. However, McMurtry glosses the passage with a revealing footnote:

It now appears that the uncle who first told me this sad story had added a few flowers of his own. What "really happened," it seems, is that the barrel of molasses had a wooden spigot, and was unloaded safely and laid across two support beams so that when the spigot was opened the molasses would drain into the molasses pitcher. Unfortunately, a sow came along one day, walked under the barrel, and rooted the spigot out. The molasses drained from the barrel and ran down a footpath all the way to the lots. The catastrophe was thus discovered and the children lined up beside the path to weep. As with many family stories, I think I prefer the fiction to the truth. (160)

The first version, of course, is the family saga. Most readers agree with McMurtry that it is by far more interesting and "better" than the literal truth of the footnote.

The noted biographer Doris Kearns Goodwin discussed the difficulties she had untangling the biography of Lyndon Johnson, a noted raconteur:

[P]oliticians present special problems to the biographer. Though they leave behind hundreds of reams of words, we can never be exactly sure which ones are theirs and exactly what they mean. It is a politician's occupational hazard that effect comes to matter more than literal truth. So accustomed are they to speaking before audiences that most often what counts most is how the audiences react. Politicians tend to regard words as verbal and temporary, rather than written and permanent. Articulation, not analysis, is the coin of their kingdom.

She goes on to say:

This lesson was painfully driven home to me, when after listening to Johnson's proud description of his great-great-grandfather's heroic death at the Battle of San Jacinto, in Texas, I discovered that the grandfather had never even been at the battle. He was a real estate trader and had died at home in bed. But Johnson wanted an heroic relative so badly that he simply created the tale, and after retelling it dozens of times, the grandfather really came to exist in Johnson's mind. (97–98)

A folklorist would classify Johnson's little story as an episode from an elaborate family saga and file it under fiction rather than deliberate prevarication.

But there is a fine line between the family saga and out-and-out lying. Texas politician and Anne Richards' protégée Lena Guerrero paid dearly for crossing this line when she openly represented herself as an honor graduate of the University of Texas and member of Phi Beta Kappa. When she gave a commencement address at Texas A&M University, she reminisced about her own UT graduation. In truth, although she attended UT, she never graduated. But no matter how appealing the fanciful biography becomes, for a public office holder deliberately to falsify her credentials is inexcusable. When Guerrero was forced to resign her seat on the Texas Railroad Commission, thus destroying her political career, her only explanation for her public indiscretion was, "Perhaps you want something to be so much that you begin to believe it is" (Burka 122).

Although Goodwin gives the same explanation for Johnson's invention of the San Jacinto veteran as Guerrero did for her putative degree, the difference lies in the context. Johnson was a known story-teller who employed traditional narrative techniques to hold audiences spellbound. He apparently told the San Jacinto anecdote in fairly private settings to establish a kind of spiritual contact with his distant pioneer heritage, the way many family patriarchs do when recounting well-worn family sagas—such as arriving at Ellis Island, coming to Texas after the Civil War, or losing a fortune during the Gold Rush. Guerrero, on the other hand, included the fraudulent degree and membership in Phi Beta

231

Kappa on her printed campaign literature and official press releases. And unlike Johnson, she was talking about her own falsified résumé, not about the exploits of a distant relative.

But what of Katherine Anne Porter? As we well know, memories, both real and imagined, are a constant thread woven through Porter's prose. It is perhaps appropriate, therefore, that I share with you some of my own memories of Porter. What I don't know is whether they really happened the way I remember them or not. Perhaps, like LBJ, these memories are my attempt to be part of Texas' cultural past. Whether they really happened or not, they're my memories, and I like having them inside my head.

I had not heard of Porter until I took an undergraduate course, "Life and Literature of the Southwest," one summer at the University of Texas. We dutifully plowed through Dobie and Webb and learned that the cliché, "When you call me that, *smile!*" is a quote from Owen Wister's *The Virginian*. We also learned that *The Virginian* was the first true western in American literature, but our teacher apparently didn't know about Mollie E. Moore Davis' realistic *The Wire-Cutters*, which was published two years before Wister's fanciful pastiche. Then, at the end of the course, for reasons that the teacher explained but that I have forgotten, we read Porter's haunting collection of short stories, *Pale Horse, Pale Rider*. I was dumbstruck. A woman writer in Texas? Whoever heard of such a thing? And her stories were so different from anything else we read in that course, so much better than anything written by the men authors we were assigned to read. When *Ship of Fools* came out a couple of years later, I bought a copy, one of the first times in my life that I blew money on a hardback instead of waiting for the paperback to come out. I wish I still had that first edition, but I don't. I remember being disappointed that it wasn't as good as *Pale Horse, Pale Rider*. That's probably why it ended up in some distant Friends of the Library book sale instead of on my sagging bookshelves.

That undergraduate course probably really happened the way that I remember it. I remember too many other details from the course—like the white socks that the professor wore with his brown suit and his illegible handwriting on the blackboard, which was so tiny and scrunched up that I never had any notes to study when it came quiz time. But for the life of me, I can't remember the professor's name. Memories are like that—they're selective.

My other UT memory of Porter is less solid, and whether it really happened or not, perhaps it *should have*, considering the twists and turns my professional academic life has taken. I swear that I remember when Porter came to campus in 1959 to discuss the university naming its new library after her. I can just see her, regal in a black dress, white hat, and gloves, walking across the mall in front of the Tower in the company of Harry Ransom and other worthies. And now, nearly forty years later, the more I think about that possible memory and the more I read and learn about Porter, the more real and detailed the memory becomes to me. Is this the way folk memory works? Is this the process by which Porter remembered so much that others dispute really happened?

Porter's visit to the UT campus, whether I actually saw her there or not, is one of the reasons this symposium and the choice of Porter as the Texas Writers Month "poster girl" mean so much. As Dick Holland has discussed, for reasons that nobody now can (or perhaps will) explain, the library at UT was not named for Porter after all (31–39). She was bitterly disappointed and ultimately left her papers and memorabilia to the University of Maryland instead of to the University of Texas, where they belonged. What a tragic loss to us here in Texas.

The literary establishment in Texas has been slow to accept Porter as one of its own, in spite of her national reputation. She was passed over in 1939 for the first Texas Institute of Letters award because she and her stories weren't considered Texan enough. As we all know, Dobie won that award instead. And Dobie is the one who ended up with the room in the new library devoted to his life and works, instead of Porter.

From my perspective as a folklorist, I recognize that throughout the last sixty years or so, a kind of academic oral tradition has grown up in Texas around these two pivotal episodes in Porter's life: not naming the UT library after her and being snubbed by the Texas Institute of Letters. Generally, these two episodes are told—with much embellishment—as anti-Dobie anecdotes, thus fitting them into a kind of elegiac Texas family saga that pits man against woman on the rugged frontier of an emerging literature. The stories are taking on an additional resonance and patina as the conclusion emerges that Porter is the ultimate winner because it is she, not Dobie, who has the national recognition for literary greatness.[4]

The variants of these two episodes are legion, both in oral tradition and in print. So in honor of Texas Writers Month, as a folklorist, let me add my bit to the growing oral tradition surrounding these episodes in Porter's life. How about this original limerick:

> There was a young lady from Kyle
> Whose temper Frank Dobie did rile.
> She left in a huff
> Won Pulitzers and stuff
> And came back to Texas in style.

Porter herself in various interviews and essays has acknowledged the literary recreation of her own past in her fiction. For example, in "Noon Wine: The Sources," she said:

By the time I wrote "Noon Wine" it had become real to me almost in the sense that I felt not as if I had made that story out of my own memory of real events and imagined consequences, but as if I were quite simply reporting events I had heard or witnessed. This is not in the least true: the story is fiction; but it is made up of thousands of things that did happen to living human beings in a certain part of the country at a certain time of my life; things that are still remembered by others as single incidents; not as I remembered them, floating and moving with their separate life and reality, meeting and parting and mingling in my thoughts until they established their relationship and meaning to me. So I feel that this story is "true" in the way that a work of fiction should be true, created out of all the scattered particles of life I was able to absorb and combine and shape into new being. . . . (Bode 36)

Such statements by Porter, in my mind, exonerate her for telling a fanciful version of what in oral tradition rather than print would simply be a family saga validating her past. Porter is the perfect example of a Texas woman writer who "wrote her own story" and "reinvented herself," not only in her fiction but in her real life. We shouldn't criticize her for this; creativity often spills over from the personal to the produced works, which is the essence of true art. I posit that Porter created a personal "truth" about her past, which provided a nurturing platform and context for her creative productions. If she had been dispassionately honest about her background, would she have become one of America's finest prose stylists? I think not.

Elsewhere in her writings, however, she remembers her Texas heritage sharply and poignantly. In 1936, after a pilgrimage back home to her birthplace and a visit to her mother's grave, Porter wrote a poem expressing perhaps her truest feelings about Texas. She wrote:

This time of year, this year of all years, brought
The homeless one home again;
To the fallen house and the drowsing dust
There to sit at the door—
Welcomed, homeless no more.
Her dust remembers its dust and calls again
Back to the fallen house this restless dust,
This shape of her pain. (Givner 295)

To her now I say, Callie, wherever you are, from all of us, welcome home. ❖

Notes

[1] The house in Kyle, Texas, was purchased in 1998 by the Hays County Preservation Associates, which is cooperating with Southwest Texas State University to raise additional funding. Upon completion of the renovation, the house will be leased to Southwest Texas State University. In addition to hosting literary events, the house will be maintained as a Katherine Anne Porter museum.

[2] Letterhead stationery of the Katherine Anne Porter House Preservation Project, Kyle, Texas.

[3] For a further discussion of this topic see: Don Graham, "A Southern Writer in Texas: Porter and the Texas Literary Tradition." In Clinton Machann and William Bedford Clark, eds. *Katherine Anne Porter and Texas: An Uneasy Relationship*. College Station: Texas A&M UP, 1990, pp. 58–71.

[4] For elaboration on this point, see: Tom Pilkington, "A Prairie Homestead: Texas Writers and the Family Romance." *Texas Studies Annual* 2 (1995): 121–29.

Works Cited

Boatright, Mody. "The Family Saga as a Form of Folklore." *Mody Boatright, Folklorist: A Collection of Essays.* Ed. Ernest Speck. Austin: U of Texas P, 1973. 124–44.

Bode, Winston. "Miss Porter on Writers and Writing." *Katherine Anne Porter: Conversations.* Ed. Joan Givner. Jackson: UP of Mississippi, 1987. 30–38.

Burka, Paul. "Lena's Lies: Lena Guerrero and the Truth about Politics." *Texas Monthly* 20:11 (Nov. 1992): 122–25, 156.

Givner, Joan. *Katherine Anne Porter: A Life.* Rev. ed. Athens: U of Georgia P, 1991.

Holland, Richard. "Katherine Anne Porter and the University of Texas: A Map of Misunderstanding." *Southwestern American Literature* 24:1 (fall 1998): 33–41.

Kearns [Goodwin], Doris. "Angles of Vision." *Telling Lives: The Biographer's Art.* Ed. Marc Pacter. Philadelphia: U of Pennsylvania P, 1979. 90–103.

McMurtry, Larry. "Take My Saddle from the Wall: A Valediction." *From a Narrow Grave: Essays on Texas.* Albuquerque: U of New Mexico P, 1986 [1968]. 141–73.

Porter, Katherine Anne. "Notes on the Texas I Remember." *Atlantic Monthly* 235:3 (1975): 102–06.

Contributors

Bert Almon, born in Port Arthur, Texas, now holds a McCalla Research Professorship at the University of Alberta and is writing a book on Texas autobiographies from William Owens to Pat Mora and Mary Karr. He has published eight collections of poetry, a critical biography of William Humphrey, and a pamphlet on Gary Snyder.

Roger Brooks was the president of Howard Payne University in Brownwood, Texas, when Katherine Anne Porter visited there. Later he served as a vice president of Houston Baptist University and director of the Armstrong Browning Library at Baylor. He now lives in Houston.

Mark Busby is the director of the Center for the Study of the Southwest at Southwest Texas State University and is coeditor with Dick Heaberlin of *Southwestern American Literature* and *Texas Books in Review*.

Terrell F. Dixon teaches ecocomposition and literature and the environment at the University of Houston. He is coeditor with Scott Slovic of *Being in the World: An Environmental Reader for Writers*, and he is the contributing editor in environmental literature for *Texas Books in Review*.

Don Graham is the J. Frank Dobie Professor of English at the University of Texas, Austin. His most recent book, *Giant Country: Essays on Texas*, won the Violet Crown Award from the Austin Writers League. He is writer-at-large for *Texas Monthly*.

Sylvia Grider is an associate professor of anthropology at Texas A&M University, where she teaches courses in folklore and Texas culture. She is coeditor with Lou Rodenberger of *Texas Women Writers: A Tradition of Their Own.*

Dick Heaberlin is professor of English at Southwest Texas State University and is coeditor with Mark Busby of *Southwestern American Literature* and *Texas Books in Review.*

Christine H. Hait is an associate professor of English at Columbia College in Columbia, South Carolina. Her doctoral dissertation explores the relationship between creativity and gender in the work of Katherine Anne Porter. Her research interests include modernist women's writing, autobiography, and film, and she recently published an essay on Kay Boyle's innovations in autobiography in *Being Geniuses Together.*

Larry Herold completed a master's of fine arts in fiction at Southwest Texas State University. He now lives in Boston.

Dick Holland, founding curator of the Southwestern Writers Collection at Southwest Texas State University, worked for many years in the University of Texas Library System and is now an independent scholar living in Austin.

Rob Johnson is a professor of American literature at the University of Texas–Pan American. He is the editor of the forthcoming collection *Fantasmas: Supernatural Stories by Mexican-American Writers* (Bilingual Press, 2001) and the author of *The Beat Generation of Writers: An A-Z Guide* (Facts on File, Inc., 2001). His short story "Box Set" is included in *Texas Short Stories II* (Browder Springs Books, 2000).

Jeraldine R. Kraver is an assistant professor of English at the University of Texas at San Antonio. In addition to her work on Katherine Anne Porter, which has appeared in *Southwestern American*

Literature and *South Atlantic Review,* she has published variously on writers including Anzia Yezierska, Emile Zola, and Henry James.

James Ward Lee, now retired from the University of North Texas, is acquisitions consultant for TCU Press and coeditor with Donna Walker-Nixon of *New Texas '98.* Among his books are *Classics of Texas Fiction, 1941: Texas Goes to War,* and *Texas, My Texas.*

Robert K. Miller is professor of English at the University of St. Thomas in St. Paul, Minnesota, and is the author of numerous books and articles. His interests include twentieth-century American literature, rhetoric and composition, and literary nonfiction. He is currently doing the research for a book on Willa Cather and the idea of virtue.

Lou Rodenberger, professor emeritus of English at McMurry University, is coeditor with Sylvia Grider of *Texas Women Writers: A Tradition of Their Own.*

Janis P. Stout is professor of English at Texas A&M University, where she also serves as dean of faculties and associate provost. Her most recent books are *Through the Window, Out the Door: Women's Narratives of Departure, from Austin and Cather to Tyler, Morrison, and Didion* (University of Alabama Press, 1998) and *Willa Cather: The Writer and Her World* (University Press of Virginia, 2000).

Darlene Harbour Unrue holds a distinguished professorship in the English department at the University of Nevada, Las Vegas. She has published the following books: *Truth and Vision in Katherine Anne Porter's Fiction*; *Understanding Katherine Anne Porter;* "*This Strange, Old World" and Other Book Reviews by Katherine Anne Porter*; *Katherine Anne Porter's Poetry*; and *Critical Essays on Katherine Anne Porter.* She has edited the Porter volume to be published by the Library of America, and she is working on a comprehensive biography of Katherine Anne Porter.

Index

244

245

247

Porter, Paul (KAP's nephew) 7, 10, 28, 96, 119, 125, 128, 137, 138, 172, 175, 176

Pressly, Eugene 45, 46, 52, 102, 103, 104

Prettyman, Barrett 118, 175, 176

Proust, Marcelle 75

Que Viva México, 63

Ransom Center (UT-Austin) 25, 96, 166, 174, 175

Ransom, Harry 78, 79, 82- 88, 90-96, 137, 138, 233

Ransom, John Crowe 72

Ratchford, Fannie 83

Raymond, Dora Neil 71

Rhys, Jean 69

Richards, Anne 231

Roberts, Warren 83, 94

Robertson, Ben 172

Robertson, Lexie Dean 70

Rodenberger, Lou xii, 122, 241

Rubin, Louis 138, 169

Scarborough, Dorothy 75,128

Schoner, Alta Ada 114, 122, 125

Shattuck, Roger 82

Shelley, Percy 72

Shrake, Edwin (Bud) 76

Silber, John 82

Silver Spring, MD 48

Smiley, Jane 151

Smith, Rebecca W. 70

Southern Review 52, 53, 104, 147

Southwest Texas State University (San Marcos TX) ix, 2, 110, 119, 137, 236

Southwestern Writers Collection

(Southwest Texas State University) 119, 137

Stock, Ernest 100, 101

Stout, Frederick 171

Stout, Janis P. 18, 20, 37, 67, 74, 77, 96, 100, 102, 104, 105, 109, 133, 138, 141, 147, 163, 171, 176, 177, 213, 224, 241

Swift, Edward 76

Sypher, Wylie 73

Tanner, James T. F. 134

Tate, Allen xii, 4, 24, 52, 53, 104, 105

Tennyson, Alfred Lord 72-74

Texas A&M University 2, 67

Texas Institute of Letters x, 67, 68, 70, 76, 78, 92, 136, 225, 233, 234

The Texas Observer 68, 77, 85, 127, 132, 137, 148

Texas Quarterly 79, 83, 84, 86, 87, 96

Thompson, Barbara 30, 37

Tinkle, Lon 75, 92, 114

Treadwell, Mary 42

Trollope, Anthony 73

University of Maryland xi, 24, 36, 50-52, 92, 96, 117, 138, 145, 177, 233

University of Texas at Austin xi, 14, 67, 68, 77-83, 85, 87, 91-93, 96, 113, 137, 231, 232, 233

Unrue, Darlene Harbour 16, 38, 53, 124, 143, 147, 148, 163, 208, 211, 241

Van Gelder, Robert 140

Vann, Billy 70

Vizcaino, Fernando 29

Vliet, R. G. 76 139, 148